INTRODUCTION TO
THE RAJ QUARTET

JANIS TEDESCO, 1950-
JANET POPHAM

UNIVERSITY
PRESS OF
AMERICA

Copyright © 1985 by

University Press of America,™ Inc.

4720 Boston Way
Lanham, MD 20706

Library of Congress Cataloging in Publication Data

Tedesco, Janis, 1950-
  Introduction to the Raj quartet.

  Includes index.
    1. Scott, Paul, 1920-   . Raj quartet. 2. India in
literature. I. Popham, Janet, 1948-   . II. Title.
PR6069.C596R3437 1985   823'.914   85-623
ISBN 0-8191-4570-X (alk. paper)
ISBN 0-8191-4571-8 (pbk. : alk. paper)

All University Press of America books are produced on acid-free
paper which exceeds the minimum standards set by the National
Historical Publications and Records Commission.

DEDICATION

We would like to thank Karen Peck, Barbara McBride and Raymond and Pat Jordan for their financial support of our project; Pat O'Brien Freeman for her editorial assistance; Mr. Bill Hendrix of Empire Office Machines in Spokane for the use of his word processor; and our typist Linda Murphy, for her dedicated and intelligent job of preparing our manuscript.

ACKNOWLEDGMENTS

We would like to thank William Morrow and Company, Inc., for
permission to quote from The Jewel in the Crown by Paul Scott,
copyright©1966 by Paul Scott; The Day of the Scorpion by Paul
Scott, copyright ©1968 by Paul Scott; The Towers of Silence by
Paul Scott, copyright © 1971 by Paul Scott; A Division of the
Spoils by Paul Scott, copyright ©1975 by Paul Scott.

We would also like to thank Random House, Inc., for permission
to quote from The Complete Essays and Other Writings of Ralph
Waldo Emerson, Brooks Atkinson, Modern Library edition,
copyright 1940.

v

TABLE OF CONTENTS

INTRODUCTION

Paul Mark Scott was born in Palmers Green, England, on March 25, 1920. He attended private (in America called public) schools but never studied at a university. In 1940 he was drafted into the army and served until 1946 as an NCO in Army Intelligence. In 1941 Scott married Nancy Avery, and eventually they had two daughters, Carol and Sally. In 1943 he was sent to India, where he remained until the end of the war.

On his return to England, Scott became an accountant and worked as a bookkeeper until he joined a firm of literary agents, David Higham Associates, in 1950. In 1952 he wrote his first novel, Johnny Sahib, and in 1960 left the firm to become a full-time writer. During the war Scott had written poetry and plays, but as a serious writer he found the novel a more appropriate vehicle. Between 1952 and 1966 he published seven novels. In 1964 he returned to India to re-familiarize himself with a country which was to dominate the remainder of his creative endeavors.

In 1966 Scott published the first volume of the Raj Quartet, The Jewel in the Crown, which he described as the book which states the theme; in 1968 he completed The Day of the Scorpion, which takes a deeper look into raj life; in 1971 he published The Towers of Silence, which is metaphysical and meditative and was the most difficult to write; and in 1975 he completed the Quartet with A Division of the Spoils, which introduces an outsider (also an NCO in Army Intelligence) who draws all the material into focus for the conclusion. In this final volume Scott uses cartoons to illustrate political developments, and he found himself wishing that he could draw like the other members of his commercial-artist family. He had come (typically) full circle.[1] In 1977 Scott was awarded England's Booker Prize for his final book, Staying On. On March 1, 1978 he died of cancer at the age of 57.

Scott hated India. He never properly understood it and felt it alien to his personality. A case of jaundice did not help his first impressions of the country, and his philosophical musings on the relationship of physical health to the raj's behavior, as voiced by one of his characters, Guy

Perron, might be traced to Scott's own experience. Yet in a few short years India became important to him, so important that he could never leave it behind. After the war he missed it, and though he read volumes on its history he still felt like a novice about India. He hoped that each of the four volumes of the Quartet would be the last, but he could not banish India from his consciousness. It was an important stimulus in his life, but he believed that ultimately the English would never really understand the Indian mind.[2]

The Raj Quartet examines British rule in India between 1942 and 1947. Scott focuses on the dramatic element within his characters, isolating the effect of action rather than depicting the action itself.

The chronology of events in over 1900 pages can be summarized as follows:

1. Ronald Merrick comes to India--1938.
2. Hari Coomer comes to India--1938.
3. Sarah and Susan Layton return to India--July, 1939.
4. Merrick first meets Daphne Manners at Mac-Gregor House--end of February, 1942.
5. Hari Kumar sees Colin Lindsey on the Mayapore maidan--beginning of March, 1942. The next day Merrick arrests him at the Sanctuary.
6. Daphne and Hari meet at MacGregor House--later in March, 1942.
7. Merrick sees Hari and Daphne together on the maidan--end of April, 1942.
8. Merrick proposes to Daphne--middle of June, 1942.
9. Merrick starts sending his car for Daphne and warns her of her association with Hari--July, 1942.
10. Hari and Daphne visit the Tirupati temple--July 18, 1942.
11. All-India Congress votes in favor of Gandhi's "Quit India" resolution--August 8, 1942.
12. Country-wide arrests and riots. Edwina Crane attacked and Daphne raped in Bibighar Gardens--August 9, 1942.
13. Edwina Crane commits suttee--October, 1942.
14. Parvati Manners is born and Daphne dies--

May, 1943.
15. Teddie Bingham marries Susan Layton--October, 1943.
16. Teddie's death--April, 1944.
17. Nigel Rowan interviews Hari Kumar in Kandipat prison--May, 1944.
18. Mabel Layton's death and Edward Bingham's birth--June, 1944.
19. Barbie Batchelor's death--August, 1945.
20. Sarah meets Guy Perron and John Layton returns home--August, 1945.
21. Ronald and Susan marry--February, 1946.
22. Nigel and Laura marry--summer, 1946.
23. Sarah returns from England to Mirat--March, 1947.
24. Perron returns to India, Merrick and Ahmed die, official withdrawal of British from India--August, 1947.

In the Raj Quartet, the British perceived their position of authority as stemming from intellectual, political, cultural, and moral superiority, all of which flowed historically from their Western Christian heritage. Once religious faith began to wane in the raj's practical, day-to-day existence, the absolute certainty of moral justification began to disappear as well. The raj would maintain its ruling position and the Kiplingesque rhetoric, but its sense of superiority would be based on racial rather than moral foundations. In truth, there was nothing the raj needed to do or to be to justify its presence or to maintain its identity except to be white.

For Scott's major characters the days of total conviction were over. They did not enjoy heaven's approval nor did they rule by divine right. If there was only a biological rather than a moral definition of the raj, there was really no code of honor or heritage of service which gave the English in India a sense of identity--as a nation or as individuals. As feelings of insecurity increased, their collective instincts took command. The raj as a group began to matter more than the raj as individuals. Collective values, psychology, and behavior determined the roles which individuals were expected to play. The distinction of their class was meant to be reflected in the caliber of their performance. If they pretended that everything was lovely in the garden, if their lives conformed to the old formulas of behavior, then (so they believed) they would survive.

But survival depended on racial purity. The raj could not contaminate themselves by becoming too closely involved with India and black natives. They cultivated, isolated, and jealously guarded their cantonments which mirrored, as closely as possible, the environment of their island homeland. And yet the raj were as isolated from the intellectual and cultural climate of England as they were from black India. They were exiles without a home, rulers without purpose or justification.

Scott establishes these facts about the raj and examines whether they or their subjects can find happiness and love, or achieve personal fulfillment in light of these facts. He explores this crucial historical period to determine what the British really accomplished for themselves and for their subjects, and how blacks and whites actually related in India. In this respect it is natural to contrast Scott's viewpoint with Rudyard Kipling's. For Scott, Kipling captured the essence of the nineteenth century mentality which pervaded raj India and which immortalized, more than anything else, the spirit of "perpetual Edwardian sunlight."

Kipling was himself from the raj caste, born in Bombay in 1865 and sent to England at an early age for a proper education.[3] In 1882 he returned to India and worked in Lahore on a local newspaper, the Civil and Military Gazette, spending a total of seven years in India. Most of his experiences centered around the important social circles of Simla after his family became personally acquainted with the Viceroy.

Kipling's famous poem, The White Man's Burden, was written in 1899, years after his Indian exper- ience. It captures the essence of his attitudes about the black native and the white man's mission.[4] In this work, Kipling characterizes the black (though not specifically Indian) subjects in Britain's Empire as sullen, silent people who behave wildly, like children or devils. They prefer their own evil or naive customs and culture to the advanced civiliza- tion of the white man. Instead of responding grate- fully, they reward England's efforts with hate and resentment. In their sloth and folly the heathens frustrate the white man's attempts to civilize them by rejecting (both spiritually and culturally) the holy light of the promised land for the dark, Egyptian nights of bondage and pagan pleasure. They judge the English and the Christian God by what they themselves accomplish or fail to accomplish.

The white man's position as ruler is not a glamorous one. Kipling sees the best of England's upper classes living a life of exile in order to serve their conquered subjects selflessly. The white man could not rule as a king, reaping pleasure and benefits for his own profit. He lives as the lowest of the low, the humble and patient shepherd. A man who wants to see and do great things could never survive as a member of the raj. In the sacred cause of freedom and civilized culture, there is no excuse for weariness and no tangible reward. The work is demanding, and where the white man sows the black will reap. The war against famine, sickness, poverty, and ignorance is hopeless, and for their efforts the raj will be blamed by those at home and hated by their native subjects. The English abroad must hide their pride and fear and abandon their personal cares and ambitions. They will be held answerable for themselves and their God after years of thankless toil. The only meaningful praise will come from their fellow raj, because only they will truly understand.

Kipling's poem adequately captures the self-image Scott's raj characters possessed: their sense of mission and martyrdom. But it does not express Scott's own judgment about the raj's true motives, behavior, and attitudes. If there was no love between white and black, it was because the Kipling rhetoric could not hide the thinly-disguised racial prejudice which shaped raj behavior.

Unlike Kipling, Scott sees the Indian as equal to the white man spiritually and politically. He appreciates the ancient cultures of the Hindu and Muslim traditions and sees their contribution as integral to the Indian character. Scott refuses to judge the native culture as "pagan" or childish, or derived from the darkness. If the diverse Indian political parties cannot rule their country peacefully, if India can never be politically and culturally united, it is more the fault of British rule than evidence that the Indians are an innately inferior race.

The parallel between Kipling's early life and Hari Kumar's early life is unmistakable. Both were natives of India; both left there at an early age to benefit from the best of England's public education system and then returned to India and worked for a local newspaper. If what Kipling believed of the English abroad were actually true, a civilized, cultured, handsome Englishman would be welcomed within cantonment life--welcomed as "one of us" whether he had black skin or white as long as he displayed the civilized, selfless, and dedicated qualities which characterized the raj. That is, any Englishman would be welcomed if the white man ruled because he was morally and culturally, rather then racially, superior.

By paralleling Kumar's life to Kipling's, Scott is experimenting to see how Kipling's world would work had Kipling been black--thereby measuring the truth of Kipling's viewpoint. Perhaps, had Kipling been black, instead of a huge legacy of poems and short stories, he would have left behind a few isolated essays written under a Greek pen name--perhaps one entitled, like Kumar's, "Alma Mater." Scott has (to use his own image) dropped Hari Coomer/Kumar into a circle of fire with only his English identity as armor to expose the real truth about the English in India and about "kiplingesque double-talk."

* * *

Although only a few pages are devoted to Emerson in The Towers of Silence and A Division of the Spoils, the impact of Emerson's influence on Paul Scott is significant. It is not within the scope of this book to explore in detail the actual interplay between the writings of Scott and Emerson in relation to the Raj Quartet. Without precise biographical information about Paul Scott and intimate knowledge of the entire body of Emerson's writings, a definitive statement cannot be made. However, even limited research reveals many intriguing similarities which in themselves may be enough to indicate that Emerson exerted a profound influence upon Paul Scott and the Raj Quartet.

It will be shown in greater detail how Emerson's essay "History" influenced and illumined Scotts portrayal of Barbie Batchelor's insights into reality. "If the whole of history is one man, it is all to be explained from individual experience."[5] This statement would philosophically justify Scott's use of imagery and symbolism which help define human nature and describe the human condition. It also would explain why Scott so successfully creates character parallels which emphasize common experiences without sacrificing the uniqueness of each character. Emerson's ideas also enable Scott to associate characters and events artistically so that everything seems to be connected, as Barbie Batchelor told Sarah Layton (The Towers of Silence, p.340). Man's power "consists in the multitude of his affinities, in the fact that his life is intertwined with the whole chain of organic and inorganic being."[6]

In Scott's complicated vision of history involving linear, single-minded fate and cyclic, repetitive patterns there emerges the power of the human will, as described in Robin White's "area of dangerous fallibility" or Ronald Merrick's "situation." Ahmed Kasim's death was fated, the result of circumstances beyond his control "which began with a girl stumbling on steps at the end of a long journey through the dark" (A Division of the Spoils, p.117). And yet Ahmed "contributed something of his own to its manner" by choosing to go of his own free will (A Division of the Spoils, p.117). In his essay on "Self-Reliance" Emerson states:

> In the Will work and acquire and thou
> hast chained the wheel of Chance, and
> shall sit hereafter out of fear from
> her rotations. A political victory,
> a rise of rents, the recovery of your
> sick or the return of your absent
> friend, or some other favorable event
> raises your spirits, and you think
> good days are preparing for you. Do
> not believe it. Nothing can bring
> you peace but yourself. Nothing can
> bring you peace but the triumph of
> principles.[7]

Men will never control chance, never master fate. Peace, says Emerson, does not mean that man controls external circumstances. It means not letting them control man. It means being in control of one's self. Ahmed attained a level of freedom and peace by going freely to his death without jeopardizing his friends--a loving, bountiful act. He did not let an unpleasant fate compromise his principles. His freedom and peace was, Scott says, his compensation (A Division of the Spoils, p.117).

In Scott's examination of raj society it is clear that to put the code, the collective identity, before the individual is to imprison the person and downgrade the contribution of society. "Society everywhere is in conspiracy against the manhood of every one of its members...It loves not realities and creators, but names and customs."[8] "I am ashamed to think how easily we capitulate to badges and names, to large societies and dead institutions."[9] Again: "Your genuine action will explain itself and will explain your other genuine actions. Your conformity explains nothing."[10] It is the collective contribution that both Sarah Layton and Ethel Manners decried as second-rate: "The world's common factor, and any damn fool people can teach it, any damn fool people can inherit it" (The Jewel in the Crown, p.476).

Scott uses light and darkness imagery to detect the presence of good and evil. God, the highest good, is the invisible lightning that struck the veranda (The Towers of Silence, p.386) and the distant but terrible fire (The Towers of Silence, p.397). Emerson says in his essay on "Spiritual Laws": "We are the photometers, we the irritable goldleaf and tinfoil [fireflies, as Sarah described them] that measure the accumulations of the subtle element. We know the authentic effects of the true fire through every one of its million disguises."[11]

In applauding Mabel Layton's natural, holistic attitude toward life, Scott supports Emerson's admonition: "Let us draw a lesson from nature, which always works by short ways. When the fruit is ripe, it falls. When the fruit is dispatched, the leaf falls."[12] And again: "There is no sleep, no pause, no preservation, but all things renew, germinate, and spring."[13] According to Scott, the natural cycle of seed, growth, flower, decay, and seed should be celebrated and lived as Mabel Layton celebrated and lived it (The Towers of Silence. p.207). This same concept was representated by the figure of the

xvi

dancing Siva: "The dance of creation, preservation and destruction. A complete cycle. A wholeness" (The Jewel in the Crown. p.152). Human history and achievement cannot be written in stone.

Both Scott and Emerson liken the unique human person and the flowering of his virtue to that of a rose. "No flower is quite like another of the same species. On a single bush one is constantly surprised by the remarkable character shown by each individual rose" (The Towers of Silence, p.207). In "Self-Reliance" Emerson says: "These roses under my window make no reference to former roses or to better ones; they are for what they are; they exist with God today....There is simply the rose; it is perfect in every moment of its existence."[14]

Without hard evidence of his interior evil, Sarah Layton distrusted and disliked Ronald Merrick without really understanding why. Emerson states: "Men imagine that they communicate their virtue or vice only by overt actions, and do not see that virtue or vice emit a breath every moment."[15] Sarah did not need to hear Hari Kumar's testimony in Kandipat prison. She sensed Merrick's evil. "A man passes for what he is worth... What he is engraves itself on his face, on his form, on his fortunes, in letters of light....There is confession in the glances of our eyes, our smiles, in salutations, and the grasp of hands."[16] Scott describes Sarah as reluctant to take the hand Merrick slowly held out. His hand felt warm and moist (The Day of the Scorpion, p.228). "His sin bedaubs him, mars all his good impression. Men know not why they do not trust him, but they do not trust him. His vice glasses his eye, cuts lines of mean expression in his cheek, pinches the nose, sets the mark of the beast on the back of the head."[17] Merrick's scarred face, his glassy, expressionless eye, and his amputated arm and artifical hand take on metaphysical dimensions and symbolic importance. Both Guy Perron and Count Bronowsky believe that the deformities suit Merrick's image so well that he would have invented them if they had not been acquired in the random course of events. Yet, according to Emerson, the scars are redundant.

The basic structural pattern in the Raj Quartet is the circle. Starting with Bibighar, the center, Scott expands in ever-widening spheres the influence

and meaning of Bibighar and examines how they apply
to issues of universal significance. Emerson believed that "the eye is the first circle, the horizon
which it forms is the second, and throughout nature
this primary figure is repeated without end."[18]
Bibighar 1942 was not the first tragedy of its kind.
The reader is faced with an image reflecting in two
opposite mirrors like Barbie Batchelor: "She was
multiplied back and front. Frontwards she was
Barbie, approaching herself, and backwards another
self retreating through one diminishing image after
another into some kind of shocking infinity" (The
Towers of Silence, p.99).

    Just as Bibighar 1942 was not the first (the
first circle can recede to infinitely smaller circles) it will not be the last. Merrick and Kumar
"had met before, countless times. You can say they
are still meeting" (A Division of the Spoils,
pp.314-15). Emerson says: "around every circle
another can be drawn....there is no end in nature,
but every end is a beginning...and under every deep
another deep opens."[19] Daphne wrote in her journal
that she had a sense of none of it happening at all
"because it had begun wrong and continued wrong, and
so was already ended, and was wrong even in its
ending, because its ending, for me, was unreal and
remote, and yet total in its envelopment, as if it
had already turned itself into a beginning" (The
Jewel in the Crown, p.467).

    Governor Malcolm detailed an adaptation of
Einstein's theory of relativity as applied to politics, in which people "sometimes found the solution
to the problem they were evading by going round in
ever increasing circles and disappearing into the
centre of those, which, relatively speaking, coinci-
ded with the centre of the circle from whose
periphery they had evasively spiralled outwards" (A
Division of the Spoils, p.332). Emerson observes:
"The natural world may be conceived of as a system of
concentric circles."[20] This description accurately
captures the structure of the Raj Quartet and
illumines Scott's philosophy of history and his study
of the workings and effects of human action and
choice.

                    * * *

                    xviii

Scott's major talent as an author is his ability
to treat a complex historical subject both intelli-
gently and artistically. He explores the interior of
his characters in their private core, their very
depths, while at the same time he describes panoramic
historical events. Scott's artistry is almost
"impressionistic." Every detail is important for the
total effect, the complete impression.

His characters are unique and unforgettable, yet
Scott structures parallel experiences between them to
such an extent that his two primary characters,
Daphne Manners and Hari Kumar, become archetypal
figures. In conjunction with these parallels, Scott
develops complicated symbols--a network of thematic
imagery and artistic associations which together
produce a forceful portrayal of what being human
really means and what constitutes man's metaphysical
condition.

Scott's literary artistry has the power to
delight the reader's mind and move his heart without
ever being maudlin or pandering to the sensational.
In fact, Scott deliberately understates especially
pathetic or violent scenes. Without preaching, the
author establishes perimeters of good and evil and
illumines universal truths which lie hidden in layers
of grey shadows cast by half-truths, lies, and
uncertainty. Scott also has the rare talent of being
able to portray women's feelings and reflections in
an authentic, convincing way.

Scott's ability to describe, to paint a graphic
mental picture and create a specific emotional
response in the reader, is a major part of his
literary ability, as is evident in the following
examples. Daphne Manners reflects, in her diary:

> I'd wake at night, shivering because
> the temperature had fallen, and lis-
> ten to the lashing on the trees, the
> wonderful rumbling and banging of the
> thunder, and watch the way the whole
> room was lit as if from an explosion,
> with the furniture throwing sudden
> flamboyant shadows, black dancing
> shapes petrified in the middle of a
> complicated movement--a bit of secret
> night-time devilry that they returned
> to the moment the unexpected light

went out, only to be caught and held
still in it again a few moments later
(The Jewel in the Crown. p.409).

When Barbie returned for the last time to Rose
Cottage she paused in front of a window and "had an
impulse which she restrained to rap on the wood and
cry: Is anybody there? and...listen for the sounds
of the years she had spent there scattering in panic
at the stranger's voice" (The Towers of Silence,
p.374).   After years of being away from India, Guy
Perron still retained his pair of chappals he wore
while touring the governor's summer residence with
Sarah Layton in Pankot. The smell of damp and grass
still seemed to be in them like a perfume, and he
remembered how he and Sarah, the substitute Governor
and his Lady, sat enthroned in two shrouded chairs
and gazed upward at the vast chandeliers enveloped in
balloons of muslin: "head thrust forward--the body
canted to achieve a position where the light on dark
varnish less obscured the detail and colour of
pigment underneath" (A Division of the Spoils.
p.348).

Paul Scott's treatment of the British in India
is primarily literary. He gathers the truth about
the subject from all aspects: historical, philosophical, and theological. But to explore and present
his final perceptions Scott chose the literary mode.
A separate book could be written about Scott's
theology, his philosophy, his history of India, or
the relationship between his ideas and Emerson's
thoughts. This book will concentrate on the Raj
Quartet as a work of literature, although it is
impossible to ignore the other dimensions of Scott's
message. It will focus on the elements of Bibighar
which are manifested repeatedly in British/Indian
relationships both on a personal and national level
and which culminate in the British withdrawal of
1947. While these elements are traced, major topics
will be explored: Scott's philosophy of history, the
interplay between fate and free will, the metaphysical perimeters of the human condition, the
effect of moral choice, and the dimensions of human
nature.

Although Scott's historical setting is very
specific, the conclusions the reader can draw from
his work are univeral in scope. It is hoped that
this introduction to Paul Scott's work will instill a

xx

deeper appreciation for his monumental contribution and great talent and stimulate others to delve deeper into the Raj Quartet and improve the body of literary criticism which it inspires.

This book attempts to preserve, as much as possible, the autonomy of each volume. This means that when discussing, for example, The Jewel in the Crown, it does not anticipate events, symbols, or themes in the following volumes. Such anticipation, however, has proved necessary in some instances and so was done in footnotes. Footnotes have been included at the end of each chapter, but rarely refer to page references or additional bibliographical material. They are substantive additions to the text utilizing material from the other volumes and must be read in order to complete this introduction.

FOOTNOTES TO THE INTRODUCTION

[1] From an interview with Paul Scott, _Publisher's Weekly_ 208 (Sept. 15, 1975): 6.

[2] Ibid., p.7.

[3] Biographical facts taken from _Rudyard Kipling_, by J.I.M. Stewart (New York: Dodd, Mead, and Co., 1966).

[4] For the complete text see _Rudyard Kipling's Verse, the Definitive Edition_ (Garden City, New York: Doubleday & Co. Inc., 1940), pp.321-23.

[5] "History," _The Complete Essays and Other Writings of Ralph Waldo Emerson_, ed. Brooks Atkinson (New York: Random House, 1940), pp. 123-24. All references to Emerson's works are taken from this collection.

[6] "History," p. 141.

[7] "Self-Reliance," p.169.

[8] "Self-Reliance," p.148.

[9] Ibid.

[10] "Self-Reliance," p.153.

[11] "Spiritual Laws," p.209.

[12] "Spiritual Laws," p.193.

[13] "Circles," p.289.

[14] "Self-Reliance," p.157.

[15] "Self-Reliance," p.152.

[16] "Spiritual Laws," p.205.

[17] Ibid.

[18] "Circles," p.279.

[19] Ibid.

[20] "Circles," p.286.

CHAPTER I

THE JEWEL IN THE CROWN

In 1964 a stranger came to Mayapore, a person who was interested in the final phase of British/ Indian history. He asked about people long dead and forgotten, and resurrected the name "Bibighar." To this stranger, and to Paul Scott, Bibighar is not an event of the past. It is a living issue, an ongoing moment of significant magnitude, a lesson to be remembered.

The plot of The Jewel in the Crown is very simple. It is treated almost as if it were peripheral to the point of the book. Most of the action takes place outside the scope of the pages. It is described but seldom depicted. When historical events are revealed, they are disclosed with a total disregard for chronology.

The closest thing to an omniscient observer is the inquisitive stranger, who functions as an impartial chronicler rather than an all-wise, all-knowing interpreter of truth. The "interview" style is developed to include numerous versions of the Bibighar incident, points of view offered by all of the main characters except Hari Kumar, who is lost, and Ronald Merrick, who is dead. Revelations gleaned from this interview style are valuable not only because they finally uncover the truth about Bibighar, but also because they reveal personal thoughts and feelings of those main characters which otherwise would remain hidden.

This step into the inner workings of the characters is essential. For Paul Scott the realm of human conscience, the ability to exercise moral choice freely, is the moving force of history and the focal point of drama. Thus Scott continually emphasizes and explores the moral drama within people rather than depicting panoramic historical events.

For this reason also the events surrounding Bibighar are alive and relevant, both to the stranger

1

and to the reader. The "why" of past history is the same as the "why" of history now unfolding and history yet to be lived. The elements of Bibighar as explored in The Jewel in the Crown involve motives and emotions which continue to plague mankind and which, if not checked, will violently and tragically determine the future.

I

To say that Scott is unhistorical in his chronology of events is not to imply that he is anti-historical. A proper understanding of history is a vitally important aspect of Scott's work, an understanding not only of the facts of this specific historical period, but also of the timeless truths about the workings of human history. Scott develops both of these aspects in The Jewel in the Crown.

It is important to remember the observation offered by Robin White, the District Commissioner in Mayapore, about recording the "blow-by-blow" account of the policies of the period. Any historian, in order to prepare his material, will adopt an attitude toward the facts. "The action of such an attittude is rather like that of a sieve. Only what is relevant to the attitude gets through. The rest gets thrown away" (pp.356-57).[1] Even in an objective historical chronology of events there is the danger of this personal prejudice selecting and interpreting facts according to its own "sieve." The relevance and truth of the sieve depends on the relevance and truth of the initial prejudice, which may not reflect the objective truth of the situation (p.357).

Ideally, an accurate interpretation of history is possible once the historian has mastered all of the facts. Paul Scott's own point of view was shaped by a first-hand experience of his subject and an in-depth knowledge of the historical background, which gave him this insight into human nature: that fear of the unknown, especially of people with different colored skin as manifested in racial prejudice, is of tremendous influence in history and was the most important element which shaped the British/Indian experience. This experience was not determined, as Kipling believed, by altruistic and magnanimous motives.

2

Kipling's supposed "sacred mission" was continually corrupted by the "primitive instinct to attack
and destroy what we didn't understand" (p.428). Paul
Scott found racial prejudice an incontestable element
of human experience despite spiritual dogmas and
influence to the contrary. In many ways World War II
India was a very religious period and place. It
would be impossible, for instance, to appreciate this
first volume fully without some knowledge of the
Hindu religion and culture which permeated Mayapore
society.

As described on pages 84-85, there are four
stages in a Hindu's journey through earthly life.
The first is early discipline and training including
the state of celibacy. The second is having a family
and supporting a household. During the third stage
those domestic responsibilities are completed to free
a person for the fourth and highest stage: Sannyasi,
when all earthly goods and relationships are abandoned, all vestiges of "self" are sublimated, and a
person earns maximum merit by living the life of a
homeless and destitute beggar. After death, a Hindu
would either be reincarnated or, if he had attained
the highest level of wisdom through Sannyasi, would
achieve heaven, which for him was total, peaceful
oblivion in a corporal state of mindless embodiment.

Lili Chatterjee, Daphne Manner's cynical and
worldly guardian in Mayapore, regarded Hinduism as a
practical rather than ascetic way of life. Sannyasi,
or the fourth stage of life, solved the problem of
society's having to take care of its old people.
Cows were sacred so that the starving masses could
not slaughter the livestock. The caste system made
class conflict and social upheaval impossible. To
Lady Chatterjee, Hindu life was not one of detachment
but one of action. Whereas all a Christian saint had
to do to attain heaven was die, she remarked, the
Hindu saint had to expend a considerable amount of
energy traveling through the realm of illusion (life
on earth) to oblivion (heaven). Violence, as a
positive manifestation of a life of action, was an
understandable and inevitable aspect of Hindu society
(p.78).

It was difficult for Robin White to understand
why Hindus involved themselves in politics if they
truly believed that earthly life was an illusion. If

3

insults, beatings, and bullets were not real, if
suffering, pain, and hunger were illusory, then there
was no logical reason for rioting and dissent. Yet
there was such violence because England would not
honor its promise to grant India political independence. In theory, as Lady Chaterjee pointed out, a
true Hindu should be indifferent to what 'should" or
"should not" be done. Such judgments presupposed a
Christian framework in which the material and spiritual worlds were real and distinct. Edwina Crane,
supervisor of mission schools in the Mayapore
district, could say that existing political policy
should ultimately reflect British moral ideals and
solemn commitments. The juxtaposition of an ideal
with the real world formed the core of Chrisian, not
Hindu morality. That was why, Lady Chatterjee concluded, Christian saints were often martyrs, because
their spiritual principles were always in conflict
with the material world (p.77).

It was inevitable that the English would misunderstand Gandhi as long as they labored within this
Christian framework. Gandhi did not conform to the
Christian conception of sanctity. He may not even
have been a Hindu saint. What he was, Lady Chaterjee
explained, was a very shrewd politician. Robin White
respected Gandhi for having the "instinct and capacity for thinking aloud" (p.344). He was misunderstood and projected an inconsistent image because of
it, but he succeeded in bringing "into the open the
element of doubt about ideas and attitudes which we
all undergo but prefer to keep quiet about" (p.344).
Robin White believed Gandhi's personal doubts stemmed
from an incident early in his life when he became an
outcast by studying law in England. He pursued his
worldly ambition instead of his religious responsibilities, and his subsequent political career reflected an attempt to work out "a personal salvation
in public" (p.344). For all his humanitarian appeal
and Christian sentiment, Gandhi was first and fore-
most a Hindu.

Gandhi's difficulty in reconciling his religion
and culture with the white man's standards and
demands also affected large portions of both the
Hindu and Muslim population. From the earliest
stages in British/Indian history, the English cited
their moral superiority as justification for the
power they held over black "heathens." It was only
natural that Hindus and Muslims would delve into

4

their own spiritual depths to endure the white man's rule, to discover reasons why this was happening, and to find solutions to their plight. Renewed fervor and moral renovations both heightened the sense of religious distinction between Hindus and Muslims and ultimately threatened peaceful coexistence between the major cultural groups. Until the religious revivals of the nineteenth century, communal problems were not considered unavoidable, and differences were not regarded as insurmountable. The British did not create social divisions, but they did deliberately pursue a policy of "divide and rule" which exploited and fueled internal difficulties and thus prolonged their own dominion (pp.340-41).

Of the two great religions of India, Hinduism was regarded by the English as the "weaker" of the two. Perhaps this indicated an unspoken discomfort with their own passive, peace-loving doctrines of the Christian tradition, which appeared effeminate or cowardly in contrast to the militant teachings of the Muslim religion. Edwina Crane found Mrs. Chaudhuri's typical Hindu behavior as the meak, docile and solicitous wife difficult to relate to, even though she realized that such a tradition enabled the Indian woman to acquire and maintain peace of mind and inner stillness (p.54).

A large portion of Hindu society was politically indifferent, even in the turbulent 1940's. Some business men like Romesh Chand Gupta Sen, Hari Kumar's uncle, were only interested in making money and being good Hindus (p.182). Many of the Indians who had attained professional and academic degrees, whom the stranger saw during his visit at the Gymkhana Club with Lady Chatterjee and the lawyer Srinivasan twenty years later, were indifferent to the toil and sacrifices of the previous generation which helped earn them the rights and privileges they enjoyed (pp.179-80).

The most religious character in the white community was Ludmila Smith, or Sister Ludmila, who ran a sanctuary for the dying.[2] She served blacks in their ultimate need, ministering to them with unqualified kindness and compassion and providing for them in death the dignity they were unable to find in life. What a waste, Ronald Merrick thought when he searched the Sanctuary for an escaped criminal, to shower money and effort on such undeserving people

5

who were better off dead (p.141). Few members of the white community sympathized with her work. Fewer still understood it. Of all the religiously-minded people in white Mayapore, Ludmila alone related to God as a person, seeing Him as someone who was happy and who thus made human happiness possible (p.128). She was a person of exceptional faith.

The other characters of the white community either did not believe in God, like Daphne Manners, or harbored vague feelings of piety directed toward an authority figure who was kindly disposed to the raj and their mission. Paradoxically, English society in India remained religious even while it became godless. The raj regarded God as a silent partner in their imperial endeavor, a partner who was historically on their side--a fact which could be deduced from England's economic, moral, technical, political, and military superiority. As long as things were going well it was natural for the raj to assume God was the champion of the white community and at their administrative disposal.

The new generation of English who came to India in the 1940's did not enjoy the same strong, religious faith of by-gone generations, a faith which Edwina's young friend Clancy knew made things a lot simpler (p.33). Answers no longer were clear-cut or obvious. The British, in 1942, did not appear deserving after being chased out of Burma and Malaysia by the Japanese. Even the faithful believers were finding it increasingly difficult to assume that heaven was still on their side. If the raj's authority was not God-given, then a new basis of legitimacy had to be found.

As God lifted his weight off the world, these concerns plagued raj society and formed the burden of its metaphysical liberation (pp.33-34). God might still exist but had chosen not to intervene in human affairs, a fact which the raj considered obvious since the war was going badly for them. God's absence caused a shift in posture, a reinterpretation of English history. Even if the raj were not God's chosen people, even if they did not witness to a superior religious tradition, they still were morally justified to rule India because they were racially superior. The raj still used "moral" arguments in their own defense but no longer deferred to spiritual standards of right and wrong in determining appro-

6

priate conduct.

Edwina Crane was a typical example of this earthly code of morality. She had been raised in genteel poverty in London. Her mother died when Edwina was very young. Her father was a school master who drank too much and who died when Edwina was twenty-one, leaving her penniless and fit for nothing (p.13). She found a position as a nanny with a well-to-do military family and came to India with them in 1906. Edwina quickly discovered that the cross of unhappiness did not belong exclusively to the realm of poverty and drunkenness. Unhappiness spread its tenacious hold even in wealthy and temperate households. Edwina realized that mere privilege did not guarantee happiness, and this truth made the world seem emotionally small just at the moment when it was physically opening up (p.14).

Instead of returning with her employers to England, Edwina chose to teach for the mission schools, even though she did not know precisely which schools were run by the Church of England (p.21). Edwina was not an ardent believer. She did not burn with zeal to save heathen souls. What faith she had was directed toward a God who was neither benign nor malign, neither destructive nor sustaining, neither creative nor destroying--merely existing and leaning his weight on the world (p.18). In her closest moments to this impersonal, featureless Presence, Edwina found him a comforter but not a redeemer, who might touch her heart without touching her soul (p.19). God affected her emotions but could not fill her with his own Life, changing and molding her to his own image. Her religious experiences were limited to the sensible order.

Edwina's attitude toward her Indian and Eurasian children was altruistic and condescending. She pitied their ignorance and hopelessness and sympathized with their hunger for free chappattis rather than for the word of God. When Edwina decided to devote her life to these children, she harbored a secret ambition. She wanted to become a source of hope for them, living proof that there was a promise of betterment and a possibility for happiness (p.25). She wanted to be a symbol like Queen Victoria, as she must have been for the first classroom of children she met, robed in her best muslin dress and seated on the dais. Edwina, like the Queen, accepted her duties altruistically. She felt a call to rid the world of the evils of poverty, disease, injustice, and ignorance (p.30). She believed, just as Hari's father Duleep Kumar did, that the world of the white man could set black children free from the chains of misery.[3] Unlike Duleep, Edwina entertained visions of playing a direct part in their liberation.

Edwina spent her life trying to prove a point: that at least one Englishman respected and admired blacks (p.11). This humanitarian, liberal "cause" was the inspiration to her sense of mission. Whatever religious faith she had did not ultimately determine her attitude toward blacks. Edwina sought to serve them in the name of her personal cause, not in the name of the Christian God. Her actions were ultimately tainted with sentimental kindness and smug generosity, a far cry from the love demanded and exemplified by a redeeming, life-giving Savior who disguised himself as a dark heathen and would be loved as such.

Years before she became district superintendent of the mission schools in Mayapore, Edwina Crane taught in a small school in Muzzafirabad. There, during the riots of 1914, she turned away an unruly and threatening mob at the door of the school house (p.26). Later, she chose to leave Muzzafirabad because the children, keeping only one eye on the blackboard and the other on the doorway, expected her to perform some other act of magic and bravery at any moment (p.26). Ironically, Edwina felt uncomfortable when the children actually associated her with the great white queen.

As a parting token of esteem the school presented her with a replica of the picture which hung in the school room entitled "A Jewel in Her Crown." It showed Queen Victoria with representatives of her Indian Empire. She sat on her throne surrounded by temporal and spiritual leaders while angels hovered overhead. An Indian prince approached the throne bearing a velvet cushion on which he offered her a large and sparkling gem--a symbol of India itself (p.27).

Edwina had mixed emotions about the picture. She knew that the image of India it projected, especially the remarkably clean and healthy-looking beggars, did not exist outside the frame. Nor did it accurately capture the true, turbulent nature of British/Indian history. The emotions which the picture was meant to conjure up were not much more than smugly pious (p.30). She was irritated by the raj habit of regarding God as a champion solely of the white community.

Yet Edwina recognized that part of this snobbery sprang from a seldom-voiced but insistent clan-gathering call to solidarity, which afforded a real enough source of comfort and protection against this frightening country (p.15). The apparently hostile environment of India, the frightening weight of limitless space and vastness heightened the raj's sense of community and instinct to survive through isolation (p.18). "There was a lot of fear in India, and it was good to feel safe," safe in the cantonment of the "charmed circle of privilege" (p.15). The raj were like frightened children who found themselves in a primitive, confusing world and chose to wrap themselves in a "magic kind of safe-guarding" and "stay within the harbour of the charmed circle" (p.33) rather than try to understand and appreciate their new environment. If the Queen Victoria picture fulfilled that need for comfort and protection, then Edwina felt there was a shadowy dignity to it after all (p.30).

Edwina did not have close friends in the white community because of her liberal sympathies, which the raj believed ran counter to their unspoken code. It mystified Edwina that she could rank as an inferior among whites and yet be regarded as superior to the highest born Indian. She believed that the raj's sense of superiority was misplaced, and that to maintain its integrity and continue its enlightened, liberal tradition, England would have to acknowledge India's ability and right to self-rule.

As an exercise in fulfilling her liberal cause, Edwina entertained a group of Indian ladies to tea once a week. These visits were not intended to be particularly friendly but they were "meaningful" from Edwina's point of view (p.44). They were gestures of solidarity, opportunities for her to exhibit her respect for and her acceptance of their skin color. The native women rightfully felt used, and when Edwina removed Mr. Gandhi's picture from her wall out of disapproval of his policies, the Indians quit coming to tea. All Edwina finally accomplished was to alienate the white community even more.

Edwina admitted to herself that she was not as unprejudiced as she wanted to be. She especially disliked Lady Chatterjee, who appeared to enjoy the best of both worlds, something which Edwina was unable to do (pp.42-43). Lady Chatterjee was a friend of several leading figures in the white community, including the district commissioner and his wife. She also entertained accomplished Indians, known for their anti-British sentiments, at MacGregor House. To Edwina it seemed as though Lady Chatterjee were playing some kind of joke at the expense of the white community.

Edwina also found it difficult to be natural with blacks. Too often she felt self-conscious, having to search for the perfect word or the appropriate English expression which the native would not misunderstand (p.51). She especially found it difficult to work with Mr. Chaudhuri, the teacher at Dibrapur. And yet both teachers were "liberals" dedicated to a cause; both were willing to make sacrifices in order to fulfill their own insignificant parts (p.30). Tragically, neither trusted the other's motives. Despite her liberal principles Edwina still harbored a hump of prejudice, "the hump, however high or low it was, which, however hard you tried, still lay in the path of thoughts you sent flowing out to a man or woman whose skin was a different colour from your own" (p.64).

In the summer of 1942 the Japanese had successfully invaded Burma while the British suffered severe losses of both men and pride. It was at this fateful moment that Gandhi attempted to mobilize his countrymen in a campaign of non-violent non-cooperation. The Indian Congress was scheduled to vote on Gandhi's civil disobedience resolution on August 8th. If the resolution were adopted and carried out, all of India would be paralyzed by strikes. The British would be incapable of moving troops and equipment to the front, and they laid plans to ensure this kind of "treachery" would not materialize.

On August 8th Congress voted to adopt Gandhi's resolution. In retaliation, the English arrested all Congressional party members along with other prominent Indian leaders, including Gandhi himself. They were imprisoned indefinitely under the Defense of

India Rules as political criminals. The English
community anticipated violent protests from the
Indian population.⁴

On August 8th Edwina Crane drove to Dibrapur for
her weekly inspection of the school. She stayed
overnight with the Chaudhuris and planned to return
to Mayapore on the 9th. Mr. Chaudhuri counseled her
to remain in Dibrapur because he anticipated serious
trouble. But Edwina insisted on driving back because
her duty was in Mayapore. She found herself
wondering how "they" always knew when things were
going to be bad (p.57). She reacted, in fact, like
a typical memsahib, and the black teacher felt
compelled to accompany her. Mr. Chaudhuri advised
Edwina to bluff her way through any crowd they
encountered along the road, and she agreed. For a
few moments Edwina felt that the two of them were
finally relating personally, as man and woman, and
not as representatives of black and white. For the
first time her virgin heart plunged into deep,
personal regard for a black person, and the experience intoxicated her.

But Edwina's exhilaration was short lived. She
could not bring herself to drive through the mob of
blacks. The ancient formulas were enacted: memsahib
Edwina could not harm the blacks for whom she felt
responsible, and the native Mr. Chaudhuri obligingly
died for the white woman whose salt he had shared.

While holding the dead teacher's hand on the
roadside in the rain, Edwina begged for forgive-
ness--for herself and her country. But there was
nothing left for Edwina (p.69). There was no
forgiveness because heaven stood vacant. There was
no hope for the children because the raj's promises
were empty. Her own cause was hypocritical and
fraudulent. She had never done anything purely for
the children, and neither had the raj. Perhaps the
children had known that all along and hoped only for
free chappattis.

In her labors against ignorance and misery
Edwina had repeatedly placed her cause ahead of
people. Her regard for blacks had never been
personal except for the brief moment in the car with
Mr Chaudhuri. She had loved all Indians dispassion-
ately in her mind, but no one Indian in her heart
(p.117). Her life had been a waste, a series of

11

missed opportunities and empty gestures (p.117).

After her release from the Mayapore hospital, Edwina returned to her solitary existence. She inquired only after Daphne Manners, as if she were a colleague (p.94). Eventually Edwina quit teaching and removed the picture of Queen Victoria from her wall because it was a painful reminder of her own years of hypocrisy. She had always believed in "simple rules for positive action" and that it was never too late to mend past mistakes (p.11). But this time there were no easy answers, no white man's magic formula to fill her life and rectify the harm she had done.

Edwina did not have the energy or the desire to sort out the moral problems surrounding the love/hate relationship between India and England (p.72). She hoped that someday white men would be able to look past the skin to the heart and know they had to keep their word. But when the young English soldiers returned to tea and snubbed her old servant Joseph, Edwina saw the same tragic thing happening again: white men distrusting and discounting a black only because of his skin color. Fulfillment of the promise seemed more remote than ever.

Lady Chatterjee once thought of Edwina Crane as a mediocre English harpy, but finally came to admire her because she had the courage to be absolutely honest (p.80). But Edwina did not have the courage or the faith to live with the truth. From a Hindu point of view Edwina did the appropriate and effi-cient thing. Dressed in white mourning garments, she entered into the state of wifely grace by becoming suttee. Mr Chaudhuri was dead and with him died her illusions and her hopes for the India she had labored so long to create. For a Hindu, her death was exemplary, the ultimate act of renunciation. But for Edwina the Christian it was the final expression of loss and despair.

Edwina Crane was a victim of the Kipling myth and of her own illusions. She had believed adamantly in the "moral drift of history." This moral drift had nothing spiritual or divine about its source, nature, or direction. It sprang from "the humane concepts of classical and Renaissance Europe" (p.33) and Edwina envisioned it as one of the great liberating and liberal forces of history. This drift was directed like

> waters of a river that had to toss
> aside logs thrown into it by pre-
> judice or carry them with it towards
> the still invisible because still
> far-distant sea of perfect harmony
> where the debris would become
> water-logged and rotten, finally dis-
> integrate, or be lost, like match-
> sticks on a majestic ocean (p.33).

England, for all its hypocrisy, had done as much as any other nation to keep the water free-flowing.

Edwina herself credited no religious impetus to this moral drift, only a social current stemming from enlightened and civilized human reason. Nonetheless, she viewed England as the party responsible, in God's absence, to ensure that prejudice did not flourish but would be swept away by the liberal policies of Whitehall. England had promised India its political freedom, and it was morally imperative that such a promise be kept. To delay or deny this freedom would signal the triumph of prejudice and the denial of the moral drift of history.

It was taken for granted in the raj community that India would be independent eventually. The issue was when and on whose terms. Robin White saw the conflict between Indian and British politicians as a kind of stubborn tug-of-war, each side demanding that the issue be resolved on its own terms. (p.357).[5]

By the time the Japanese were moving across Burma, the British sense of moral superiority had drifted from a religious to a racial basis. Without spiritual inspiration and justification, the white man became weary of his burden, but simultaneously more and more impatient with India's demands for freedom. After all the British had done for the Indians, it should not be unreasonable to expect Indians to remain loyal to the Crown during time of war, or so the English believed. But Gandhi remembered all that India did for England during the Great War, after which spoils for the black man consisted of even more repressive measures culminating in General Dyer's slaughter of hundreds of unarmed men, women and children at Amritsar in 1919.

13

From then on, Gandhi knew that the solution, the way to freedom, would be an Indian answer, and not a British one (p.346). As White observed, it was ultimately a case of a healthier and more vital Indian morality outlasting and outweighing a weaker and wearier British one (p.357).

British home government never lost sight of the inevitable goal of Indian independence. Whitehall did not retract its liberal policies even during the war. The difficulty was that day-to-day practices in India often did not reflect the official policy of England. There was a time warp between the British who made the decisions at home and the British who carried out those decisions in India. As Scott repeatedly observes, the raj still lived in the nineteenth century. They were little Kiplingites who strained official policy through the sieve of their own prejudice (p.357). Robin White and the Indian lawyer Srinivasan both referred to this time warp, this gulf between policy and practice, as the "area of dangerous fallibility between a policy and its pursuit" (pp.200, 357). No matter how honorable the official policy, no matter how sincere Whitehall was in its dedication to liberal goals, the application of those policies and the realization of those goals depended upon the Englishmen in power in India. In this "area of dangerous fallibility" between principle and action, between official position and practice, between decision and individual application, reigned the human conscience.[6]

Although White did believe in a moral drift of history, he did not assume, like Edwina Crane, that it would be propelled or directed infallibly to its proper end. "The impetus behind that drift stems in the main from our consciences" (p.357). Human choice ultimately directed the moral flow of history. Without a God to intervene, the flow of historical events depended entirely on men. The right or wrong of its direction was no longer determined by supernatural truth but was ultimately only a matter of opinion. The justice of Whitehall's official policy may have been self-evident, but in this dangerous area where the human conscience could shape events to its own prejudice, there was room for spoilers (p.462). One of those spoilers was General A.V. Reid.

Reid was not a villainous character. He was

14

simply a typical member of the raj with a Kiplingesque point of view. When he became an officer of
the Realm he accepted every one of the responsibilities of that way of life (p.296), which for him
meant performing his duty to country before fulfilling his personal obligations. Since he was willing
to put aside his private concerns during a time of
crisis, he expected blacks to do the same. The mere
promise of independence should have been enough to
guarantee Britain's good will and sincere dedication
to that ultimate goal. In time of war even Gandhi's
policy of non-violent noncooperation had to be
regarded as seditious.

Reid disliked Gandhi's type of Indian, educated
and westernized, with all the advantages of white men
but treacherously ungrateful in their political
attempts to rid India of their benefactors. Perfect
black subjects, according to Reid, were docile,
single-minded workers toiling to survive. Reid could
be deeply moved by the sight of pregnant women and
small children tending fields in the scorching sun
while vigilant memsahibs stood by to help the women
who collapsed. This was the real India, the way
things were meant to be. These natives understood
the value of work, appreciated what was done for
them, and were willing to leave sophisticated political issues to the superior white mind (pp.313-14).

General Reid's flaw was that he saw things only
from a British point of view. He was sensitive to
the greater emotions like patriotism, duty, and the
satisfaction of a job well done. The War Week
Exhibition held on the Mayapore maidan in April of
1942 had been Reid's inspiration. The raj needed an
emotional boost, needed to hear the stirring fanfare
of military marches and see flags waving proudly and
freely. But Reid was totally insensitive to the
needs and feelings of blacks as individuals. He did
not actually respect or admire them and assumed they
were incapable of handling the complicated machinery
of democratic forms of government. In light of this
posture toward the blacks, he was willing to postpone
Indian independence indefinitely and eagerly retal-
iated against any overt action of dissent or violence
against the Crown with quick and absolute reprisal.
When Reid said Indians and British must sink their
differences in time of war and work together for the
common good, what he really meant, in practice, was
that Indians should do all the sinking for Britain's

good (p.339). As White learned from working with
Reid during the August riots, Reid tended to bear the
proportional weight of a sledgehammer to a pin in his
daily contact with people (p.338).

Reid's India was not the true India, black
India. His Mayapore was not Hari Kumar's Mayapore.
When Reid was posted to Mayapore, images sprang to
mind that would occur only to a white man: quaint,
nineteenth century Indian architecture, duck-shooting
on the lake, access to Darjeeling during the hot
season or train connections to Calcutta if he managed
some time off. As new military commander, Reid moved
the native troops back on the plains and transferred
the white Berkshire regiment to Mayapore where the
men could be billeted in decent housing, eat decent
food, be waited on by servants, and otherwise enjoy
the privileges white soldiers of the Realm deserved.
In his private journal, Reid commented: "Conscious
of the problem involved in appearing to make a
distinction I nevertheless felt that Johnny Jawan
would be less uncomfortable in Banyaganj than was
Tommy Atkins" (p.286).

In contemplating the white sector of Mayapore,
the orderly cantonment and eye-pleasing maidan, Reid
reflected on the wisdom, serenity, and enduring
nature of British rule. The white quarter functioned
as a living symbol for Reid, as he believed it should
for all of black Mayapore as well. It set an example
and indicated the course to which natives should
aspire (p.290).

This cantonment, the site of physical isolation
of white from black, was a prerequisite to the raj's
psychological survival.   The sea of nameless black
faces, the endless spectacle of misery and disease,
and the sense of vast space and immense weight and
flatness oppressed white exiles, even Edwina Crane
and Daphne Manners (pp.9,18,193,209). Despite their
liberal sentiments, they both experienced these
frightening aspects of Indian life and needed to
enjoy the comfort of being among their own kind
(p.115).

The cantonment served as a safe harbor, a
reassuring refuge not only for new-comers like Colin
Lindsey but for raj who enjoyed a long-time Indian
connection as well.   This exclusive section was a
little bit of India transformed into an image of

16

their English homeland where the whites lived in "protective purdah" (p.346). There the raj created their narrow, insular, segrated, tight little circle where they would not be bothered by any blacks except clean and respectful servants. Among their own kind, whites did not have to guard their tongues or seek the perfect, literal expression they so often had to use in dealing with the natives. Even Daphne needed this respite and recognized herself, or at least part of herself, in this neat, enclosed green oasis of the maidan.

By creating their cantonment, the raj sustained an illusion of English life which spread like a thin, protective veneer between them and the real India. Their sense of racial superiority dictated this isolated life, a life which kept the black world across the river shrouded in mystery--still a foreign land. This isolation fueled the white man's primitive fears and his instincts to attack what he did not know and did not understand. In this refuge the raj inevitably became trapped by their own prejudice. Their white skin was a sign of moral superiority, of identity, and of purpose. To open up their world and to abandon their illusions and prejudices meant they would have to rely on an essential, interior dignity to justify their presence (p.171). But a sense of this kind of dignity vanished along with a sense of the presence and intervention of God. So the raj guarded their cantonment against all native trespassers, even against Hari Kumar, who needed such a refuge as much as any other Englishman but who would never be allowed to experience the security, ease, and privileges of white Mayapore because of his black skin.

What was impossible for Hari was impossible for all Indians. They would never be allowed into the white man's world as equals. This truth formed the core of Edwina Crane's despair. The false hope represented by the Queen Victoria picture was an example of truth as perceived (sieved) through the white man's prejudice. The dignified princes in the picture were really petty despots, and the wise politicans were shrewd economists who exploited India for their own profit. God could not possibly approve of such a transaction, assuming He was attentive to man's activity in the first place. The picture did not capture the ugly power struggles, the violence, injustice, distrust, and hatred of the real India.

For all its advantages, Daphne came to recognize
life within the cantonment for what it really was:
small, ingrown, and hateful (p.115). The benefits of
white solidarity were soured for her by the accom-
panying spirit of conformity and the incubating
atmosphere for racial hatred. After she met Hari,
club life impressed her more and more as boring and
shallow. What particularly oppressed her were white
women's attitudes toward black men. To regard
themselves as racially superior they mentally had to
emasculate and shame millions of black men, even
muscular, handsome men like Hari Kumar, in every-day
dealings (p.427). Daphne found such an attitude
unnatural to feminine psychology and destructive of
women's natural sexual responses.

II

Duleep Kumar came from a wealthy, landowning
family in the United Provinces. At an early age he
resolved to break away from this Hindu, land-locked
tradition and study law, so that he would one day
grant favors like the white sahibs (pp.212-213).
Duleep failed in his own life to achieve his
professional goals because his "passion for achievement was always just that much greater than his
ability to achieve" (p.214). He believed his failure
resulted from remaining too Indian. Power and
influence in India did not mean having land or money
or many sons. Real power resided in the ability to
speak, to think, and to act as an Englishman (p.215).
Initially, Duleep regarded his marriage as disastrous
to his personal goals. But the birth of his son Hari
gave him new hope. Perhaps Hari could achieve what
he himself never could. Duleep's wife died in
childbirth, but he still had to remain in India two
more years to take care of his mother since his
father had become sannyasi and left the family home
months before. Finally, with all his familial duties
discharged, Duleep fled from India with his two-year
old son.

In England Hari enjoyed the best public schools
and houses full of servants. Duleep was careful to
stay away so that Hari would not be "contaminated" by
his still too-Indian father, and later so he would
not be ashamed of him. In a sense, Duleep achieved
his primary goal: he made Hari a true Englishman in

every way except his skin (pp.210-231). Duleep knew, from his own experience, that there was no future for an Indian in an Anglo-Indian world (p.225). What he failed to understand was that there was no future for any black man in India, no matter how "English" he was on the inside. All that counted was skin color. And for the mistake of being an English-Indian there would be an especially high price to pay.

In 1938 Duleep lost his fortune and committed suicide. He was unable to face his son or his son's fate. Hari, having no money to finish his education at Chillingborough, was forced to join his Aunt Shalini in Mayapore and face life on the black side of the river. In the four years before Bibighar, Hari changed from a carefree, pampered English athlete to a bitter, tortured black man trapped by the color of his skin. Everything about Hari's life was ugly and squalid (p.240), from the stench of the river bank where the untouchables emptied their bowels, to his own starkly furnished bedroom with iron bars on the windows and cockroaches running free on the floors and walls. The apartment complex at Chillianwallah Bagh was twenty years old, "modern" by Indian standards. It was a typical example of Hindu construction with native bathrooms piped to the outer walls, which permitted human waste to drain down the walls to the ground. At night Hari could hardly breathe from the heat and the stench, and in the morning he would be awakened by the sound of crows.[7] To face life in black India he had to debase all his civilized instincts (p.241).

For the first few months Hari remained in his room, sickened by the nightmarish illusion which had become his life. But he was not by nature a coward, and eventually resolved to force this impossible situation to its unimaginable but logical conclusion (p.239). He tried working in his uncle's warehouse, but his sahib manner evoked envy and suspicion from his black co-workers. Hari found the common Hindu variety of the English language appalling, and the reader can imagine him moving aside lest a native brush against him.

Facing the threat of an arranged marriage, Hari resolved to end his financial dependence on his uncle and strike out on his own, hoping to find a job in the white man's world. He applied with the British-Indian Electrical Company, and after his initial

interview with a fellow Chillingboroughan felt hopeful that he would be hired in a managerial position
and sent to England for training. But his interview
for the technical aspect of the postion was with a
man of inferior accent and education who did not like
"bolshie black laddies" on his side of the business
(p.258). After Hari expressed ignorance to all the
questions raised, his interrogator taunted him:
"Where are you from, laddie? Straight down from the
tree?" (p.258) Hari walked out of the interview and
did not get the job, because he would not crawl for
the white man (p.258).

At first Hari shared his father's belief that
once he became the kind of Indian Englishmen recognized, he would be welcomed into the white man's
world. But Hari's Englishness was a hindrance rather
than a help. His ability to speak superior English
and his public education threatened and infuriated
blacks and whites alike. Instead of being recognized
as one of their own and being welcomed into the white
world, Hari met only with contempt. The more he was
rejected in the white man's world the more he feared
falling into the black and clung desperately to his
Englishness which was being stripped away layer by
layer (p.239). At night Hari would lie in bed and
speak aloud to himself to detect traces of a
contaminating accent.

As the memory of England and his sense of
identity continued to slip away, Hari depended more
and more on Colin Lindsey's letters. His relationship with Colin was his one source of assurance that
his former life had been real and that he still
counted as an Englishman. But Hari could not bring
himself to be honest with Colin about what life in
black India was really like. He could not unburden,
even to his closest friend, all the fear and shame
which filled his days.[8] Hari's silence misled Colin
to believe that his friend was doing well and that
nothing had changed substantially in Hari's life or
in their relationship. Colin's letters reflected his
illusions, and this one remaining life-line to
England served to heighten Hari's sense of loss and
isolation.

Hari finally admitted to Sr. Ludmila that he and
Colin no longer spoke the same language (p.277), an
ironic statement since all they held in common was
language. What Hari began to realize, though he had

20

not fully faced the painful truth, was that unless he
continued to share cultural experiences with Colin,
the bond of common language would not prove strong
enough to sustain their friendship.

But Hari did not want to share his new world
with Colin. And Colin, once he had witnessed what
life in black India was really like, did not want to
be touched by such an existence. After being in
India for several weeks, Colin's unit was stationed
in Mayapore in late February, 1942, but Hari received
no friendly summons from Colin. By chance they
encountered each other on the maidan while Hari was
reporting on a cricket match for the Mayapore
Gazette. Hari waited for a sign from Colin, a sign
of recognition, of acceptance, of affirmation, but it
did not come. Underneath the babu clothes was a
person Colin should have known, but did not (p.282).

Hari discovered, in this final rejection, the
lie that Edwina painfully uncovered, the source of
their mutual despair. No black would ever be
accepted by white men in India. There was no future
for Hari, no hope, and no pardon from this fate. In
England the color of his skin had been an asset, if
anything, because of Whitehall's liberal policies.
But between England and India, between this policy of
right reason and its implementation, was the "area of
dangerous fallibility" dominated by the spoilers who,
through moral choice, ruled according to their own
prejudice, ignorance, fear, and cruelty.

Hari finally understood that white and black
could never meet on equal terms in India. He did not
blame his father's illusions or his wasted life. He
blamed the English for fostering and then denying
that hope. Ethel Manners admitted that a man like
Hari Kumar was an English creation and responsibility, the "loose-end of our reign" (p.475). Hari
had no place in either white or black world. He was
not allowed in the white world and its safe,
reassuring cantonment, though he found black India as
hateful and foreign a place as any other white man.
Even if he had wanted to become a productive member
of black society, Hari had no clear idea of how to be
a "good" Indian. It could mean he should toil in the
fields like a peasant and care only about filling his
stomach. Or it might mean joining the Indian army to
fight with the British against the Japanese or
enlisting in Chandras Bose's Free Indian Army to wage

war against the Crown. He could be a rich prince and share tea with white officials while his black subjects starved or demonstrate with Mohammed Ali Jinnah for a separate Muslim state (pp.273-74).

There seemed to be no answers for Hari Kumar. The Englishman with black skin had to accept the truth: he was invisible to white people, even to Colin. Despite his English manner, speech, education, and pride, he was nothing at all (p.282). By the time Sr. Ludmila found him drunk on the river bank, anger was etched clearly in his facial expression even when he was unconscious. He had reached a point of personal crisis when the darkness inside him triumphed. He hated the whole stinking country, the people who lived in it and the people who ruled it (p.425).

Hari's determination to reject (p.283) the Englishness he used as a protective armor and his refusal to know "his place" as a black native made him a perfect target for the darkest spoiler of all: Ronald Merrick. It would perhaps surprise Edwina Crane to say that her absentee God helped create and empower a person like Merrick. But the absence of supernatural norms in human conduct gave free rein to Merrick who, if he had his way, would redirect and ultimately deny what Edwina envisioned as the moral drift of history.

On the surface Merrick appeared to be a typical member of the white community, like General Reid. He was born of a poor but hard-working family. Through his own efforts he completed the education appropriate to his social class. As a child he bore the brunt of ridicule and harsh jokes, having to fight his way out of many confrontations. Such a life was lonely and humiliating for an intelligent boy whose ambitions would only be frustrated if he remained in England.

India offered Merrick the kind of opportunities that would never have been his at home. He rose quickly through the civil ranks and within a few years became District Superintendent of Police, neither a glamouous nor heroic distinction, but important nonetheless. General Reid respected Merrick's attitude and talents, and privately commissioned him to ferret out the secret but true leaders of Gandhi's movement who hid behind Congress's apron

22

strings (pp.292-93). He was a competent, energetic policeman, and even Robin White thought Merrick a capable and reliable officer.

In India Merrick could socialize with a class of people who would have had nothing to do with him in England. Like Edwina Crane, he found himself suddenly regarded as superior for the first time in his life, superior to millions of natives because of his white skin. For this insecure man from the lower middle class who was unprincipled and irreligious it was easy, even necessary, to believe that the white man's superiority was racial instead of cultural and moral. That was why color mattered "like hell." "It's basic," he told Daphne (p.417). It was basic in all of Merrick's dealings, an excuse, a "cause" which justified all his mean, small and overt acts of cruelty and prejudice.

It was no accident that Daphne came to associate Ronald Merrick with club life. He was an adamant, vigilant guardian of the cantonment's physical isolation and the white man's biological purity. Lady Chatterjee described Merrick as handsome were it not for a perpetual sneer in his eyes (p.91) which was directed at all blacks, even the daughter of a Rajput prince. He took himself and his position seriously yet he bent the rules, turned his back, and used the law as a cloak to hide his own private acts of cruelty. This was the "quantity left out of the official equation" (p.200), that area where Whitehall's policies gave way to personal passion and prejudice.

In The Jewel in the Crown Paul Scott begins to develop an image which he will employ and expand throughout the entire Raj Quartet: the image of light vs. darkness. In parts of the world further away from the equator than India, the rhythm of light and dark determined one's sense of time, "the way it expands and contracts and organises the seasons" (p.428).[9] Within the perimeters of Scott's work, light and darkness take on moral dimensions as well which roughly coincide with good and evil.

There was the darkness of shadows cast by Englishmen who were very conscious, as they walked in the Indian sun, of their length or shortness (p.168). There was the darkness of India's immense, featureless landscape at night, and the deeper shadow cast

by the Bibighar wall (p.9). After the death of her
father, Edwina's own future looked as dark and
mysterious as the black, featureless plains of India
(p.20).

Daphne thought of her unborn child as a "creature of the dark, a tiny living mirror of that awful
night" of fear, violence, and pain (p.390). Duleep
Kumar's fatal flaw was the dark root of compromise
(p.220), and Edwina believed that Gandhi's policy of
nonviolence must have a "dark side" if he thought the
Japanese would be better masters than the British, or
if he wanted the Japanese to do his violence for him
(p.10). Letters from Colin darkened Hari's day
(p.239) because they only reminded him of the
hopelessness of his life, which appeared more and
more to be a product of the disastrous designs of a
malign spirit (p.245).

The most important image of darkness is that
which surrounds and describes the two main antagon-
ists. Hari Kumar was a "black-haired deep brown boy,
a creature of the dark" (p.133). The image of
darkness described his inner state more than the
color of his skin. Sr. Ludmila thought of it as a
"darkness of soul" (p.159) emanating from bitterness,
anger and despair.

Merrick, too, was a spirit of darkness, but his
was a darkness of the mind, heart, and flesh (p.159).
There was a wall between himself and everyone else, a
veil of physical and emotional coldness which revealed itself in a lack of true candidness (p.113).
He was never open or honest and never really gave of
himself even with Daphne. The motive for his actions
could inevitably be reduced to jealousy, suspicion,
and hatred, all complicated by a mixture of social
inferiority and racial bigotry. Merrick had locked
himself away from black India and from any rewarding
human relationship. He was a prisoner inside his own
skin, much like Hari Kumar.

Sr. Ludmila witnessed the first meeting between
Kumar and Merrick. Both were handsome and muscular,
though the black man was more handsome than the
white. Both were well educated, though the black was
better educated than the white. One stood quietly
buttoning his cuffs while the other watched him, a
gun slung across his hips, smiling in a way "that
keeps you out of his thoughts" (p.142). They were

drawn together, these two spirits of darkness (p.146). Their meeting was not accidental. It was destined from the beginning (p.139). "Two such darknesses in opposition can create a blinding light. Against such a light ordinary mortals must hide their eyes" (p.146).

There was no way of retreat. Merrick chose the tragic, twisted path (p.144) because the old resentment was there, between the haves and the have-nots. But in this case both Kumar and Merrick had experienced two sides of the coin. In England Hari had enjoyed all the privileges which were denied to Merrick. In India the tables were turned. In the confrontation between this cultured, educated English gentleman of black skin and an ambitious white man from a deprived background there was only one possible ending: the tragedy of Bibighar. Merrick would have it no other way.

Hari Kumar threatened Merrick's sense of racial superiority and shallow identity. Hari regarded the color of his skin as an accident of birth, irrelevant to his true identity as an Englishman. Merrick believed skin color was so essential to a person's identity that it made any other "accidental" quality, such as speech or education, irrelevant. He hated Hari Kumar because Kumar would not bow to the truth of this prejudice. And yet, as Sr. Ludmila sensed, there was something else involved in Merrick's response to Hari, what she regarded as Merrick's darkness of the flesh (p.159). There was the attraction of white to black, the attraction of an opposite, but in an unnatural context. Merrick desired as well as hated the black man. He was excited by Hari's hatred, repulsed by and yet drawn to Hari's blackness and to the kind of westernized, educated, handsome Indian he was.

At that crucial moment in the Sanctuary Ronald Merrick stood "high and dry on the sterile banks" (p.159), defying Edwina's moral drift of history, anchored down by the prejudices of a small man of inferior position and by a private compulsion he as yet had not acknowledged (p.159). In the "area of dangerous fallibility" where human choice determined Hari Kumar's destiny, it was a tragic, twisted course of events which placed Hari in the path of a man like Merrick. Nothing came to Merrick spontaneously, easily, or happily (p.406). He could not love, only

25

punish (p.165). This was the man who chose Hari
Kumar as his victim, and who later, because of
Bibighar, punished him with all the force of the
white man's law.

III

        MacGregor House was originally built in the
eighteenth century by an Indian prince who fell in
love with a singer of classical music. He installed
her in the house where she sang for him morning and
evening; a Scheherizade performing to save her honor.
Eventually the prince came to love only her voice,
that part of herself she gave to him. When she died,
the house was closed and fell into ruin (p.75).

        The prince's son despised him for harboring an
attachment that was never consummated. The son built
his own monument to love a mile away, which he called
Bibighar, meaning "house of women," and installed
his private brothel. He watched his father's house
fall into ruin and thought, "Such is the fate of love
never made manifest" (p.147).

        The son was a selfish, lecherous despot who
squandered his fortune and tyrannized his subjects.
After an Englishman was poisoned in his court, the
prince was imprisoned and his lands impounded.
Thirty years later a Scotsman named MacGregor bought
the older house, the house of the singer, and rebuilt
it for his bride. It became known as MacGregor
House, the place of the whites, a mile away from
Bibighar, the house of black courtesans.

        The English version of the story related that
MacGregor burned Bibighar because it was a place of
abomination in his eyes and in the eyes of the Lord.
But the Indians believed that MacGregor had fallen in
love with one of the Indian girls who spurned him for
a black lover, and that both the courtesan and her
lover perished in the fire (pp.149-150).

        MacGregor, his wife Janet, and their baby were
later murdered by mutinous sepoys. The young wife
was said to haunt MacGregor House, to warn white
people that this was not a good place for them to be
(p.150). But Lili Chatterjee was never bothered by

ghosts. During her years of habitation she continually filled MacGregor House with white and black guests. It was one of the few places in Mayapore where Indians and English could mix without too much embarrassment on the part of the English and too much caution on the part of the Indians (p.41).

Bibighar was never rebuilt. The garden strayed wildly, the way Indians liked gardens to be. Daphne's first response at seeing Bibighar was "How Indian!" And yet it reflected something broader about "human acts and desires that leave their mark in the most unexpected and sometimes chilling way" (pp.413-14). Bibighar was not just a place, it was a condition, a state of "something having gone badly wrong at one time that hadn't yet been put right but could be if only you knew how" (p.413). Bibighar, in ruins, was the sign of love made manifest and a reminder of the possible consequences.

There was a special relationship between the house of the singer and the house of the courtesans. Between them flowed dark currents of human conflict, the flow of an invisible river which might have been traced by following the route taken by the girl running in the darkness from one to the other. No bridge was ever thrown across this current to stand between the house of the white and the house of the black. To get across one had to "take your courage in your hands and enter the flood and let yourself be taken with it, lead where it may" (p.151). This, observed Sr. Ludmila, was the kind of courage Daphne Manners had.

Daphne was born in Punjab but, like Hari, moved to England when she was very young. Daphne's mother hated life in India and for her sake, her father took up medical practice in Wiltshire. But Daphne believed he always regretted leaving India and was never truly happy in England. She sadly watched him methodically work himself to death. Shortly before the war Daphne's mother died of cancer, and later her brother was killed in France. For a brief time she drove an ambulance during the Blitz, but when a doctor warned her to quit because of her heart, Daphne was forced to join her only living relative, Mrs. Henry (Ethel) Manners.

Henry Manners served as a provincial governor in India some years before, and his administration was

27

remembered as just and benevolent. While he was
governor, Henry and Ethel became good friends with
Sir Nello and Lili Chatterjee. For the two women,
this friendship survived beyond the deaths of their
husbands.

After spending a few months with her Aunt Ethel
in Rawalpindi, Daphne came to live with Lady Chatterjee in MacGregor House. The young English girl felt
responsible to love India for her father's sake. But
loving India did not come easily. Daphne, like many
newly-arrived Englishmen, was overwhelmed by the
physical vastness, the stinking millions, the foreign
culture, and the heat. She was repelled and
frightened, and suffered from a "permanent sinking of
heart" (P.114). She had a recurring nightmare of a
sea of black, nameless faces, all individuated but
unknown to her. Daphne, like Hari, found herself a
stranger in a foreign land in returning to her
birthplace. Her defensive reactions involved hating
everything around her (p.115).

But her hatred quickly dissolved into an attraction, and that attraction into love. Even then a
pure, unqualified love for India proved difficult to
maintain. Like Edwina, Daphne found it difficult to
be perfectly natural with the Indians she met at
MacGregor House. To her shame, there even were
moments when she mistrusted Lady Chatterjee (p.115).
Daphne had vowed never to patronize the exclusively
white club because of its narrow prejudice and smug
self-righteousness. But Daphne soon discovered that
club life met a need she had not anticipated: a need
to be among her own kind (p.115). Like Edwina, she
craved contact with someone or something familiar,
dependable and proven (p.114). Her relief in finding
it at the club was so intense that it took her
several visits to realize that the whites there did
not entirely trust her because she lived at MacGregor
House.

There were several parallels between Daphne and
Edwina. Both women had lost their immediate families, neither approved of the raj's prejudiced
attitude toward blacks yet did not feel entirely at
ease with natives. But Daphne was not just another
Edwina Crane doomed to a tragic end. The important
difference was that Edwina's posture toward India was
essentially a political statement--a sacred duty, a
liberal cause. Her life was full of impersonal

28

gestures: having native women or English soldiers to tea, displaying Gandhi's picture with honor or removing it with disapproval, staying with but not enjoying the Chaudhuris in Dibrapur.

Daphne's response to India was personal, not political. She did not make "significant" gestures. For all her failings, Daphne did not end her life in empty despair. She never divided her life into parts like Edwina did, one set of liberal responses on the outside and another more reserved, withdrawn set on the inside. Daphne had no causes; she only lived a full and whole existence (p.152). She wanted to give all of herself, all her resources to the world, not just a small portion of her thoughts or a little piece of her heart. That kind of holistic, complete response demanded courage, the courage to leap into the current between black and white worlds which spanned the distance between Bibighar and MacGregor. Daphne resolved to meet Hari Kumar in the current, preferring a fleeting moment of being fully alive before drowning to remaining safe but empty and unloved on the bank (p.151).

Loving Hari proved as difficult as loving India, and in a sense they began as the same kind of love. Rather than being attracted by his handsome, Western appearance, Daphne was excited and yet frightened by his blackness. She was drawn to the Other, the Unknown, and grew to love and desire his black body (p.439) despite Hari's lukewarm response. From the moment they first met at MacGregor House Daphne recognized a sadness in Hari, a sadness which made him uncommunicative and distrusting. He was also "prickly" and easily offended (p.381). There was an anger inside him which made him misjudge her good intentions (pp.380-82). He did not, as many blacks would have, set out to cultivate her affections.

When they met for a second time on the maidan during the War Week Exhibition, Daphne experienced a yearning for meaning beyond the boring and super-ficial existence she led at the club. She sensed that she could find that meaning with Hari. Ever since her ambulance-driving days in England, she felt that her time was short (pp.373-74, 385, 389). She now knew how and with whom she wanted to spend her remaining days. With Ronald Merrick looking on, Daphne extended an invitation for Hari to come to MacGregor House, to enter into the fullest and most meaningful few months of her ill-fated life.

In his four years of exile Hari had learned that
the English did not solicit the friendship of blacks
except out of pity, or for selfish purposes. For
many weeks Hari assumed Daphne's gesture of friendship was calculated and hypocritical. He had been
invisible to whites for so long that he had despaired
of ever being recognized as a valuable person, let
alone as an attractive man, by anyone in the white
community. This prejudice, combined with intense
bitterness and anger, made it impossible for Hari to
express any softer feelings or physical affection for
Daphne. Small, natural gestures like holding hands
became a major issue because of his distrust.

Daphne understood that the initial expression of
desire and defiance had to come from Hari or it would
not be natural or human; it would not be appropriate
to their sexes (p.425). She did not take charge or
force the issue like a typical memsahib. But the
longer she waited for a sign from Hari, the more
fearful she became that he might be associating with
her for all the wrong reasons. She was not beautiful
after all, but tall and plain, near-sighted and
clumsy. All the prejudices and suspicions of her
race, which she rejected in principle, surfaced and
fueled her own feelings of insecurity. Still, she
waited for a sign from Hari which never came because
Hari did not trust her. He believed, until the night
they visited the Tirupati temple together, that
Daphne knew all long Merrick was the officer who
arrested him, and by seeing them both, was playing
him for a fool (p.425).

Their relationship was riddled with other difficulties. From the beginning, they were too self-conscious. In raj society such a friendship could not
develop naturally. Whenever Daphne and Hari were
together in public, they felt disapproval and animos-
ity press around them. They were forced to meet in
isolated, out-of-the-way places such as Bibighar and
the Sanctuary. There were few places where they
could otherwise see each other. Hari was not allowed
in establishments reserved for Englishmen, and he
would not subject Daphne to places fit for his kind.

But the obstacle between them, even more damag-
ing than their own personal reservations or social
condemnation, was India itself. On the evening they

30

met to visit the Tirupati temple Hari tried to turn
Daphne against him by behaving like a "typical"
Indian male. He was rude and self-centered, he ate
with his fingers and ignored the house servants.
After playing Indian music on the phonograph for
Daphne, he took her to the temple in a bicycle tonga.
Everything Indian was part of Hari's personal prison
and objects of his hatred. But Daphne not only
accepted these aspects of Indian culture, she appreciated and preferred them. She was not simply
willing to overlook Hari's transparent attempt to
offend her. She had cultivated a love for India which
Hari would never share. If Daphne sought to find
India by loving Hari, she would never possess either
of them.

Paradoxically, in cultivating a relationship
with Hari, Daphne discovered the world of black
Mayapore. This was not the same black society she
met at MacGregor House--the world of Lady Chatterjee,
Judge Menen, or Srinivasan the lawyer. Through Hari,
Daphne met Aunt Shalini and became involved with Sr.
Ludmila and her work at the Sanctuary. Knowing Hari
expanded the horizons of her experience.

At the same time, as she grew to love Hari,
Daphne isolated, interiorized, and protectively
guarded her love from the spoilers. Loving Hari
added meaning and happiness to her life--a tiny spot
of interior joy (p.405). That small piece of
territory, where she was most comfortable and most
herself, became her own enclosed circle, her own
inner cantonment which no one else could share.

Daphne's life fragmented into three parts
(pp.411-12). Her most private and joyful part was
the life she shared with Hari. She was another
person at MacGregor House, only partially herself,
living with and loving Aunt Lili, and being involved
in the movements of important Mayapore society. Then
there was her life at the club, where she could relax
in a familiar and proven atmosphere. The world of
the club was Ronald Merrick's world. It signified
flag-waving and the security of white man's law,
English superiority, and responsibility.

In the scenes between Daphne and her white
suitor, the reader sees the best aspects of Merrick's
character, aspects which would never again be manifested. The intimate dinner they shared at his

31

bungalow was filled with touching coincidences, sensitivity, and poignancy. Merrick's home was spartan yet tasteful, with an underlying vein of sensuality. It would have been a perfect evening and a perfect match, except that the entire episode was orchestrated, step by step, to lead up to the moment when Merrick proposed to her, a moment devoid of warmth, candor, or passion. Even in his most vulnerable moment, he was a calculating machine, intent on pursuing and destroying Hari Kumar and whoever else stood in the way.

It was impossible that these fragments of her life would remain separate. Destiny drew Merrick and Kumar together, those kindred spirits of darkness, and Daphne was caught in the middle of their conflict, the third angle to this "dangerous geometrical arrangement of personalities" (p.140), this triangular web with all its twisted and tragic turns. After Merrick warned her about her imprudent "association" with Hari, Daphne recognized that the white man's prejudice was cruel and ignorant no matter how it was manifested. Merrick was not really a conscientious friend and officer of the law. He was the Dark Shadow just on the edge of her life (p.405). Merrick's brand of prejudice as manifested in club life meant conforming to an idea, "a charade played round a phrase: white superiority" (p.427). Daphne realized that the moral issue had gone sour. "We're back to basics, the basic issue of who jumps and who says jump" (p.427). The motivation for men like Merrick was lust for power and the primitive instinct to attack and destroy what he did not understand (p.428).

When Daphne and Hari finally made love in Bibighar Garden on that fateful night of August 9, 1942, their coupling was not a pure, selfless experience of love. "This was not me and Hari. Entering me he made me cry out. And then it was us" (p.433). Both wanted desperately to be loved, to be alone no longer. But Bibighar, with its violent and lecherous past, was no Eden where a man and woman could walk innocently with God. The couple's time to savor paradise in each other's arms was tragically short. For a moment they lay peacefully together while Daphne traced the miracle of Hari's black ear. "They came....Suddenly. Climbing onto the platform. My nightmare faces" (p.433). Their love was doomed just as her very life was doomed. Raj society made it virtually impossible for their relationship to thrive. And when they finally jumped into the current together, they were caught up in far-reaching historical events which devoured them in their tumultuous and impersonal wake.

After her attack, Daphne was tortured by uncertainty and guilt. In the moment of crisis she had resorted to that hateful memsahib posture just as Edwina had. She presumed that she knew how to deal with the situation better than Hari, and that her judgment was the correct one. She thought Hari lacked the white man's cunning necessary to save himself and refused to let him take charge and deal with the dangers threatening them as a man should. Later, Daphne was haunted by the knowledge that Hari was being punished because of her lies. But the truth would damn him as well. There was nothing Daphne could do to intervene between the man she loved and his cruel and unjust fate in an Anglo-Indian world.

Daphne was indifferent to the political repercussions of the Bibighar "outrage." The attacks on both herself and Edwina Crane had alerted and mobilized the white community against the ultimate danger and basest form of civil disruption: violation of white women. Young blacks like Vidyasagar were quick to use the fate of the six Bibighar "martyrs" as an excuse for rioting and armed confrontation with the British. The situation was further aggravated by General Reid's belligerent show of force and the absence of Congressional leaders who perhaps would have shepherded the mob's energies into non-violent confrontations.

During the first few days of rioting, the raj regarded Edwina and Daphne as martyrs, as innocent victims. But as it became apparent that neither would identify her assailants (and Daphne even threatened to suggest that her rapists could have been English soldiers with their faces blacked) the whites began to regard the two victims as traitors. A rumor, which could be traced back to Ronald Merrick, detailed a cruel account of how Hari had wanted to attract Daphne for vain and egotistical reasons, and how Daphne, plain enough to be flattered, fell into his trap. In Bibighar Hari attempted to show Daphne which was the master race and arranged for some of his anti-British friends to do the same. The entire incident was as much Daphne's fault as Hari's. Both she and Edwina had been very naive in their personal associations with blacks. It did not surprise anyone in the white community that they got what they deserved.

Daphne's courage never failed her. Despite the social pressures and the scandal, she adamantly resolved to keep her baby. She was willing, even eager to accept all the consequences of jumping into the current and all the consequences of loving an Indian. She wanted to have his baby like a nameless black peasant. She did not want to play raj and be saved from an unpleasant fate because she could afford a clever doctor.

It is possible that Daphne subconsciously willed to die just as Edwina chose to die. She had the courage to love Hari but not the will to live without him. There was nothing she could do to save him. "There's nothing I can do, nothing, nothing" (p.436). Her words echoed Edwina's as Daphne faced the same feelings of despair, violation, and futility. She had thought she was running free, chasing the sun-god, when all the time she was rooted clumsily in the earth (p.390).[10]

Yet during the months she carried her baby, Daphne was like a woman in the state of grace (p.165). Despite the curiosity and slander surrounding her name she discovered, through the pregnancy, the fullness of a meaningful and loving experience. Her child would be a sign of her defiance to white prejudice and a witness to a forbidden love: Daphne's "typically ham-fisted offering to the future!" (p.376)

Ethel Manners watched Parvati's birth, the birth that killed the young mother. Despite all the worry, disapproval, and sorrow at her niece's difficulties, she felt that she was "begin born again myself. It was a miracle and it made you realise that no miracle is beautiful because it exists on a plane of experience where words like beauty have no meaning whatsoever" (p.472). Out of all the sorrow, the courage, the love, the misunderstanding, and the heartache came this child with light brown skin and a tint of red in her hair. Ethel Manners retreated into silence because she could not find words for this momentous and significant event.

Silence plays an important part in this first volume. Daphne observed that "behind all the chatter and violence of India--what a deep, lingering silence" (p.468). The silence of India was the silence of the Lord Siva dancing in a circle of fire (p.468). In his hands he held the powers of order and chaos, of creation and destruction.[11] His entire body was poised as if he were about to take flight--the left leg held in the air, the right leg tensed to spring into action, and wings ready to ascend. His figure was action carved in stone with the right foot planted firmly on the ground: of this world yet not (p.410). The Lord Siva smiled in his dance.

The silence of India was the silence of the Lord Vishnu (p.468), sleeping manifestation of Lord Venkataswara the preserver. His body lay in peaceful repose like the country of India itself. He, like Siva, smiled in his pose as if ready to awake at any moment, again like India, when the fear of white skins and the weariness of subjection wore too thin (p.468).

The silence of India was the silence deliberately broken by and punctuating its music. It was the only music Daphne knew that consciously broke silence or retreated back into it when it was finished, as if to prove that every man-made sound was an illusion (p.468). The singer in the first MacGregor House broke the silence and used her music to protect her honor. Later, a young Eurasian singer also broke the silence, closing The Jewel in the Crown with a morning raga.

The silence of India was the soundless laboring of black peasants for long hours under the scorching sun. It was the rebuke never spoken by black lips after an insult from white. It was the helpless response of an affluent India to the endless and crushing sorrow, shame, and hopelessness of poor India.

Daphne's arrival startled both black and white India out of their silence and repose. Even twenty years later MacGregor House echoed with the sounds of the clumsy young girl: glass shattered, flower beds violated, an endless flow of nervous chatter. After Bibighar, Daphne was surrounded by attention, gossip, and disapproval. Yet within herself she felt the

oppressive burden of her own trap of lies and webs of
silence which had surrounded her throughout her
association with Hari.

Silence, as developed by Scott, is many-faceted.
There was the strained silence between Edwina Crane
and Mr. Chaudhuri, a silence laced with distrust,
misunderstanding and prejudice. After her attack
Edwina clothed herself in a veil of silence, refusing
to identify her assailants, resigning from the
school, and withdrawing from Mayapore society.

There were times when words could adequately
convey neither meaning nor message, as when the old
servant Joseph sank to his knees at Edwina's funeral
pyre. "Oh Madam, Madam," he gasped (p.123), just as
Daphne moaned only "Oh Auntie," as she fell to her
knees after running up the steps to MacGregor House
(p.122). There were Anna Klaus's silences about her
years in and flight from Hitler's Germany.

There was the silence, innocent enough in
motive, which drew the web more tightly around the
two lovers. Lady Chatterjee admired Daphne's courage
but distrusted Hari's motives. She felt responsible
for introducing them and could foresee only frustration and heartbreak for the couple who dared to defy
the longstanding taboos. But she did nothing to help
or to hinder their relationship, silently watching
with growing concern and worry.

Hari was guilty of silencing the truth in his
letters to Colin. He never revealed what life was
like in black India and thus contributed to the
degree of dismay Colin felt when he finally discovered the truth for himself. If Hari had been honest
from the beginning, perhaps Colin would not have been
so blinded by the squalor and misery of India and
would have been able to recognize Hari on the
Mayapore maidan.

Daphne, too, was a guilty party in this conspiracy of silence. She segregated her life in the white
community from her life at MacGregor House, and both
of those from her life with Hari, as if they were
three separate realms (p.411). She was dumbfounded
and felt like a fool when she discovered that her own
white and black worlds had already clashed violently.
Yet she still kept Ronald Merrick's marriage proposal
a secret, which complicated the entire Bibighar

episode and helped assure her own destruction. And there was the determined silence of Ethel Manners, perhaps not so innocent, as she resolved to abandon Hari to his own fate, believing that she could do nothing for him, and dooming him to his bitter end (p.475).

Daphne's refusal to identify her rapists involved a complicated ·network of lies intended to protect Hari and to keep the truth hidden. But she found herself trapped by her own lies, a trap sprung even as she crawled up the steps of MacGregor House in the dark (pp.438,444). She could not swear that the innocent boys whom Merrick arrested were not her assailants because she had to keep insisting that she did not get a good look at anyone. If the police were ever to capture the real criminals, they might plead for mercy on the grounds that they were driven to madness by the sight of a black man and a white woman making passionate love in Bibighar. Daphne knew that Hari was suffering from her silence, but she clung to the belief that he would suffer even more if the truth were known (p.440).

Hari took her demand to say "nothing" quite literally. Daphne thought he might be using this silence as a new way to mock himself (p.468), a joke he could play on himself as the invisible man. But the inquisitive stranger saw an added meaning to Hari's silence: "Kumar was a man who felt in the end that he had lost everything, even his Englishness, and could then only meet every situation--even the most painful--in silence, in the hope that out of it he would dredge back up some self-respect" (p.355).

In his desperate cry to Daphne at the gate of Bibighar Hari uttered his last recorded public words: "I've got to be with you. I love you. Please let me be with you" (p.436). It was the last time his voice would be heard in the streets of Mayapore, a voice so English that if a witness were to close his eyes he would imagine only white skin. Hari was Kumar by skin but Coomer by language, and by his silence Hari finally shed the remnants of his English identity and his illusions: the silence of a desperate man in search of the hard core of himself.

The complicated web of silence in The Jewel in the Crown was a symptom and product of racial prejudice. It came from years of misunderstanding, distrust, hatred, fear, and ignorance. Only courage and love would break that silence. Daphne's journal told the truth. It was a message from the grave, an "insurance against permanent silence" (p.373). In it she finally expressed the full story and measure of her love which she could share with no one in life.

IV

Through structure and theme, Paul Scott explores the nature of history in The Jewel in the Crown. In a sense, the reader of the Raj Quartet enjoys a God-like perspective[12]because, for Scott, historical events have no definite beginning and no satisfactory end, "as if time were telescoped...and space dovetailed...so that at once past, present, and future are contained in your cupped palm" (p.133). Specific historical events, such as Bibighar, have an "eternal" dimension with roots stretching far into the past and repercussions extending into a never-ending future,[13] "as if Bibighar almost had not happened yet, and yet has happened" (p.133). Bibighar is continually present to the reader as to God, in an ever-present "now."

To reinforce this viewpoint, Scott employs a structure based on reminiscences: different people tell different stories from their own points of view about a past event. The actual story-telling is in the present, but the subject within the story is unfolded as if it were happening now instead of in the past, giving the illusion that the result is still to be determined.[14] This illusion is shattered only by Scott's casual, one-line references to outcomes even before they occur. The reader is told that Ethel Manners died in 1948 (p.82) and Merrick died in 1947 (p.334) and is informed of Edwina Crane's suicide (p.82) before knowing of the events leading up to her death.

The effect of imposing the future suddenly on the present creates an overwhelming sense of destiny. To support this sense Scott continually prophesies future events in his reminiscences. Bibighar is described as "the affair that began on the evening of August 9, 1942, in Mayapore, [and] ended with the spectacle of two nations in violent opposition, not for the first time nor as yet for the last" (p.9).

38

When Edwina Crane's father died she did not weep; "although there would come a time when she did once more it had not arrived yet" (p.19). Sr. Ludmila believed that Kumar and Merrick were destined to meet at the Sanctuary. It was "written on the walls when I first came here and saw the tumbledown buildings and recognized that they would serve my purpose" (p.139).

Human beings, as part of their metaphysical condition, are caught in a pre-determined, linear flow of impersonal forces. One aspect of these forces was Edwina's "moral flow of history." As a liberal, she interpreted this force to be directed, by its nature, toward the goals of right reason. But there seems to be no such guarantee in Scott's framework. What "is" is not necessarily more just or more wise than what "could have been." The course of history denied Lili Chatterjee, of the ruling Rajput class, the role which was rightfully hers (p.42). From Scott's analysis of the raj, the reader could not be certain that the white man's rule was a sign either of right reason or divine Providence. Daphne herself was doubtful about the course of events: "I felt as if the club were on an ocean-going liner, like the Titanic, with all the lights blazing and the bands playing, heading into the dark, with no one on the bridge" (p.389).

Destiny is not only linear in pattern (e.g., event at point A in the present directed to point B in the future) but also cyclic, where point B in the future is an echo of the past. On the night of Bibighar when Lili Chatterjee thought that Daphne and Hari were meeting at the Sanctuary, the place where it all began, she believed that disaster was inevitable because the situation had come full circle (p.121). Thematically, Scott uses this pattern repeatedly. When Daphne echoed Edwina's lament: "There is nothing I can do, nothing, nothing..." (pp.69, 436), it is more than coincidence. The personal tragedies produced by violence and hatred are a recurring blight in human history. The reason, according to Scott, has little to do with chance or luck, as Sr. Ludmila's mother believed (p.130). The real cause and originating impetus to impersonal historical forces is the free human will exercising moral choice in the "area of dangerous fallibility" (p.357). On the evening of August 9th when Daphne was missing, Merrick again came searching at the

Sanctuary as he did the February before. Sr. Ludmila realized that:

> ...everything fitted into place, fitted back into that dangerous geo-metrical position I had had warning of, with Merrick and Kumar as two points of a triangle, with the third point made this time not by Rajendra Singh but by Miss Manners. I had that sensation which sometimes comes to us all, of returning to a situa-tion that had already been resolved on some previous occasion, of being again committed to a tragic course of action, having learned nothing from the other time or those other times when Merrick and I may have stood like this, here in this room where I am bedridden and you ask your ques-tions, with the name Kumar in our minds and the name of a girl who was missing and who had to be found (p.158).

Escape from their "cycle of inevitability" (p.159) which spiralled through time depended on free choice or accurate judgments. If Sr. Ludmila had guessed that Daphne was more than a friend to Merrick, if Colin had recognized Hari on the maidan, if Merrick had not chosen the "tragic and twisted way," then the cycle could have been broken and another direction established in the course of historical events.

But the cycle was not broken. Merrick was a man of violent passions and of emotions lacking any subtlety, just like the Scotsman MacGregor (p.150). They both were opinionated, insensitive, arrogant, and strong-willed. Merrick had designs on Daphne (which could not masquerade as love) just as Mac-Gregor desired a black courtesan. Both men were spurned for black men, and both destroyed their native rivals, consuming their "beloveds" as well.

The violence and hatred surrounding the Bibighar incident was at least the second of its kind. Events came full circle and outrages were repeated because nothing was learned from the other times.

After this second Bibighar, a dark-skinned child

was born, a girl who studied the art of singing classical Indian music. She lived in MacGregor House just as had the other singer who was loved by an adoring prince and who sang "the same songs perhaps that the girl is singing now" (p.75). Parvati now picked the flowers which Daphne had picked before her (p.86). The cycle is completed and the stage is set for men to remake or reject the moral choices which lead to or away from another Bibighar.[15]

The structure of The Jewel in the Crown supports this cyclic theme. Through each successive account, the same events are recounted. Each time, Scott digs more deeply into the meaning of those events so that by the time the story line catches up, the reader has a deeper understanding than he had with the first reference.

Within each section of the book Scott brings the subject around full circle, either back to the starting point of the section, or to an important subject in earlier pages. In Part I, "Miss Crane," the reader is informed (within two pages from the beginning) that Edwina was hosting English soldiers to tea. After reading about her life and tragic experience, the reader again is told that the soldiers returned for tea (within two pages of the end of the section). Events come full circle. On the surface, nothing has changed.[16] Part II, "The MacGregor House," opens with a description of the garden. Throughout the section the reader enjoys Lili Chatterjee's random patterns of thought and countless digressions from the subject so that it is not clear whether she intends to talk about Edwina Crane or her niece Daphne. The two seem inseparable, as if their fates are intertwined, at least in the mind of Lili Chatterjee and now in the reader's consciousness. The section ends with the description of guests in MacGregor garden at a party given for the stranger. Eighteen years do not separate the garden from Edwina's old bungalow where, in the mind of the stranger, "the fire that consumed Edwina Crane spurts unnoticed, licks and catches hold. In this illuminated darkness one might notice this extra brilliance and hear, against the chat and buzz of casual night-party conversation, the ominous crackle of wood" (p.123). A new image is forever added to the view of MacGregor House.

Part III, "Sr. Ludmila," opens with a descrip-

tion of Sr. Ludmila's weekly trips to the bank with
one of her youthful, native bodyguards, a story
repeated halfway through the section. Preceding and
following this second rendition is her description of
Daphne waiting for Hari to meet her in the Sanctuary
on the evening of August 9th. In each instance
Daphne is described as having light falling on her
face. As Sr. Ludmila discusses the petrified circle
of the dancing Siva and the cycle of tragic events
and choices (and in so doing thematically develops
the on-going nature of Bibighar), Scott structures
the section to return the reader again and again to
the same points in the past, the most important of
which was, in Sr. Ludmila's mind, finding Hari drunk
in the river wasteground, which she mentions three
times (pp.133-137). In Part IV, "Evening at the
Club," the stranger consciously compares and contrasts club life in the present to club life eighteen
years in the past. The clientele is different, but
the fixtures, decor, and atmosphere of social and
racial snobbery are the same. When the stranger sees
the signature of Ronald Merrick in the Club records,
it seems almost as if the infamous character had
visited with Daphne only the evening before.

In Part V, "Young Kumar," Scott develops the
details of Hari's background, moving through the
events of Duleep's life, Hari's experiences at
Chillingborough and his friendship with Colin
Lindsey, his coming to India, and the meaning for
Hari of Colin's rejection. The section ends with the
fifth account of Sr. Ludmila's finding Hari drunk in
the wasteground. But now the reader has a deeper
understanding, a better grasp of the significance of
that event by coming full circle.

In Daphne's journal (Part VII) the cyclic
structure reaches its climax. Many important subjects are repeated: Hari and Daphne's relationship
never had a chance (pp.376,415,426); Daphne did not
know that Merrick was the man who first arrested Hari
(pp.377, 407, 424); the lovers' tragic fate was
sealed by a conspiracy of silence (pp.379, 411, 435,
438, 468); Daphne questions whether Hari could ever
really love her (pp.379-80, 408); Daphne's nightmare
faces (p.383) materializing in Bibighar (p.433);
Daphne's sense of wasting time (pp. 385, 389);
Daphne's being introduced to Sr. Ludmila (pp. 407,
409-10); the trap of lies closing in (pp. 438, 447);
Hari's echoing Edwina's prayer for forgiveness

(pp.430, 435); and Daphne's repeating Edwina's lament that there was nothing she could do (pp. 430, 436, 467).

This confusion of linear time, this cyclic recurrance of events and thoughts, helps realize and dramatize what Scott considers to be the nature of history. For Daphne, the end of white man's rule was "unreal and remote, and yet total in its envelopment, as if it had already turned itself into a beginning" (p.467). The first destruction of Bibighar was such a beginning. And "MacGregor House was built on such foundations" (p.467). For Scott, history forms an organic whole. The way he "telescopes time" and "dove-tails space," the way the reader holds the past, present, and future in his cupped hands, is like the wholeness of dancing Siva, representing the natural cycle of life: creation, preservation, and destruction (p.152). In this sense, there is truth to Lady Chatterjee's observation that all reality is one. During her well-traveled life she saw the Taj Mahal, which brought a lump to her throat, the floating palace at Udaipur, the view from the Arc du Carrousel, London on Sunday morning, the Malayan archipelago and the toe of Italy from the air, New York at night, Manhattan from the deck of a liner coming up the Hudson, an old woman drawing water from a well in a village in Andhra Pradesh, and Parvati playing the tamoura and singing a morning raga (p.80). "These are not divisible, these sights and people" (p.80). All was one. If there is no clear demarcation between historical events, their causes and conclusions, then all human events comprise a historical and moral unity. That is why Scott admonishes the reader that Bibighar can only by understood in relation to the "moral continuum of human affairs" (p.9), and never in isolation.

In this context the reader must examine the meaning and importance of Bibighar, 1942. All Scott's main characters in The Jewel in the Crown made an attempt to love and affirm something outside themselves. The tragedy of the book lies in the fact that all such attempts ended in failure. For some, like General Reid and Ronald Merrick, failure meant witnessing India achieve political independence and the passing of the white man's empire. For Edwina Crane, it meant seeing a life built on magnanimous attitudes and wasted opportunites, and having a heart which never lost itself to love except for one short,

violent moment. For Lili Chatterjee, failure was
betraying a friend's sacred trust by not manifesting
concern or offering guidance and support from long
years' habit of facing problems with stoic cynicism.
For Robin White, it was being unable, in a crises
situation, to ensure black Mayapore of the just and
benevolent workings of the white man's law.

For Hari and Daphne, failure was much more than
falling victim to social prejudice or not handling
their problems in a cunning enough way or telling
lies. As Daphne admitted in her journal, their love
never had a chance (p.376). Part of this failure was
the fault of raj society which refused to tolerate
authentic love between the two races, either on a
personal or national level. The premise of such love
was the equal dignity and value of both white and
black skins and the ability of each race to offer
something worthwhile to the other.

Because of historical circumstances Hari and
Daphne's friendship could never develop naturally.
They were always painfully aware, self-conscious, and
deliberate in breaking each social taboo. The
would-be lovers found themselves continually scrutin-
izing themselves and each other, never being quite
capable of fully trusting, loving, or believing in
each other. Physical attraction and good intentions
could not surmount all the barriers between them.
They were never really friends because "such a
friendship was put to the test too often to survive"
(p.426).

Daphne's personal failure was loving the wrong
man. Their Englishness formed a common bond but she
could not love Hari without loving his skin and his
Indian heritage. As the world of black Mayapore
opened up to her through Hari, it appeared that by
loving him, Daphne could embrace and possess all of
India. The tragedy was that she was more "Indian"
than Hari. If Daphne wanted to accept India and its
culture, she would have to reject Hari. She could
not love or have them both.

Black skin did not play a part in Hari's
self-image. It was only a surface characteristic.
The essence of Hari Kumar was Harry Coomer, Englishman. After realizing that such an image could no
longer be sustained, when Colin did not recognize him
on the maidan, Hari was unable to fill the void. He

44

never found himself, never delved down to the hard
core of himself to realize that being white or black,
English or Indian, did not determine his value and
identity.

The reader cannot help but be overwhelmed by the
pathos of such love lost and be frustrated by such a
need for love denied. "Human beings call for
explanations of the things that happen to them and in
such a way scenes and characters are set for
explanation, like toys set out by kneeling children
intent on pursuing their grim but necessary games"
(p.123). The "whys" of Bibighar are traced to the
moral choices of the main characters and back even
further into the past. The prejudice did not
conclude with Hari's imprisonment or Daphne's death.
The same prejudice that determined the events of
Bibighar continued to shape larger issues, especially
the relationship between England and India. "It was
no longer possible for them to know whether they
hated or loved one another, or what it was that held
them together and seemed to have confused the image
of their separate identities" (p.9).

Perhaps there had been love between the two
nations somewhere in the past when each reaped
"moments of significant pleasure" from the other
(p.476). But the affair had been stormy for too
long. The love/hate faces of the coin blended into
one truth: that the white man's "savagely practical
and greedy policy" (p.476) gave free rein to the
spoilers who used India for their selfish pleasure.
When they tired of the sport and were no longer able
to fool even themselves with worn-out arguments of
moral justification, they claimed incompatibility and
withdrew from India's body (p.476).

The wasted opportunity, of which Lady Manners
spoke, marked a bitter loss to both black and white.
Isolated from India in their own small, enclosed
circle of safe harbor (p.33), the whites pretended
"the world was this small. Hateful. Ingrown"
(p.427). And blacks, bereft of the white man's
influence and denied entrance into his world, were
like Hari Kumar, left only with Aunt Shalini's
well-meaning but narrow affection which could not
reach him or encourage him outside "the ingrown
little world which was the only one she knew, one
that stifled him and often horrified him" (p.260).
Daphne tried to occupy that uncertain ground outside

45

the prescribed little circle, learning from past
mistakes but keeping the lessons to herself and
hoping others would learn as well (p.378). Her love
for and physical union with Hari was the "logical but
terrifying end" of the attempt to break out of the
circles and live together (p.379). Her personal
tragedy stemmed from the fact that she had established her "own little circle of safety," which was
Hari (p.462), and from the existence of the white,
judicial robot which destroyed him.

This judicial robot did not mark the triumph of
true moral law or right reason. Once set in motion
no one could stop its working, and bystanders like
Robin White and Jack Poulson, although plagued by
personal doubts and fears, remained inactive and thus
created an atmosphere of moral anarchy (p.345) in
which the judicial robot functioned. This robot
could not make the moral distinction between love and
rape (p.453). Whites could therefore persecute Hari
for loving, and they themselves could systematically
rape India with impunity and clear consciences.

Scott obviously believed India should be independent because her people were capable of self-rule
and deserving, like any other nation, to fail or
succeed on their own. It is equally evident that
Scott saw England's actual withdrawal and the motives
behind it as a disastrous moral failure. The
political division of India on religious grounds was
a particular sign of failure because it meant England
would withdraw at any cost--to India. Britain must
accept the blame for allowing a favored religious
minority to seize a political opportunity (p.276) to
the detriment of the majority. But by then England
had washed her hands of all responsibility and all
moral pretensions (p.476).[17]

Scott also believed that it was a moral failure
for India to deny the religious foundation of its
culture and character, and declare itself a secular
state. Congress may have wanted to keep its new
country free of a priest-ridden autocracy, but what
they admitted by this action was that there were no
moral differences between India and England, and that
India was as morally bankrupt as its Western partner.
Therefore, their "cohabitation" was lawful because
India did not deserve its freedom on the grounds of
moral superiority after all (p.79).

46

Ultimately Scott is saying that the reasons why Hari and Daphne's love ended tragically are the same reasons why the English/Indian relationship failed: someone or some group of individuals made the choice to hate instead of love. That choice multiplied by millions of individuals is the history of the two nations, and reduced by millions is the story of Bibighar. The real animus, as Ethel Manners understood, was fear and dislike between white and black (pp.204, 476), or as Edwina Crane thought of it, it was the question of who was who and why (p.15). There would be violent conflict and heartache until people learned from misunderstandings and injustice (p.378) and saw past a person's skin into his heart (p.73). "I'm not sure,..." Hari bitterly commented, "That the conflict isn't one that the human race deserves to undergo" (p.277). The tragedy of Bibighar emerges again and again through the remaining volumes of the Quartet, but its culmination is the callous withdrawal of England and the bloodbath of a divided India.

For all of their failures there is something positive to be said about Daphne Manners and Hari Kumar.[18] Their love and brief moment of union were not as exalted and selfless as they could have been, but Daphne and Hari labored under tremendous handicaps. They were not the young, innocent Adam and Eve walking with God in the Garden of Eden. Bibighar Garden was no Paradise. God had fled earth, and the Garden was overgrown, vacant, and unattended. Yet Hari and Daphne tried to love, and to try and fail was far preferable to not trying at all.

MacGregor House was the site of love never made manifest (p.149), the house of the white, a museum of dry and lifeless artifacts and ghosts, and a symbol of the hazards of colonial ambition. It was a repository of the past just as all of India would be for England (p.480). Bibighar was the place of love made manifest; while it was certainly over-indulged in the house of courtesans and hastily seized in the ruins where Daphne and Hari possessed each other, it was love (in an authentic form) nonetheless. MacGregor still stood but Bibighar, even in ruins, was immortal. Scott sees loving union and physical communion as the most important and fulfilling aspects of human life. They alone can effectively challenge prejudice.

Scott describes Daphne during her pregnancy as
being "like a woman in the state of grace" (p.165).
This fruition of love was like an earthly order of
sanctity, the fullness and elevation of all that was
good and worthwhile. The birth and blossoming of
Parvati is as close to a happy ending as the reader
will come in the entire Quartet, the "promise of a
story continuing instead of finishing" (p.479). It
is certain, in light of Scott's linear and cyclic
interpretation of history, that this story will
continue with the same possibilities and the same
choices between love and hate. If the choices are
made again as with Bibighar, there will be tragic
consequences. Robin White was correct about there
being a "cumulative, impersonal justice...The kind of
justice whose importance lies not only in the course
apparently and overwhelmingly taken, but in its
exposure of the dangers that still lie ahead"
(p.358).

These dangers are built into Scott's metaphysical premises. If God has withdrawn from the world,
if human conduct must no longer conform to a divine
moral code, if there is no absolute standard of right
and wrong, then men like Ronald Merrrick must be
judged according to a new standard. If human
consciences act autonomously in determining what is
right and wrong, then Merrick was not contemptible.
Given the fact that Hari Kumar was the antithesis of
what Indians should be, according to raj standards,
then Merrick's actions were commendable. If right
and wrong are only matters of opinion, then Merrick
needed no excuse to hate or punish anyone.

It is obvious that Scott intends Merrick to be
understood as villainous and his choices to be
regarded as morally contemptible. There is, in The
Jewel in the Crown, an ultimate though not spiritual
standard of right and wrong. Scott is not addressing
what it means to be a saint, whether Hindu or
Christian. He is dealing with what it means to be
human. In this first volume it is clear that
prejudice, hatred, anger, bitterness, and cruel abuse
of another person demean the spoilers just as surely
as they injure the victim. Hating is being not fully
human and being hated is a fate no human being
deserves. Scott's idea of ultimate evil is to deny
another his personhood. The solution is to give
everyone the opportunity "to be explained by yourself, by what you are and what you do, and not by

48

what you've done, or were, or by what people think you might be or become" (p.431). The alternative is the lesson of Bibighar. Daphne asked Anna Klaus, "What am I to do, Anna? I can't live without him." Anna responded, "This you must learn to do. To live without" (p.469).

FOOTNOTES TO CHAPTER I

[1] All page references in this chapter, unless otherwise noted, are from Paul Scott, The Jewel in the Crown (New York: Avon Books, 1966).

[2] During her childhood Ludmila had been one of the poor and disdained. Her mother was a prostitute who suffered a poor and lonely existence punctuated by intermittent periods of financial prosperity during which she would be generous to those less fortunate. Ludmila had a vivid recollection of the good nuns refusing her mother's offering for the poor, a gesture which the child first interpreted as a sign of God's own displeasure. Surely, Ludmila thought, these nuns were His favored spiritual instruments. Their religious habits distinguished them as such. But she came to realize that by rejecting her mother's offering, the nuns condemned the poor and hungry to even deeper misery. God could not be pleased with them or their self-righteous behavior. Perhaps, Ludmila concluded, their religious habits of modesty were really signs of punishment and divine displeasure (p.131). Later, when she came to Mayapore, the widowed Mrs. Smith donned her own nun-like habit. She may have been subconsciously exorcizing guilt she carried all her life for being the daughter of a harlot and so wore the nun's habit as a symbol of penance. She might have offered comfort to the destitute and untouchables of Mayapore to compensate for the comfort never offered to her outcast mother.

[3] Edwina was honest enough to recognize, however, that although the children were taught to respect the white man's law and system of justice, they were not encouraged to develop personal relationships with Englishmen.

[4] This course of action was a bitter bone of contention between General Reid and District Commissioner White. White believed that if all the leaders who preached non-violence were arrested, the populace would then be left in the hands of less honorable hoodlums (p.303). Reid thought White was naive to assume Gandhi's followers would not turn into a violent mob given the opportunity for action.

[5]Scott obviously admires the character of Robin White. Behind White's lean, stoic face was a man who genuinely admired and respected blacks and believed them deserving and capable of self-rule. He did not feel racially superior to his subjects, only responsible for them, a trait which lent an air of inner confidence and dignity to himself and his position (p.202).

[6]This is one reason why Scott emphasizes the inner workings and moral disposition of his characters and sees them as the focal point of drama. Scott reveals important action facts casually, with a disregard for accurate chronology, letting the reader assemble his own jig-saw of facts, and concentrates on the motives, feelings, and beliefs of his characters.

[7]The crows' monotonous chanting was like the cries of creatures "only partially evolved, not yet born, but sharpened already by desires the world will eventually recognise as hunger" (p.95). From Scott's numerous references, crows were all-pervasive in India. (See references on pp.18,242,95). Only on the maidan did the crows cease to appear predatory to Hari (p.250). To the stranger these "wheeling, sore-throated" crows were the "one sure animated connexion," the "familiar spirits of dead white sahibs and living black inheritors alike" (p.170). There are also several other bird images in The Jewel in the Crown: the crane (p.85), the flamingo (.171), a prehistoric bird (p.127), and a canary (p.95). Edwina Crane imagined the humane concepts of classical and Renaissance Europe as migratory birds that rose in the air and flew to wherever they were welcome. Clancy heard the faint rumble "which was all that was audible to him of the combined thunder of centuries of flight" (p.33). In the The Day of the Scorpion there are fewer bird images (of crows and vultures; see pp.71,125,184). Scott again develops his bird imagery more seriously in The Towers of Silence and A Division of the Spoils.

[8]Like a true Englishman, he refused to be cowardly and reveal his pain to his friend: "it would be foreign to the scale of values he knew he

must hand on to" (p.239).

[9]This systematic change of seasons helped to emphasize the temporary nature of man's existence (p.130). Perhaps that is why the English were conscious of the length of shadows cast as they walked in the sun, needing proof of their existence, of the mark they had made and of the ever-shining presence of the Edwardian sun: "...To make sure we're never lost in that awful dark jungle of anonymity" (p.428).

[10]In Greek mythology Daphne was the daughter of the river god Peneus and was Apollo's first love. In an act of malice Cupid shot an arrow into Apollo to make him fall in love, and another arrow into Daphne to make her reject love. Apollo pursued her like a hound pursuing a hare, with jaws open ready to seize. Daphne called to her father, to change her form so that the sun-god would no longer desire her. He changed her into a laurel bush. She would be eternally green and experience neither death nor decay. Roman conquerors wore her as wreaths on their brows. (See Bulfinch's Mythology [Toronto: Thomas Crowell, 1970], pp.20-23).

[11]The major Hindu deity is Brahma. His attributes are creation (as manifested in the person of Brahma), preservation (Vishnu), and destruction (Siva). Buddha is the incarnated form of Vishnu.

[12]The airplane traveler enjoys such a perspective as well, in contrast with the grounded observer. From the air the patterns of buildings and streets become more intelligible (p.208) or stand revealed as they truly were: "random and unplanned, with designs hacked into it by people who only worked things out as they went along" (p.478). If men truly perceived as God did, they would not pick out the white current from the dark: "as from a cliff, the sea, separating itself stream from stream and drift from drift, but amounting in God's Eyes to no more than total water" (p.282).

[13]Such a future Edwina envisioned as "an image seen in a series of mirrors that reflected it until it became too small for the eye to see" (p.18).

[14]Daphne also observed how the war was just beginning to affect Mayapore, as if her brother David was to be killed all over again (p.107).

[15]This cyclic pattern is also demonstrated by the literal way in which the stranger participated in Daphne's experiences. He stared out her bedroom window in the same way and at the same sights as Daphne did (pp.100,104), listening to the ever-present calling of crows (p.96). He walked across the bedroom floor wondering if Daphne, too, played the childish game of avoiding the cracks (p.101). He laughed about the lions in the WC, like Daphne did (pp.102,104) and bathed in her tub, and by "closing the eyes against the contrary evidence of the sex" attempted to re-enact the ritual of Daphne refreshing herself at the end of a long day (p.102). The stranger took his shoes and socks off when visiting the Tirupati temple just as Daphne did (pp.205,423). He traveled the route between Bibighar and MacGregor that Daphne must have taken, and smelled the aroma of the land, an aroma which he loved and which Daphne at least came to need. Before leaving MacGregor House, he viewed the reality for himself and "the dream for others" (p.479).
This type of sharing falls short of the symbolic and mystical participation which Sr. Ludmila (p.282), Sarah Layton (The Day of the Scorpion, p.360) Barbie Batchelor (The Towers of Silence, pp.170,175), and Guy Perron (A Division of the Spoils, p.351) experience.

[16]There is, of course, a linear flow to Scott's structure as well. In Part I the reader knows only that there was an attack on an English girl. In part II the reader learns that the attack was on Daphne Manners and reads of Hari Kumar, first only as a name in Daphne's letter to her aunt and then mentioned by Lili Chatterjee as a figure of mysterious and unknown importance in the Bibighar affair. In Part III Sr. Ludmila reveals all the intricate details of Hari's personal tragedy. Robin White's testimony discloses the date of Merrick's death and the fact that Hari had been released from prison. Daphne's journal lays bare the truth which Sr. Ludmila had guessed: that she and Hari had made love in Bibighar. Only in the final pages does the reader learn, in Lady Manners' letter to Lili Chatterjee, of Daphne's death.

[17]The theme of the illusion vs. reality is crucial to understanding The Jewel in the Crown. The primary illusion was not Duleep Kumar's belief that in India a black Englishman and a white Englishman could meet on equal terms (p.260). Nor was it Edwina Crane's empty and starved attraction for Lieutenant Orme (p.17) nor the private fantasy world into which Duleep's mother entered in her final months (p.282). It was not even Daphne's circle of safety in no man's land, a circle of illusory protection based on Hari's presence and love (p.462). The primary illusion was the English imperial mystique which glorified "savagely practical and greedy policy" and enabled such policy to masquerade as humane, enlightened, and moral. This was the basis from which other illusions sprang. For many months Hari could not accept his life in black Mayapore as real. It seemed more like a waking nightmare (p.238). There was a "powerful element of fantasy, sometimes laughable, mostly not; but a fantasy that was always inimical to the idea of a future stemming directly from it" (p.245). Only after his interview with the British Indian Electrical Company did he accept the situation as real (p.261).

By "real" Scott does not mean merely what is empirically verifiable. The true nature of things often takes on supranatural dimensions. What Scott refers to as "magic" was a very real aspect of life. Upon hearing one of her favorite hymns from childhood Edwina "might have been borne down by an intensity of feeling, or regret and sadness for a lost world, a lost comfort, a lost magic" (p.24). The memories of Edwina's childhood did not contain those safe and magical feelings which Sr. Ludmila's did. Sr. Ludmila retained very vivid recollections of "gloves and warm coats and stout shoes...of crystallized fruit lying in a nest of lace-edged paper" (p.130). All the good things about her young life seemed encapsulated in that one new year's day of the new century when "the magic of Christmas was still in the streets" (p.130). Sr. Ludmila's strong sense of childhood magic is similar to Barbie Batchelor's. There must have been that same kind of magic between Hari Kumar and Colin Lindsey, Sr. Ludmila believed. She imagined "young Kumar and young Lindsey as boys, running home across chill fields to come and toast their hands at a warm grate" (p.282). "...Such safety. Such microcosmic power. To translate, to reduce, to cause to vanish with the breath alone the sugary fruits in their nest of lace-edged paper. To know that they are there, and yet not there. This is a magic of the soul. But it was a magic Kumar could not conjure, on the maidan that hot evening, to make Lindsey disappear" (p.282). There was another kind of magic at work, which Colin referred to as Nemesis (p.271) and Hari thought of as the malign spirit (pp.245,271). It was the kind of magic that Sr. Ludmila also remembered, symbolized by, gathered up, pressed together, and contained in the day "the Sisters refused to take my mother's charity" (p.130). This dark magic, this cruel fate designed by a malign spirit, became the theme of Hari's life, of his relationship with Daphne, and ultimately of the entire British/Indian enterprise. That was why Janet MacGregor's ghost still lingered in her husband's house, to warn people with white skins that it was not a good place for them to be (p.150). And that was why MacGregor still echoed with the presence of its second ghost: of tinkling glass and clumsy feet bespeaking the continuing presence of Daphne Manners. The survivors must now "view the reality for themselves and the dream for others, and to make up their minds about the precise meaning of what lies beyond" (p.479).

[18]While Edwina Crane, Robin White, and Daphne all tried to harmonize black and white in the outside world, Hari had to deal with the same problem within himself. His failure was like the Hindu journey through life: passing through illusion (his life in England) to oblivion (his life in India). But he did break through his own anger and bitterness in the end of his final words to Daphne testify: "I love you" (p.436). Ronald Merrick was never able to break out of himself.

55

CHAPTER II

THE DAY OF THE SCORPION

In The Day of the Scorpion Paul Scott abandons the journalistic mode of the first volume for a more difficult, highly symbolic style. This new approach enables the author to study the significance of Bibighar and subsequent events more deeply and to explore his characters with omniscient vision. In this volume, as in the first, Scott concentrates on developing the interior drama of his characters and the effect of events rather than the events themselves. Scott continues to disclose the course of events in an off-hand, random fashion, as in the revelation of Teddie Bingham's death (p.324).[1]

Scott introduces several new characters whose involvement in Bibighar grows from passing curiosity into a living, formative element of their consciousness. One of these characters, Sarah Layton, functions as a moral guide much like Dante's Virgil. In interpreting Sarah as a moral guide, the reader must remember that she is plagued by emotional peaks and valleys as she travels along paths alternately illumined by light or consumed by darkness. With each successive appearance she seems to have undergone a substantial change of heart as a result of some unrevealed cause. Initially the reader sees her in England, longing for India. Then the reader sees her disillusioned with India and longing to return to England. After Susan Layton's wedding, Sarah feels on the threshold of a new life, an illumined way. But when she is unable to escape Pankot because of her sister's pregnancy, Sarah is caught up in darkness more than ever before.

The Day of the Scorpion explores the aftermath of Bibighar. It reveals the truth about Hari Kumar's arrest and monitors Ronald Merrick's festering, interior darkness. It also continues Scott's historical exploration of the relationship between England and India.

I

The origins of India's caste system, dating from

before the birth of Christ, were not purely religious. One of its main objectives was to guarantee
the racial purity of conquerers, e.g., to keep dark
skins from mingling with light. It is no wonder that
India's caste system thrived and solidified through
its turbulent history and the constant advent and
passing away of conquerers. The Moghuls and Mahrattas controlled India's more recent past until the
coming of the European trading companies.[2] The
Portugese, French, and British all vied for economic
supremacy until the early nineteenth century when the
British connived and manipulated themselves into a
position of political and economic dominance. In
1857 nationwide riots against the trading companies
erupted when the natives tried to reclaim their land.
The violence achieved little except to convince
Whitehall that if England were to maintain political
supremacy and continue to reap economic benefits,
control of India must pass into the hands of the
Crown itself. This was accomplished in 1859--osten-
sibly to protect the peace, but actually to protect
England's investments and profits (pp.445-46).

The question why the British kept coming to
India becomes more complicated at this point in
history. There were still the greedy who exploited
India for profit. There were also adventureres and
soldiers who came seeking glory and fame and the
prospect of a life both savage and dangerous. The
missionaries came ("blue-eyed Bible thumpers," as
Jimmy Clark called them, p.445) along with humanitar-
ians ("noble neo-classicists"), who came to save the
black heathens. Clark cynically judged these types
of people who could not stand the commercial pace at
home and who veiled their endeavors abroad with pious
and hypocritical rhetoric (p.445).

These moralists, in the name of reason and
revelation, helped to create the myth of the sacred
mission of the white man, who (they said) was morally
bound to spread civilized standards to all reaches of
the Empire. This mission meant imposing British
standards of politics and government, religion,
economics, language, and culture upon subject
nations. The English were in India primarily to
"serve," as John Layton believed, and as Mabel Layton
so bitterly remarked when she sent money for the
black victims at Amritsar to Mohammed Ali Kasim's
father: "The choice was made for me when we took the
country over and got the idea we did so for its own

58

sake instead of ours" (p.64).

Policies designed to form India into its own political image created a dilemma for England. On the one hand, to create a democratic nation capable of self-rule would be counter-productive to Britain's economic interests. The British insisted on (or encouraged, in the case of princely states)[3] adoption of certain democratic forms of government on a provincial level. But on a national level they adopted a policy of "divide and rule" and worked deliberately to discourage and destroy feelings of national solidarity. They encouraged and fueled religious conflicts between Muslims and Hindus and later claimed that India was incapable of self-rule because of irreconcilable differences. By doing so they justified their continued presence. They divided and ruled and hung on like grim death (p.16).

1937 marked a major step in federal rule. An "All-India" Congress was formed, an experiment to see if the diverse Indian groups could make decisions collectively or whether India could only be governed by British fiat. The majority of local represent-atives to the Congress were Hindus. Mohammed Ali Kasim was one of the Muslim exceptions. In 1939 the congresssional party, itself not directly answerable to the populace, demanded that its members resign their position after the English Viceroy declared war on Germany in the name of India without consulting the Congress. Many Muslim League members were voted into those vacant seats, thus strengthening their own party and ensuring the eventual birth of Pakistan (pp.16-17). Scott sees the existence of Pakistan as the moral responsibility of England. Pakistan marks the failure of all the noble goals and benevolent policies to which the raj paid lip-service.

Whether the English ever had the right to rule India is a fruitless question. As Clark would say, England had the right because England had the power (p.448). But a valid question, and one which Scott explores in detail, is whether coming to India was a good thing, good first of all for India and secondly for England.

Its technology helped England efficiently de-velop and exploit India's natural resources, although the white man was never bashful about helping himself to the economic spoils. In India, Western civiliza-

59

tion confronted an ancient and slowmoving culture. It
was the case, remarked Clark, of the internal
combustion engine confronting a creature evolved from
the primeval slime (p.438). To the "blue-eyed Bible
thumpers" and "noble neo-classicists," England made
significant and lasting contributions during the
years of her dominion by leaving a legacy of
religion, language and law, buildings and monuments,
a sophisticated communications network, and their
cantonments and graves.

Yet Scott, during his return trip to Ranpur in
the 1960's, observes a lamentable fact: the British
reign did not fundamentally change life for the
inhabitants of the native town (p.3). The British,
for all their years of de facto and official
domination, remained a foreign element. They lived
as exiles, regarding an island thousands of miles
away as their homeland and the source of their
identity. They never came to think of India as their
home, and they never embraced Indians as their fellow
and equal neighbors.

As an occupational force the British ruled India
like a police state. They lacked the finesse,
dedication, sensitivity and foresight to understand
Indians and their problems. Mohammed Ali Kasim (MAK)
accused the authorities of being relieved when riots
broke out in August, 1942, after Congressional
leaders were arrested. The raj could then answer
violence with violence, an easier and less demanding
task than working through the situation with diplo-
macy and in peaceful cooperation (p.36).

Scott is careful not to pass judgment on his raj
characters. They were, generally speaking, well-
intentioned and sincerely dedicated to the Kipling
myth. They frowned upon blatant greed and hunger for
power. Even Count Bronowsky was suspect in raj
circles because he "feathered his nest" (p.124). The
English might use blacks to make their lives more
comfortable and make their task of "serving" a little
easier, but they would never consciously use India
for their pleasure. Gaiety, happiness, and joy were
not words in the raj's vocabulary. As Sarah told
Mabel in Surrey, reality was not to be enjoyed
(p.79).

The English at home often misunderstood what
life in India was really like. Colin Lindsey's mental

image of leopard hunting and dark, bearded maharajahs
costumed in turban and sword changed radically when
he witnessed life on the other side of the river for
himself. Even Susan Layton, who spent her early
childhood in Ranpur, bought piles of impractical
clothes to dress like the heroine in the Garden of
Allah for her romantic encounter with the outpost of
the empire (p.86).

Newly-arrived exiles became "consciously
English" once in India (p.286). They could not do
anything or be anywhere without consciously representing an ideal, performing a duty, or achieving
some noble service. This deliberate performance was
given not only for the natives, but (sadly) for their
own kind as well. English males turned either thin
and pale or red and beefy, but they all labored under
the same collective responsibility: to protect
English women (p.149). Once the male had singled out
a mate to enact the timeless ritual of breeding and
to perpetuate the racial speciman, he approached her
with that same collective, representative state of
mind. His enthusiasm was not for her as a person but
for her as an embodiment of an ideal and for the
prospect of fulfilling a necessary and patriotic
function (p.150). Sarah, however, could not enter
into this ritual with Teddie Bingham or anyone else.
She realized that a "dead hand lay on the whole
enterprise" (p.139).

One of the most conscious efforts at being
English was the creation of the cantonment, that area
of Indian cities and towns where the British lived.
This segregated, orderly ghetto was dotted with trees
and parks, with neo-classical colonnades and bunga-
lows all built to remind the English of home.[4] The
cantonment was the white man's public stage. It was
the physical expression of England's attempt to mold
India to its own image. Within its boundaries the raj
felt secure. Life in the cantonment was what life was
meant to be. It was an environment they could live
with (p.3).[5] India's vast, physical expanses permitted the English to sprawl comfortably, to expand
and rule according to their talents, which (in their
sin of pride) seemed as endless as the land itself.
And yet this limitless space oppressed these island
natives of pygmy stature (p.422). Much of the land,
especially the limitless Indian plains, was not
hospitable to human occupation. The horizon, in this
hot, flat expanse, would forever recede from the

traveler, as if the land itself were stretching to overwhelming dimensions, dwarfing any human beings who in their hubris sought to stride across the land like giants (p.123). The English could not exploit and mold the free spaces as they hoped. As a defensive reflex they fortified their cantonments against the Indian vastness, and turned in on themselves (p.3). Their haven became a prison.

From these insular, prison walls life back home in England seemed transformed, reduced, miniaturized. Fellow countrymen without "the Indian connection" seemed like foreigners after a few years. Most children, like Sarah and Susan Layton, were educated in England to ensure claim to their cultural inheritance (p.434), yet those years were filled with unhappiness, loneliness, and a yearning for their Indian home.

But "home" for the raj was also "home" for millions of blacks who had no cantonment, no protective quarters to ensure survival. Having the British establish and dictate acceptable norms of behavior and achievement spurred young, educated Indians to "ape" the white man's manner of speech and dress. Normally capable of displays of extreme emotion, Indian men mimicked the sophisticated coolness and non-violent veneer of Englishmen to the extent of losing their own vitality (p.95). This mimicry, combined with the British policy of "divide and rule," hastened the eclipse of an Indian sense of identity and nationhood, an Indian consciousness, an Indian sense of value and importance. Blacks had no collective identity in the face of the raj's collective obsession.

The goal of Mohammed Ali Kasim's life and political labors was to help create a united India. As important as it was to achieve self-rule, it was just as vital to create an Indian nation capable of functioning collectively, as a unified people. That was the ultimate political goal of the Congressional party and why MAK's loyalty remained with the party rather than with Jinnah's Muslim League, despite its errors in judgment and application. MAK was "looking for a country" (p.18) because a unified India as yet did not exist.

This goal, to help Indians feel that they were before all else Indians, was possible despite religious differences. MAK believed such differences were neither irreconcilable nor fundamental.[6] Social and cultural integration had been a fact before British occupation and might be again, according to Scott's description of the Muslim natives in the Pankot hills who offered sacrifices to the old Hindu gods and enlisted to fight Allah's holy wars against the enemies of the Christian King-emperor (pp.53-54). Scott values the contribution of both Hindus and Muslims in Indian life. He laments the separation of Pakistan and the passing of a diverse and thus richer Indian character (p.3).

Politics was the only acceptable means MAK found to change the system, the only way for him to rebel against what the British were doing to his country. But MAK's brand of politics was only the kind that the English found acceptable, and it did not include violence or self-serving opportunities (pp.40,494). MAK's younger son Ahmed harbored vivid scenes from his childhood of gatherings at his father's house. Famous Indian statesmen and public figures would quibble among themselves like children in private while the common people waited expectantly on the other side of the wall. "They are saving India from the British," his older brother Sayed explained (p.105). But the British remained day after day. The only difference was that his father was imprisoned for making a speech at the request of one of those great Indian statesmen (pp.105-106).

Indians were bound to lose as long as they played according to British rules. Gandhi's great political gamble of non-violent non-cooperation did not result in negotiations with the Viceroy as the Mahatma and Congressional leaders hoped. Instead, the British reacted ruthlessly and imprudently to this native act of "moral blackmail," a game which whites themselves had been employing for years (p.95).

The truth was that England would give up India only when India no longer fit into England's present image of itself (p.40). Or as Clark explained, India's gangrenous and draining presence would be amputated from the body of the Empire when the liberal leadership in Whitehall realized that it had become an economic embarrassment, a millstone around the over-extended neck of Imperial England[7] (p.446). Edwina Crane might have believed in a "moral drift of history" and in England's obligation to honor its promise of independence, but as faith in God and in the white man's moral superiority waned, the rhetoric and the bold-faced lies appalled those with a conscience and spurred those without one (p.446).

The foundations of the British Empire in India paralleled the foundation of Fort Premanager. Both were "ruined strongholds" (p.4). Their basic premises and starting points were all wrong, as much of a violation of human rights and dignity as walling up promising young Hindu men and their child brides. Both were elaborate misadventures (p.4-5), and The Day of the Scorpion indexes the raj's growing realization of this fact, anticipating the day when the British would come to the end of themselves as they were (p.4).

For Sarah Layton, this truth took many years to learn. Her earliest memories of India were of a secure and warm environment where Mumtez the ayah slept protectively across the bedroom door. Sarah remembered all the native servants with affection, especially the old man Dost Mohammed, who demonstrated what a scorpion did when surrounded by fire.

Sarah and Susan migrated to England for their education, to claim their cultural inheritance as most raj children did. Sarah's English experience was not a happy one, but she kept her own feelings hidden for Susan's sake, who on the surface seemed to conquer her environment with self-centered charm. The most significant event during their years in England was their great-grandfather's death in Surrey. Millie, John and Mabel Layton had come home for their long leave. It was then that Sarah first felt alienated from members of her family.[8] Susan confessed to her parents that she was miserable in England and wanted to go home. Sarah suspected that Susan's emotional outburst was simply an attempt to monopolize her parents' attention, but she still felt betrayed that Susan had never confided in her. It was a self-imposed taste of personal failure, and from then on Sarah distrusted public displays and calculated use of emotion.

Both homesick Layton girls disliked their mother's sister Lydia because she spoke ill of India. Lydia believed it was an "unnatural place for a white woman" (p.78). The heat and strain of duty sapped women of their vitality and beauty. But Sarah had not yet witnessed this phenomenon for herself, and resented Lydia's attitude. She began mentally to compare her family in England with her family in India.[9] While Lydia vocalized her opinion about her business and everyone else's, the Indian branch of the family was reticent and secretive (p.80). Aunt Mabel was especially withdrawn and made no effort to help others feel comfortable in her presence. She was like a rock. There was a hard streak in Mabel, and yet her interest in Sarah was substantial and challenging (p.78).

Climate, Sarah theorized, could contribute to a nation's superiority. It had originally toughened Englishmen, enabling them to conquer and subdue less "seasoned" or developed peoples. But in recent times the hardships caused by environment had been minimized, and such superior conditioning passed to Englishmen who lived in the demanding climate and topography of India (pp.119-120). India obviously changed people, and, while she lived in England, Sarah believed it changed them for the better.

Sarah found leaving England strangely painful. It was her second experience of feeling torn between her identification with India and her identification with England. Before leaving for India in 1939 Sarah burned a pile of relics of her years in England. As she stood before the bonfire she mused on the paradoxical demand of the raj life made upon herself and her family (pp.85-86). They had to learn to accept continual changes in location, traveling between England and India, and within India itself. It was a nomadic existence in the name of duty. That same duty imposed a tradition upon them which they had to maintain and embody.

Both Sarah and Susan quickly realized that the India of their memories was not the real India, that the India of their childhood was not the India they confronted as adults. The real Pankot and Ranpur were not misty or magical but solid and far larger than the girls remembered. They seemed to be spread too thinly and yet too thickly over the landscape (p.71). There were servants to make their life easier, but no devoted ayah to make their sleeping nights secure.[10]

Susan was the first to feel the darkness press around her. She had not felt secure in England and expected that at "home" in India she would finally count, she would belong, become "indelible" (p.356).

But India never helped her feel welcome. The land and natives appeared hostile to the insular white community, a community which in turn placed specific demands on its own members before they "counted." The Layton and Muir names were excellent references, but Susan would have to fulfill other matrimonial and reproductive requirements to be fully accepted.

Years earlier, when John Layton returned to India after his education at Chillingborough[11] and enlistment in the Pankot Rifles, he too felt that the real India did not fulfill his expectations. His experiences in World War I and the death of his father James tarnished the vision, although it was still "splendid enough" (p.63). As he wandered among the natives in the hills surrounding Pankot, recounting his war tales to attentive audiences, John felt that being "home" in India was not a place but a state which lodged mysteriously in the heart (p.69).

It was a noble sentiment but one which could not sustain his daughters. While Sarah and Susan lived in England, they longed to return to India, but once back they felt like foreigners. They were exiles with no home, no sense of security, and no formula for happiness. Sarah realized that it was time for her to leave India because the raj would never find real happiness there (p.422).

This was one of many interior changes Sarah experienced. She longed for India, and her disappointment and disillusionment were as intense as her longing. The reader is not privy to the process which brought Sarah to this point. After three years of raj existence (1939-1942) she was clearly unhappy and looked to her family for the security and safety that India did not afford her (pp.71,157,230). Until her sister's wedding Sarah felt comforted and supported by her family, which abided in the "geometric pattern of light and the circle of safety" (p.230).

But this raj light surrounding family and tradition was stale and stifling, based on pre-World War I attitudes and expectations. The code of the raj and of the Layton and Muir families was "preserved in perpetual Edwardian sunlight" (p.444). It was out of touch with the real needs of whites and blacks. Family duty and social responsibility became sources of oppression rather than comfort for Sarah, who, unlike Susan, questioned any code imposed upon her before absorbing it into herself. Sarah realized that Lydia was right after all, that India bled white women of their vigor and beauty. They wilted like hothouse plants exposed to a ruthless environment. In most cases only stoic husks and empty shells were left, with but a few hearty exceptions like Mabel Layton, Lady Manners, and (Sarah speculated) Daphne Manners (pp.139-140).

After Susan's wedding the burden of familial responsibility increased dramatically for Sarah. She had wanted to train as a nurse and participate more actively in the war, contributing something in her own right. But Susan was pregnant, and Millie transferred even more of the burden onto Sarah while John Layton remained a prisoner of war in Germany. Although Sarah and her mother had never been close, Sarah believed that family obligations were more important than her own desires. The suffocating atmosphere of this burden brought Sarah to withdraw more and more into herself, causing her family to regard her with "alarm and affection" (p.456). On the outside, Sarah conformed to the raj code of conduct. She was the dependable one. Yet she found her environment more and more hateful. She now recognized that the source of security she experienced as a child really sprang from snobbish solidarity and prejudice. Her family, along with the entire raj community, functioned and responded collectively. Whatever they contributed to India would be second-rate because they would never give their best until they gave of themselves as individuals and not as a crowd (p.146).

The raj's fatal flaw was its blind and paranoid group consciousness. The English were scrupulously aware of their position of authority and privilege, of responsibility and duty. Life in India was like a play with the raj's code as the script, their formula for proper conduct. The English gave their performance every moment of every day (p.229), playing the role of Kiplingite martyrs. Incidents like the thrown-stone or the suppliant woman in white only heightened rather than diminished this awareness (pp.171,173-174).

Teddie was cast in a particularly nobel role. He loved the game of playing raj. He loved the people and the theme, the regiment and its mythical virtues. He was, in Ronald Merrick's terms, an amateur. And if

67

the code had accurately reflected life, Teddie's performance would have become legendary. But there was nothing lyrical about treachery, and Teddie's noble gesture could not bring the tale back to life (p.411).[12]

Because life was a play, it became remote--one step removed from reality. "Performing" rather than living kept the raj detached, capable of stiff-arming life away. Millie Layton was an expert at enduring, at keeping life in abeyance. She struggled just to get through each day by shifting most of the family burden onto Sarah and drinking to dull her loneliness, or as Clark put it, getting her screws out of a bottle (p.455). If Millie could not deal with a situation, she disassociated herself from it, withdrew from the game, and gave the impression that for her it did not exist or never happened (p.355).

Sarah also held life in abeyance. She was courageous in facing raj shortcomings and in acknowledging truth about herself and her family. But she could not cope with emotions, neither her own nor other people's. Since her grandfather's death Sarah regarded displays of emotion as superfluous, deceiving, and faintly menacing. This defensive posture made India a particularly difficult place to live because India was a land where people felt, or pretended to feel, extreme emotions (pp.95,106). Nothing was simple or self-evident (p.184).

The combination of emotional detachment and intellectual censorship is symbolized by what Sarah came to think of as her "funny turns." When she was young she thought of them as hallucinatory growing pains during which she was incapable of perceiving things properly. She felt gigantic in relation to everything else, which seemed small and far away. Even her own body, sensations, thoughts, and feelings seemed unrelated and distant.

Her first adult experience of this kind occurred while she galloped across the palace grounds in Mirat with Ahmed Kasim. She felt, as the horizon drew away with every stride of her horse, that the land was pulling away, leaving them dwarfed on the same small patch of ground instead of striding like triumphant and confident giants across the land (p.124). Her second such experience as an adult came after she visited Merrick in Calcutta. As her train pulled into the Ranpur station on her return journey she had another "funny turn" when the sights and sounds of the city seemed far away (p.461).

Because Sarah withheld herself from the raj's play she appreciated its true nature: a charade rather than an inspiring performance.[13] This vision of comic/tragic reality was especially pronounced during the Bingham wedding reception, when guests moved like puppets and Susan preserved the raj's respectability with a curtsy to the Nawab. This impression returned to Sarah when she met Count Bronowsky on the railroad platform in Ranpur. As he carried her hand to his lips and regarded her with his nocturnal eye, speaking with an accent she did not recall being so pronounced, she had a "sense of charade, of puppet-show; of dolls manipulated to a point just short of climax" (p.464).

Susan Layton was the person most suited to this atmosphere of "performance" and the person most vulnerable to its trap. Both she and Sarah returned to India with their childhood memories and illusions. Even during her years in England Susan showed an aptitude for pretending, which prepared her for the game of the raj playing raj. Reduced to its single cell, it was the game of Susan playing Susan (pp.145,345). But once in the habit of pretending, she found it impossible to distinguish between the role and real life, between illusion and reality.

Susan's talent, which attracted so many, was her ability and courage to create the illusion of being the center of a world without sadness, a world which allowed others entry (p.182). But the illusion did not suffice, and in the end, after Susan despaired of ever belonging, of finding a happy, secure place in life, she foresook the real world for the world of madness (p.500). At least there her family, obliga-tions, and empty frustration would not follow. She was judged "dangerously withdrawn," but Sarah thought Susan looked truly happy for the first time in her life (p.504).

The consummate actor in The Day of the Scorpion was Ronald Merrick. Instead of discovering the real state of Merrick's mind and heart, the reader confronts the truth which made Daphne Manners recoil: there was no way into Ronald Merrick. He was neither candid nor honest. He assumed whatever posture was necessary in dealing with a person or a situation in order to create the appropriate facade or impression. What Merrick chose to reveal about himself and Bibighar cannot be trusted, because he acknowledged no truth outside his own arbitrary criterion.[14] Merrick's ability to perform corresponded to his attitude toward life in India. "When I got out here it all seemed so unreal, like a play" (p.221). But the scenario of Merrick's play was substantially different from the raj's. The script was not "the code" but "the situation" which Merrick enacted and thereby became a creator, an instigator, an active agent in the flow of historical events (p.309).

The desire, the need to be the moving force in a situation, was symptomatic of Merrick's self-obsession (p.353). As much as this lower-class, insecure man wanted to belong, he could never participate in the raj's play because he could not accept their moral frame of reference (p.414). Merrick's approach to life was self-centered rather than group-centered. He valued nothing above himself and his own standards. His obsessive self-awareness spot-lighted only his own existence. His twisted self-definition included no one else except "all the people whom he chose as victims [who] lay scattered on his threshold" (p.415). What the raj viewed as a vulgar display of emotion--the suppliant woman falling at Merrick's feet--Merrick simply regarded as appropriate.

II

Scott employs a "wall" image to describe those artificial barriers constructed or conceived between people. Mabel erected a wall between herself and all others, by which she guarded her secret self (p.368). A wall divided Ahmed from all those people, elite and common alike, who believed in and were excited by the power of politics (p.105). Sarah felt a barrier between herself and Susan in England when Susan exploited and reveled in her emotions and Sarah had to hide her own. The sides of the wall were a matter of perspective, depending upon who felt left out or who felt lacking.

As a young child in India Susan had been afraid of the servants who lived at the other end of the

garden beyond the wall. She believed that she no
longer would be frightened, that she would be happy
and whole like everyone else seemed to be, if she
could only cross to the other side of the wall
(pp.356-57). Then she could lay claim to the secret
world of self-assurance, of moral certainty, of
individual and collective identity, and of selfless
and fulfilling love (p.427). Susan could finally
enter the secret garden of happy center where she
would be self-assured like Sarah and be certain of
her worth. She believed that following the code and
playing the game faithfully would transport her to
the other side, and so she adamantly pursued the path
which led to marriage and pregnancy (p.355).

Teddie's death compounded her insecurity. The
prospect of raising his child alone terrified her.
Try as she might, Susan could not earn that secret
garden because the code guaranteed no magic formula
for happiness. There was only "Susan crying to be
let in and building the likeness of it for herself
because she believed the secret garden was the place
they all inhabited, and she could not bear the
thought that she alone walked in a limbo of strange
and melancholy desires" (p.346).

All her efforts to build a life that would
"count" in other people's eyes only made Susan
realize the hollow and deceitful character of the raj
myth. Her source of despair was the same as Edwina
Crane's, her crisis of identity the same as Hari
Kumar's. "What am I? Why--there's nothing to me at
all. Nothing. Nothing at all" (p.345).

Susan did not realize that no one was as happy
and secure as they appeared. Most people were
frightened and lost but were less honest about their
condition. Susan deliberately used her beauty and
charm as "fearful armour against the terrors of the
night" (p.346). But others wove their own kind of
armor, even if they did not consciously acknowledge
their fears and insecurity.

Every major character in The Day of the Scorpion
assumed some kind of protective shell, from Major
Tippit who buried himself in the past because he
found no value in the present or hope in the future,
to Millie Layton, who needed alcohol to buffer the
cares and worries of each tedious day of waiting.
Millie's drinking gave her a "vagueness and general

air of distraction" (p.127) which disappeared only momentarily when she shouldered her rightful burden as head of the household immediately after Teddie's death.

While Susan changed for her short honeymoon in the Nanoora hills and Aunt Fenny chattered away about Merrick's involvement with Daphne Manners in her typically shallow and insensitive way, Sarah peeled off her peach bridesmaid dress and was relieved that she would never wear it again (p.214). It seemed like a symbol of the demands of breeding duty which Susan had accepted but which Sarah found meaningless and degrading. She shed the dress like a layer of unwanted skin, a husk-like prison, and imagined her inner self liberated and illumined by light. "Perhaps, she thought, I am no longer in darkness, perhaps there is light and I have entered it" (p.214).

Yet Sarah was still very much the colonel's daughter, a fact which was obvious to the Sister Prior in Calcutta, to Ronald Merrick, and to Jimmy Clark. Sarah had rejected the content of the raj code but could not find anything to replace it. Her veneer was still that of a memsahib. Her instinctive reactions, as when she recognized Lady Manners in the bazaar and turned hastily away (pp.373-74) still reflected her class and upbringing.[15] Her regimental skin, however thin, could not be so easily shed like the bridesmaid dress.

Sarah was a prisoner of her past, of her family, and of her countrymen. Pandit Baba shrewdly observed this truth while discussing Hari Kumar's unjust incarceration in Kandiput prison within walls of "defeat and apprehension" (p.237). Who, he asked Ahmed Kasim, was on the inside of a prison? "For what is outside in one sense is inside in another" (p.107). As a Hindu, Pandit Baba advocated action which would free his countrymen and their raj jailers, though his motives could scarcely be considered humane. "In time we must break the walls down. This duty to break them down is our sentence of imprisonment. To break them down will be to free ourselves and our jailers. And we cannot sit back and wait for the orders of release. We must write the orders ourselves...I speak metaphorically" (p.107).

Imprisonment was a relative state, a matter of

degree. For Lady Manners only death would release
her from the chains of ostracism and unbelief. She
could not challenge the raj's blindness and hypro-
crisy in any other way except to offer love and a
home to Parvati for a few short years.

For reflective Sarah, prison walls enclosed her
at every turn. Prison meant to be ordinary, to lose
sight of her personhood, to be enveloped in interior
darkness, to be chained to an environment not of her
choice or making (pp.140,86,121). But Sarah was a
timid rebel who did not have Daphne's courage to
embrace. In her mind she rejected the abuses and
prejudices of the raj world, but she still clung to
the Edwardian twilight and the safety of her family
and class because there was nothing else.

In one sense, the raj code of conduct was a
noble and proud tradition. It sprang primarily from a
need to belong, a need to elevate and justify the
presence of a conquering nation who came originally
for economic reasons and stayed for political ones.
Stemming from a Kiplingite sense of mission to spread
civilized standards to all reaches of the Empire, the
raj code serviced its own members and "edified" (at
least in theory) the subject race. It gave whites a
sense of collective dignity, identity, and purpose,
and (as in the case of the stone-throwing incident) a
sense of noble stature. Even Teddie, who Sarah
believed had no real depth (p.139), assumed an air of
calm dignity despite the piece of plaster sticking to
his cheek.

Teddie achieved the height of his stature in
dealing with the INA traitor, Mohammed Baksh. Teddie
was shattered to discover the INA soldier was an
ex-Muzzy Guide. But he pulled the weeping man up from
where he had fallen at Teddie's feet and told him, "I
am still your father and your mother"[16] (p.403). It
was vitally important to Teddie that the Man-Bap
tradition be true. It was his back-bone, the core of
his identity.

Whereas the stone did no real damage to the
wedding party's spirit,[17] the INA phenomenon destroyed
Teddie's sense of equilibrium. The stone incident
did not shatter the raj's sense of inviolate truth:
that the black man owed allegiance to the white man
whose salt he had eaten. To witness large numbers of
the Indian army taking up arms against the King-

Emperor, breaking their sacred oaths and betraying their fathers' regiments, was a fatal blow to the raj's belief in the sacred tradition they exemplified. It turned their world upside down.[18]

When Baksh told Teddie there were two more INA's in the field who wanted to give themselves up, he wasted no time in attempting to retrieve the lost sheep back into the fold. He drove out in a jeep and called them by name like God: "Aziz Kahn! Fariqua Kahn!" For one magical moment it seemed they might come to Teddie's call of reconciliation, drawn by the very power of his voice, or his presence, or the idea he symbolized.

It would have been a legendary scene, Merrick cynically commented, except for one thing. Teddie's courage could not revive the myth, and he died with no one but Merrick for consolation in his final agony.

As he lay beside Teddie's burned body, Merrick was impressed by the similarity between Teddie's death and Edwina Crane's act of suttee. Both had tried to sustain the same belief: Man-Bap as depicted by Edwina's stylized picture of Queen Victoria. Both made the same, noble, hopeless gesture: Teddie going out to save the INA traitors, and Edwina guarding the school house at Muzzafirabad. Teddie walked into a trap, and Edwina imprisoned herself in and set fire to a shed--both desperate acts of embattled believers (p.413). They met the same fate as the scorpion in a ring of fire: death by burning.

Man-Bap was the raj at their best, and both Sarah and Lady Manners wished that their best would be remembered (pp.318,358). But their best was past history. Their worst "is the lives we lead" (p.318) and that, to Lady Manners, was what really mattered. As the raj saw it, Man-Bap was the traditional relationship, the age-old pledge from a superior, parental race to an inferior, child-like people. But it had become an excuse, a compulsive need on the part of the English to deny India's right to come of age in order to ensure their continuing sense of security and identity.

The worst about the raj was not only how they victimized Hari Kumar, insulted Ahmed Kasim, postponed Indian independence, or dealt high-handedly with the native population.[19] The worst was also how the raj betrayed their own. As a group, the raj had no interest in or means of fostering and encouraging members to flourish as individual persons. Private life and interior vitality were neglected because the raj had only a public face (p.145). The code, the form, the "good show" was what mattered. The whole was greater than the sum of its parts (p.171) and more important than any one individual. The code of group responsibility dictated that Susan marry the proper type from an acceptable family and background.[20]

To Susan, armored in her wedding dress with the veil symbolically pulled over her face (p.214), the raj extended all its resources of approval, affirmation, and support. But her honeymoon was a disaster. She had expected to find happiness and love, sexual fulfillment and unitive pleasure if she followed the code. All that had been the implicit guarantee, and "all that was on the other side" (p.355). For three days Susan let Teddie do things to her body and almost came to believe that there was something to her after all (p.357). But she never truly gave herself to Teddie. She did not know how to love or how to learn (p.360).

When she was informed of Teddie's death Susan let out a "drawnout shriek, a desolate cry of anguish" (p.335). It was the first honest expression of her life. Madness, grief, and despair were the substantial truths about her, but faced with these truths the raj had no response. It had no place for a lost individual, nor could it help Susan find herself. "It did not know her and had no answer..." (p.346). If Susan could not count as a member of the raj then she did not know how to count as a person.

"I used to feel like a drawing that anyone who wanted to could come along and rub out" (p.355), Susan confided to Sarah. When Susan came to India she hoped she could make a life that the raj would recognize and approve of. She would finally be at home, finally count. "Then no one could come along and rub me out..." (p.357). After Teddie's death Susan was devastated by the realization that she could never make it to the other side of the wall, never feel secure in that secret garden of happy center. Something inside had been left out: There was no love deep down for anyone (p.357).

75

Without a father, Teddie's baby would only have her, and Susan could not face it. "There is nothing to me at all. Nothing. Nothing at all" (p.345). She could no longer hide her feelings of fear, insecurity, and unhappiness. The armor of her fine looks, good family, and proper life could not protect her against the increasing heat of the encircling flames. She flushed: "I'm out in the open. Like when you lift a stone and there's something underneath running in circles" (p.355). Susan, too, was the scorpion in a ring of fire. Her raj defenses were ineffective against the light and heat of this truth: that the Edwardian sun had set. Susan withdrew from the game completely. Like Hari Kumar, she wrapped herself in a shroud of silence.

Unlike her sister, Sarah was much more critical of the role she was expected to assume. On the surface she had become a pillar of the raj community (p.331), having shouldered her familial duties in John Layton's absence. But she could not take "it" on trust like Susan and Teddie. She resented being made love to in a representative state of mind. She was not an embodiment of an ideal. She was a person who would not be thoughtlessly implicated in the raj's code--until it was defined and justified to her (pp.123,150).

The ladies of the Pankot military community realized that Sarah's intricate brooding did not stem from a simple case of self-absorption (p.49). Sarah worried them. Her aloofness gave the impression that she did not take "it" seriously, as seriously as she should, and that she was privately laughing at them. That was why, the ladies cattily concluded, that Sarah Layton still had not found a husband. Such attitudes made her unsound (p.133). That possibility had occurred to Sarah. She waited and longed for someone to fall in love with her enduring Layton face and unclaimed body (p.423). She suspected that, if she continued to question and examine, she might never be happy (p.124).

Sarah was honest to the bitter end. Once she rejected the raj code, she had nothing to replace it, nothing positive to fill the empty shell. Claiming none of the moral certainty and illumination proper to the Edwardian age, Sarah found herself questioning basic standards and values. Her conversations with

Merrick shed light on Sarah's interior doubt.

> "There are times," Sarah said, "when
> I think I don't know what a human
> being is." Times--she told her-
> self--when I look up and see that
> heaven is empty and that this is an
> age when all of us share the know-
> ledge that it is and that there has
> never been a god nor any man made in
> that image (p.223).

Standing outside the moral certainty of perpetual
light, Sarah found herself wondering if there were
such a thing as "great love" (p.451). Perhaps, she
reflected as she left Merrick's hospital room in
Calcutta, the real world was simply an amalgam of
chemical reactions for the purpose of giving some
lucky few experiences of sensual pleasure or creature
comforts (pp.93,421).[21] Sarah was no longer certain
whether men had souls, or whether there were such
things as right and wrong (p.403). For Sarah, as for
Lady Manners, the years of belief were over and the
years of disbelief had begun (pp.51,358). Once Sarah
entered into this state she realized "that this kind
of knowing isn't knowing but bowing my head, as you
[Ethel Manners] were bowing yours, under the weight
of it" (p.503).

The age of the raj was passing away. The war
postponed the day of Indian independence, but the end
was inevitable nonetheless because the raj was dying
from within. Even the most stalwart members kept the
form but no longer had faith in God or their own
sacred history and moral guidelines. Even Susan
suspected the truth: "...people like us were
finished years ago, and we know it, but pretend not
to and go on as if we thought we still mattered"
(p.358). This last generation of raj was not "bone
of India's bone" (p.358). It was a foreign,
unwanted, and dissatisfied element on the fringes of
its own dying history. They betrayed the tradition
of their fathers, and out of a sense of guilt, of
defeat, and of inadequacy hated one another, hated
the country they were a part of, and hated their own
changing history (p.358). The heritage of Man-Bap,
created and cherished by generations of raj families,
had vanished with the Edwardian age. Sarah understood that:

> We live in holes and crevices of the
> crumbling stone, no longer sheltered
> by the carapace of our history which
> is leaving us behind. And one day we
> shall lie exposed, in our tender
> skins (p.415).

All that was left, contended Jimmy Clark, was to cut
off the stinking limb of India and set it free. It
would do no good to fan the dying flames. All that
was left, for people like Hari Kumar and other
trainees in Chillingborough's liberal school of
imperial administrators, was to play "tomb attendant"
(p.445).

Ironically, it was Sarah, fair blossom of the
respected Muir and Layton regimental tradition, who
stood poised, with the power to drive a nail into the
coffin. She chose not to license another generation
of jailers her Uncle Arthur was cultivating (p.422),
despite a dream she had about her father. In this
dream Teddie visited her and advised, "Of course,
Sarah, it'll be up to you really" (p.324). Then her
father told her in a supportive but obviously
disappointed tone, "I suppose you did your best"
(p.325). Sarah felt, as the colonel's daughter, an
obligation to keep the code alive for her father, if
not within the family circle then at least within her
own life (p.461). He would want her to hold back the
tide of changing circumstances, to hold in trust the
days of perpetual-seeming light that once belonged to
him (p.458).

But as much as she loved her father, Sarah could
not face the claustrophobic atmosphere of duty, the
weight of the crumbled stone. Balanced between the
call to stay and preserve or the need to run and
rebel, Sarah chose to crawl out from the broken
carapace and brave the scorching truth. Suspended
between a meaningless past and an uncertain future
(p.369), Sarah preferred to exist as a firefly,
illumined dimly from within by her own interior light
instead of prolonging the days of "perpetual light."
It was more seemly for a generation of exiles to
carry their family and past as an interior illumination of mind and heart than to pretend the gathering
darkness outside themselves did not exist (p.228).
Sarah chose to leap into the darkness rather than
hold it back, and the catalyst-like agent for this
decision was Jimmy Clark.

Their sexual encounter was not an act of love. It did not even have the air of desperate need that Hari's and Daphne's union had. Clark challenged Sarah to enter into something for its own sake, to do it for sheer enjoyment and pleasure, and to give herself over to it entirely (p.122).[22] Such an act meant breaking out of the raj prison, an order of release of sorts. The key to Clark's bedroom door opened "a prison of a kind" (p.458). But their union was an incomplete gesture, before which Sarah had "a dim recollection of an empty gesture that had something to do with wrenching the reins of a horse" (p.457). Clark could not offer Sarah his love. He only wanted to possess her body even though he was well aware and appreciative of her expansive and substantial interior dimensions.

Sarah abandoned the raj's code "to enter into her body's grace" (p.461).[23] It was a feeble act of liberty by a fledgling individual. Sadly, she chose to fill her shell with an inadequate gesture rather than waiting for the gesture to develop a meaning and value of its own as she did while riding with Ahmed (p.125). Release from the raj prison on any terms would not liberate her. She had first to determine what she wanted to escape to and be saved for.

In choosing to sacrifice the raj code for what she perceived as true, Sarah realized that she was giving up the "collective illusion of a world morally untroubled...a world that thought it knew what human beings were" (p.346). She did not believe in God (p.360), and she was glad no one in her family did either (p.82). Sarah was perceptive enough to realize what a world without God meant: "it is an intensely bleak discovery because it calls our bluff on everything" (p.223). No moral definition of man, of justice, of right and wrong could be assumed. Only God's presence guaranteed rightful authority (p.173); only He justly deserved and instilled devotion to a cause and sacred obligation.[24]

Even for those who still believed in a higher power, the world seemed constricted and consumed in darkness. The retired missionary Barbie Batchelor was self-righteously judgmental about the entire Bibighar incident, and especially about Daphne's baby. The meaning of Parvati's name, the fact that she had never "been brought to God" (p.367), and that she had been conceived through an act of fornication

horrified Barbie as much as did the thought of a
white woman being freely intimate with a native.
Barbie was quick to add, in acquiescence to a
somewhat embarrassing tenent of her faith, that of
course "we are all God's children" (p.367).

Lady Manners was a believer, but her faith gave
her little reassurance in the face of the injustice
and social censorship she lived with. Her soul, she
knew, would achieve some state of happiness after
death, but that end was unimaginable and unintelligible and therefore a kind of oblivion (p.319). The
prospect of finding mercy in this life, and even in
the next, seemed almost hopeless (p.43). She
believed

> We must remember the worst because
> the worst is the lives we lead, the
> best is only our history, and between
> our history and our lives there is
> the vast dark plain where the rapt
> and patient shepherds drive their
> invisible flocks in expectation of
> God's forgiveness (p.318).[25]

The union of the raj's history with the Christian tradition crystallized with Teddie's memorial
service. Rev. Peplow's sermon should have been
inspiring, but Susan found it lacking that spark of
illumination which would provide comfort and lend
meaning to Teddie's tragic death. The out-dated, pat
religious formulas were not enough (p.345). Even the
hymns sung during the ceremony registered the growing
mood of alarm and despair: "Oh God of Comfort, hear
our cry--And in the darkest hour draw nigh" (p.340).
And again: "Hold Thou Thy Cross before my closing
eyes;--Shine through the gloom..." (.341).

If there was a God he would be much like
Claudine, the blind seamstress who created and
captured beautiful butterflies in lace. God, as a
blind creator, imprisoned men in a web of darkness
and duty, so that they would never enjoy life, never
make love in the sunshine. "As yes, poor butterflies. They are one of my prisoners" (p.371).

If God was blind to the fate of men, then man's
environment was indifferent also. If God did not
rule over the affairs of men, then the world was like
a circle of threatening flames, "a repository only of

80

occasions and conditions of despair..." (p.429). Nature harbored a sweet indifference to man's problems (p.395). Without God there was no "great chain of being" marking the metaphysical communion between the state of man's inner being and the material order, a fact which Sarah realized during the storm in Calcutta: "The Furies were riding across an uninhabited sky, to their own and no one else's destruction" (p.421).

If it was expedient for Sarah to cast off the vestiges of a meaningless past, it was also necessary for her to reject the religious traditions of her people. She was not only left with the shell of her regimental skin but with antiquated relics of her religious inheritance, like her baptism gown made of lace-imprisoned butterflies. The gown was a work of vanished generations (p.370), a relic of a promise unfulfilled, a symbol of transformation and rebirth, of participation in a God-man relationship, of a caring and loving providential protection (p.450).

When Mabel knelt beside the storage trunk and unwrapped the gown, Sarah noticed that her posture was the same as when she pruned her rose bushes. It was appropriate, Sarah reflected, that decayed husks, whether religious or historical, should be pruned away. Only then could people and roses be coaxed to their vigor and ripe old age, "with the removal of those decayed relics of its former flowering" (p.370).[26]

Even though Sarah did not believe in baptism, she agreed to be baby Edward's godmother. Susan insisted that the old religious (and now social) custom be exercised. On the day before the baptism, Susan dressed her son in his (formerly Sarah's) gown of captive butterflies, as if this relic of former flowering, this echo of Paradise, would be his best possible protection, the best possible armor if there were any truth left to the raj code at all.[27] She carried the child to the end of the garden next to the servants' wall, the barrier between them and the secret garden of happy center. Taking the can of kerosene which Mahmoud used to burn the "accumulation of unwanted years" (p.504), Susan poured the liquid in a wide, geometrically perfect circle.[28] Then, reenacting Edwina's and Teddie's deaths, she set a match and watched the flames enclose Edward: a scorpion in a ring of fire.

One of the richest symbols in The Day of the Scorpion is Scott's use of light and darkness, which occurs no fewer than forty-seven times. In the simplest examples, Scott uses light to illuminate faces. Jimmy Clark's face, when he rode with Sarah in the taxi after abducting her from the rest of the group, was illumined by "odd, distorting lights" (p.437). The photograph of Hari Kumar which Nigel Rowan showed to Lady Manners revealed a two-leveled density of a dark face in artificial lighting (p.235). At the Binghams' wedding reception Count Bronowsky's black eyepatch made him look like a nocturnal animal caught out in the sun (p.181). Merrick's face in bright sunlight showed his age (p.181), but in darkness his features and form did not fade or diminish. His presence seemed intensified, taking on an added dimension of density (p.218) because he was in his own element.

There was the light of the sun, shining brightly on the day of battle (p.395) and after Teddie's funeral service (p.343), producing a glare on the lawn at the wedding reception in the midst of which Teddie and Susan stood together (p.176). There was the sunshine which reflected off the palace lake in Mirat into which Sarah gazed, "letting that milky translucence work its illusion of detaching her...floating her off into a sea of dangerous white hot substance that was neither air nor water" (p.156).

Scott also uses the light image as a metaphor for what is good and healthy. The government of Mirat was brought out of darkness into the light of day (p.98). Sarah, when feeling pressured and trapped, needed air and light (p.337). Susan's grief after Teddie's death could not be shared, could not emerge into the light of day. Sarah walked in the twilight back to the veranda where her family waited in a "geometrical pattern of light and the circle of safety" (p.230).

Light is used to symbolize the ability to understand. Sarah comprehended Merrick's words as "if a whole light shone on it" (p.220). It is used to mean a life-giving, liberating force. Sarah felt happy after the wedding, as if she had found herself, or found an answer. If there was a light, she wanted to enter it (p.214). "Truth is a fire few of us get scorched by" (p.411). The raj's code and moral certainty was preserved in "perpetual Edwardian sunlight" (p.444) and yet was ending like "this hearth with its dying fire" (p.411).

There are highly visual images such as Susan's kneeling on the grass, the halo of her hair glowing against the red brick of the servants' wall (p.358). Uncle Arthur stood in the colored light of the stained glass window at Susan's wedding, praying to be delivered from the "perpetual shadow of professional neglect" (p.171). With his posting to Calcutta he reached the end of his dark rainbow (p.374). Count Bronowsky spoke of the golden youth Ahmed falling into the arms of some deserving Diana and "the day was properly divided from the night" (p.167).

As he develops his light imagery, Scott brings another strand into his complicated pattern: the imagery of darkness. It symbolizes many things, the first of which is death. Death was a darkness which would engulf everyone just as it claimed the Muirs and Laytons buried in the Pankot graveyard (p.341). There was also the darkness of Susan's madness, which frightened the raj community. Sarah told her, "We sense from the darkness in you the darkness in ourselves, a darkness and a death wish. Neither is admissible. We chase that illusion of perpetual light. But there's no such thing" (p.501).

Darkness is also used as an image of evil. The unknown rapists sprang out of the darkness at Daphne (p.307). Randiput prison was a triumph of interior darkness, a place of cruelty, injustice, despair, humiliation, and isolation (p.237). Sarah sensed that Merrick was the dark, arcane side of the raj (p.415) as she walked with him "in the swiftly encroaching dark through wich he was beginning to loom" (p.221). Merrick's line between blacks and whites determined his behavior "like a blind man with a white stick needing the edge of the pavement" (p.224).

There are images of darkness which are not blatantly evil but simply a statement of an unfortunate truth. Between the best of the raj's history

and the worst of their individual lives lay a vast,
dark plain (p.318). For Daphne and Hari darkness
fell across the constellations (p.305). John Layton
waited patiently in Germany for his passage through
the night (p.421).

Darkness is also used as either an indifferent
or benign element of life. The night air was India's
only caress (p.228). The raj were light fireflies
emitting faint interior flickerings in a sea of
darkness, "signal lights of souls" (p.477). Ahmed
emerged from the dark interior of the Nawab's guest
house when he and Sarah first met (p.156). Barbie's
constant chatter and rendering of opinions gave
issues of the past the "dark, ponderable glow of
living issues" (p.367). Daphne would flare up out of
Sarah's darkness (p.158), or thoughts of her and Lady
Manners appeared to Sarah "like vapours casting
actual shadows" on a sunlit scene (p.183). The
bedroom where Sarah gave herself to Clark was dark,
and she felt safe in the oblivion of her own private
darkness (p.456). Both Mabel Layton and Mohammed Ali
Kasim were solid, real, and cast shadows of their own
(p.333). Ahmed, tired of living in the darkness of
his father's shadow, longed to cast one of his own
(p.494).

There are also occasions where light and not
darkness is the malevolent image. Sarah observed
that "what light there is, when it comes, comes
harshly and unexpectedly and in it we look extraordinarily ugly and incapable" (p.501). For English
exiles in India, the enemy was not darkness of the
unknown but the light and certainty of their own smug
prejudice (p.422).

It is clear from these examples that Scott's use
of light imagery does not consistently align the
"good" with light and "evil" with darkness. In
"perpetual Edwardian sunlight" the purpose of life
might be clear, moral perimeters defined, and choices
clearly illumined, but the perception of reality was
narrow and limited. This light became a prison, and
dimmed to darkness in the face of the brighter and
scorching fire of truth. The coming light would be
more honest, "whose heat would burn the old one to a
shadow" (p.458).

The image of darkness associated with Ronald
Merrick is clearly evil. But darkness is also a sign

for the unknown and unexplored, such as Sarah's own inner self. It symbolizes the incomprehensible and unintelligible, which was how Sarah regarded Daphne's love for Hari, or the details of Ahmed's life. In cases such as these, the darkness is not absolute but relative. Daphne's love was not senseless in itself but merely incomprehensible to Sarah. Ahmed's life was not engulfed in absolute, metaphysical evil like Merrick's, but it seemed dark to Sarah who could not imagine or understand it. Here darkness manifests a condition of the perceiver rather than of the perceived.

Light makes sight possible, but in the case of Sarah's encounter with Clark in the dark bedroom, other senses were at work even though her vision was symbolically hindered. Light illuminates, makes things understandable and intelligible, yet it is not the ultimate measure of reality. In the case of a person casting a shadow, like Mabel Layton or Mohammed Ali Kasim, the important reality is the figure, not the light which is displaced or absorbed. Mabel and MAK knew who they were; they had an unshakable sense of self outside the raj's "perpetual Edwardian sunlight." Perhaps, in casting their shadows, they absorbed outside light: "negative and positive were aligned on top of the other" (p.235). But perhaps that outside light was scorched by their interior illumination (not fireflies but beacons), scorched by the truth of their personhood. Their shadows were a perceptible measure of their being, of their interior stature. In this symbolic sense Merrick, who could absorb darkness without being diminished, would never absorb light and thus never cast a shadow of his own.

Light and darkness are not polar opposites. They are vehicles Scott uses to convey a truth by comparison. Edwardian sunlight is brighter than Merrick's darkness, but dimmer than the scorching light of truth. As light and dark are only comparison, so also are white and black and (in some cases) even good and evil. Differences, Scott seems to be reminding the reader, may often be a case of degree. There is such a thing as truth, but the way people tell it is always relative to their own experiences and points of view. "It shows where people's hearts lie" (p.197). In day-to-day living moral choices are exercised, not in arenas of absolute good and evil, but in infinite shades of grey.

But this was not true in the case of Ronald Merrick, whose moral guideline was absolute and to whom the gulf between black and white was sacrosanct. If "there has never been a god nor any man made in that image" (p.223), then Ronald Merrick had his own answer to the problem of what it meant to be human, a definition shaped largely by his own prejudice and life history.

After the wedding, Teddie shunned Merrick's company. He resented being involved with common signs of vulgarity as in the incidents of the stone and the suppliant woman. Teddie's best man was not really "one of us," not of his class or social background, and Teddie never forgave Merrick for dragging the wedding party into his own sordid problems (p.354).

Because of the vacuum of Merrick's "anonymous history" (p.392), Teddie did not trust Merrick to deal with the INA prisoner. At least that was how Merrick interpreted Teddie's insistence on going up with him to interrogate Mohammed Baksh. Although Sarah believed this of Teddie, it is clear that Merrick could not have interpreted Teddie's coolness in any other way. Merrick himself was neurotically conscious of class difference. Viewing all human relations according to that factor, he was unable to walk into a room without measuring himself against every other white or black man. Merrick reduced all forms of rejection, dislike and mistrust to social prejudice and believed Teddie did the same.[29] As an insecure, lonely man from a deprived background, he envied Teddie for being born into a privileged position and class and into a superior family lineage which gave him the opportunity to participate in the legend, to warm his hands near the raj's hearth and its dying fire (p.411).

Merrick was a man apart, living in the cold and darkness. He was the perfect man to deal with the INA problem, and it was natural for him to make the problem his specialty because it signified a personal triumph over all the superior amateurs and their emotional approach to life. It shattered the raj's faith in Man-Bap and made them look like fools. It suggested that blacks were not capable of a white standard of behavior after all. They could not

sustain feelings of loyalty, bravery, and faithful-
ness to the Crown and their own sacred oath. Once
information about the INA's became common knowledge,
whites found it increasingly difficult to keep up the
charade of respecting blacks for pulling their own
weight and for reflecting the attributes and abil-
ities white men valued most.[30]

For Teddie, the INA question was a moral one,
and the issue illuminated the social differences
between himself and Merrick (p.391). It mattered
deeply to Teddie because it determined his self-image
and the image of his people. He could not leave
Mohammed Baksh in the hands of Merrick the
unbeliever, Merrick the outcast, Merrick the persecuted. He offered forgiveness to Baksh, then went out
to find his two colleagues, calling them by name
(p.406).[31]

That Merrick would eventually be embraced into
the fold as "one of us" (p.367) was indicative of the
raj's moral decline. Merrick's attempt to save Teddie
from a firey death won him the sympathy of the Pankot
community and the Layton family. Susan felt
"beholden" and commissioned Sarah to visit Merrick
and invite him into a god-relationship with their
family. In this way the Laytons were forced to
approach Merrick just as the suppliant woman had. In
depending on Merrick for the truth about Teddie's
death, the Laytons looked to him to relieve their
suffering and anxiety (pp.361-62). After her visit to
the hospital, Sarah was informed by Aunt Fenny that
she had the family's approval if she was interested
in Merrick, because he "counted."

Merrick was very much like members of the raj,
but not in a way most of them would have recognized.
Only Sarah did:

> You are, yes, our dark side, the
> arcane side. You reveal something
> that is sad about us, as if out here
> we had built a mansion without doors
> and windows, with no way in and no
> way out. All India lies on our
> doorstep and cannot enter to warm us
> or to be warmed (p.415).

What was wrong about Merrick was wrong about the raj.
He simply pushed their assumptions and attitudes to

their logical conclusions.

If there was no God, if the raj had no basis for
its attitude of moral superiority, then it needed
another justification for its ruling position. Whoever believed Indians to be innately inferior,
incapable of self-rule and not to be cultivated as
friends, were manifesting aspects of Ronald Merrick's
creed. Whoever believed that India should be
administered according to the old ways of Generals
Dyer and Reid or doubted that blacks could ever be
modernized sufficiently to master Western civilization's intricate technology or believed that a black
man could only diminish a white woman, believed as
Merrick did (p.227). According to Merrick, social
pressures which kept blacks and whites sexually
separated were the same as biological pressures.
British and Indians by nature were not meant to be
lovers, friends, or intimate associates in any way
(pp.226-27).

The raj as a whole, whether they ever discussed
the issue publicly or not, would agree with or live
according to Merrick's code. The basic premise was
that whites were biologically, and therefore culturally and morally, superior. That was the line,
Merrick's line. It separated blacks from whites,
right from wrong, and defined what it meant to be
human. This line was as necessary to British conduct
as a white walking stick was to a blind man following
the edge of the pavement (p.224). It gave Merrick a
sense of purpose, of identity, a "moral term of
reference" (p.224). He knew who he was when he got
up in the morning.

Merrick's line replaced the worn relic of
Christian morality based on revelation and reason.
There was nothing the raj needed to do or to be in
order to maintain its identity except to be white. No
code of honor, no heritage of service, no rules for
people living together existed except Merrick's rules
of contempt. Teddie's honorable actions were meaningless. Daphne's relationship with Hari was "like a
direct challenge to everything sane and decent we try
to do out here" (p.202).

Merrick admitted to Sarah that his line was
arbitrary, e.g., not based on any authority other
than his own (p.224). Merrick's line could function
only in a godless world. Most of the raj needed a

god-like authority to justify their position and behavior. But Merrick was his own authority and would be incapable of implementing his philosophy of hate in a Christian world. In fact, Merrick blamed liberally-minded Christians for corrupting the "calm purity of their contempt" which whites naturally felt for black (p.311). Merrick's contempt for the liberal policies of Whitehall knew no bounds. He believed the real criminals of Bibighar were those who pretended there was such a thing as universal brotherhood and equality (p.310). He felt straight-jacketed by policies concocted by people who did not know anything about the real India. The disadvantages of such a system were twofold: 1) Merrick could not act or judge according to his own instincts. He had to be a rubber-stamp administrator, and 2) he believed that as such the system would back him up no matter what he did, that he could literally get away with murder. Merrick's objections were legitimate. To be able to function in a truly human way a person must be able to act freely and to be held responsible for his actions. But a man like Merrick with no conscience enjoyed and functioned under the white man's protective cloak and could abuse the law and the purpose of the raj's code for his own twisted purposes.

According to Merrick, when the British feigned admiration for the Indian military and servant classes, they were really manifesting perverted sexuality and feudal arrogance. What the English really admired were blacks' attempts to imitate white political ideas or expressions of bravery and loyalty exercised on their behalf (p.311).

Raj solidarity, according to Merrick, was not based on common tradition, equality of position, love of regiment, or a call to service. What bound whites together was their contempt for Indians as men (p.312). For Merrick this did not simply mean a belief that a black was more stupid or lazy or less competent a soldier or statesman. Blacks were inferior not in degree but in kind--as men, essentially inferior as human beings.

This was Merrick's godless definition of what it meant to be human. Relationships between people were based on contempt, not love. Contempt was the prime human emotion because without divine fatherhood "men are not born equal, nor are they born brothers" (p.114). There was no such thing as the brotherhood of man (p.311). Contempt and envy, not love and hate as Edwina Crane believed, were the two faces of the British/Indian coin. Merrick believed that man's personality, his unique stamp, existed at the point of equilibrium between the two (p.312).[32] A man's identity was not based on his relationship with a loving savior or with another human being about whom he cared. His personhood depended on how and when he balanced his envy and contempt within himself. To be human he did not need anything or anyone else. It was a closed definition of being human, a prison. To be human would ultimately mean to be self-obsessed, like Merrick himself, who wanted to stand in the spotlight, but would have to stand alone.

In practice the Raj's self-righteous and bigoted presumptions of superiority created a barrier against blacks as surely as did Merrick's policy of contempt. With God dead the old moral standards no longer applied. Instead of absolute truth there were only opinions or instincts, or Merrick's arbitrary line between black and white. "Vulgar" replaced "evil"; society and its relative, bigoted standards usurped a god-governed world.

For a moment, while he lay with Teddie in the jungle and contempleted Edwina Crane's death, it seemed to Merrick that "it" might be true, that there really was devotion, sacrifice, self-denial, a sacred code of conduct, something higher and more noble than the merely human (p.413). Teddie almost made a believer out of Merrick, but not quite. Because, after all, Teddie was dead, Teddie was the fool, not Merrick. Merrick was alive though grossly (and symbolically) disfigured--looking barely human (p.418). But Merrick emerged from the experience assured that the legend Teddie exemplified was an "impossible, nonsensical dream" (p.414). There was no final moral definition of the raj or of man in general, no "environment some sort of God created" (pp.413-14).

Merrick felt responsible for Teddie's death. If Teddie had believed Merrick was his own kind, if he had trusted him to deal properly with the INA prisoner, he would have not followed him and he would still be alive. "It was the stone all over again" (p.387): Teddie's being victimized by Merrick's presence. It was not intentional, Merrick confided to

Sarah. He had not chosen Teddie, but "afterwards he haunts you, just as if he were on your conscience. The irony is that you don't really have him there. You can question you conscience and come out with a clean bill. But he sticks, just the same" (p.386).

For Merrick, to speak of having a conscience was the ultimate defilement of truth. The point of the persecution after Bibighar was to convince him of his terrible mistake and make his life unbearable because he could do nothing to chanage it (p.220). Many people came to realize that Bibighar was a total and unforgivable disaster, one with which no conscience could cope (p.304). But Merrick was not one of them.[33] "I think that I shall believe they were [guilty,]" Merrick informed Count Bronowsky, "until my dying day" (p.199).

Sarah knew that Merrick was a man without a conscience:

> Perhaps that was the way into him, to become his victim and then to haunt his conscience. But if so, it seemed to her that it was an approach without access in the end. There was, for some reason, no way into him at all, and all the people whom he chose as victims lay scattered on his threshold (p.415).

Sarah found Merrick appalling. She sensed his self-obsession and instinctively distrusted his "calculated candor," as Daphne called it. What she did not yet fully understand was that the Laytons were Merrick's victims too. Perhaps it was a way of punishing an outstanding raj family for perceiving him as not quite decent enough, a little too vulgar, too humble in origin. Perhaps it was a way Merrick could force his way into the raj's good graces. But because Merrick did not let Teddie "fry," the Laytons felt "beholden" (p.361). Merrick succeeded in forcing Sarah to approach him and to witness his burden.

Merrick did not accept the offer of being godfather to Teddie's child. He sensed Sarah's reluctance and had already triumphed over her by forcing her to ask him in the first place. Sarah did not want this man tied to her family in a god-rela-

tionship (p.362). Perpetual Edwardian sunlight may
have been dimming to total darkness; the majesty of
her inheritance might be in its dying moments. But
Sarah, the colonel's daughter, wanted the raj's ruin
to be a noble one. To die with honor meant to die
without Merrick's infiltration, without his demonic
influence. [34]

It was to Sarah's credit that she sensed
Merrick's appalling interior without witnessing him
in his true form, as described by Hari Kumar in his
interview with Nigel Rowan. It is primarily during
this interview that Scott lays bare Merrick's real
disposition, his true feelings about Bibighar and
about blacks and whites living together. It was also
during this interview that Hari revealed Merrick's
philosophy about "the situation."

It is clear in The Jewel in the Crown that
Merrick hated Hari from the moment of their first
encounter. [35] "Merrick spoke to me as if I were a lump
of dirt," Hari recalled during his interview (p.268).
Merrick's version of their meeting was that Hari
responded to him with "dumb insolence" (p.201) and
harbored designs to avenge himself on the white
community for not accepting him as an Englishman
(p.208). But until Bibighar their relationship was
only "symbolic," according to Merrick. Hari's arrest
gave Merrick the opportunity to make their relationship "real" by enacting "the situation."

For Merrick, history was a series of events
whose significance had never been realized. Because
people were afraid to accept responsibility for their
actions, they preferred to view these events as part
of an impersonal drift. By pretending they had no
control, people ironically contributed to the random-
ness of history's flow. But the direction of history
could be corrected, redirected, by understanding and
enacting ideas, thus establishing their proper significance (p.309).

Comradeship, to Merrick a lame and pitiful
catchword, was impossible between black and white.
The only true emotions were fear on the part of
Indians and contempt on the part of the English. To
make these real one had to enact "the situation"
(p.310). The first phase was degradation. While he
slowly sipped whiskey, Merrick contemplated and
inspected Hari's naked body. During the second,

"persuasive" phase, Merrick tied Hari over a trestle and caned him. It was during this phase that Merrick, while stroking Hari's genitals, said: "Aren't you enjoying it? Certainly a randy fellow like you can do better than this?" (p.302) [36]

During these first two phases Merrick's words and actions were unhurried and deliberate. He wanted to extract everything possible from the situation while Hari was in his power.[37]Hari and Merrick were finally face to face, with everything in the white man's favor (p.293).

During the "charitable" third phase of the situation, Merrick offered Hari a glass of water. It was a reminder of the white man's power to be kind, to be magnanimous. Such action was not an affirmation of any innate dignity of the black, but functioned as a tool to emphasize the two great dimensions of human interaction: fear and contempt. It would only degrade Hari if he continued to pretend equality, and it would corrupt Merrick himself if he pretended anything other than hatred (p.310).

What Hari realized and Merrick forgot about this play, this performance of "the situation," was that it existed only if Hari participated (p.315). Once Hari detached himself from Merrick's game and from those feelings Merrick tried to instill, he would no longer be in the white man's power. By the next morning it was evident that the case was not going as well as Merrick expected. He was sure of Hari's guilt and could not understand why the white man's law would not quickly condemn him (p.316). Perhaps the liberal policies which Merrick despised impeded the process of swift and absolute punishment. But Merrick still singlemindedly tried to trample Hari's dignity and illusions: "What price Chillingborough now?" (p.317) How did liberal illusions measure up against the situation in the real world?

But Merrick did not defeat Hari Kumar. Months of prison life had subdued Hari's body. His face was pale, his cheeks hollow. His head hung low and his back curved from lonely hours of sitting and holding his head between his hands. But his eyes were alert, and his voice conveyed not only an impression of Englishness, but a sense of his interior dignity and spirit (p.243).

Hari had matured since his petulant days of
bitterness and disappointment in Mayapore. "My behaviour at that time left a lot to be desired," he
admitted to Rowan (p.261). In 1942 being intimate "in
mind" with Colin had been Hari's way of maintaining
his inner sense of Englishness. But he had realized
how ridiculous the effort was when Colin did not
recognize him at the cricket game on the maidan
(pp.263,286). He was even suspicious of Daphne's
overtures of friendship. After years of being invisible to English people he could not believe that she
regarded him as an equal or could be interested in
him as a man (pp.260-61).

Hari was ashamed for half-believing Merrick's
lie that Daphne had accused him of attacking her,
just as he was ashamed of thanking Merrick for the
glass of water. Merrick wanted Hari to feel grateful
to him, "beholden" as Susan would say, for any
gesture of kindness, and to depend on him to
delineate faithfully his proper place as an Indian in
the white world (p.313). For a few brief hours
Merrick succeeded. In his cell that night Hari wanted
Merrick's approval, wanted his acceptance and forgiveness, because in that prison cell Merrick was
master. Hari recalled the nightmarish first evening:
"I called out for help. The name I called was
Merrick" (p.313).

The shock of his own prayer of supplication
jarred Hari to his senses. Rather than give in to the
forces intent on destroying him--the threatening
flames pressing him on all side--he wondered if he
should not destroy himself like the scorpion stinging
itself rather than be overpowered by outside enemies.
It seemed the only act of free will open to him. And
what would be lost, except a ridiculous amalgam of
Duleep's ambition and his own preferences and prejudices? Hari felt like "a nonentity masquerading as a
person of secret consequence" (p.314).

Merrick's contempt almost destroyed whatever
remnant of dignity and pride Hari had salvaged
through his years in India. Then it occurred to Hari
that "nonentity" was a comparative term. To establish
his identity by comparison was playing Merrick's
game, doing what Merrick's own consuming inferiority
complex forced him to do. Hari realized, "I wasn't to
be compared. I was myself, and no one had any right
in regard to me....Whatever kind of poor job I was in

94

my own eyes I was Hari Kumar....there was no one anywhere exactly like him" (p.314).

Gradually Hari's illusions, his support system, his self-concept had been stripped away. He was left with an undeniable sense of the hard core of himself without any other qualification. Take away the exterior details--his color, race, religion, education, cultural background, talents, manners, and abilities--and there was still the unique and incomparable person of Hari Kumar. His Englishness was accidental to his person. He did not have to be a good Indian or a good Englishman to be himself.

Wrapped in a towel and pacing his cell with the cup of water Merrick had left, Hari realized he had come to the point his Hindu grandfather had reached years before: Sannyasi. In a way similar to his grandfather's, for his own salvation, Hari stripped himself down to bare essentials, answerable to and defined only by himself. "Here I am, a good Indian at last" (p.315). Hari's grandfather gave up everything to lose himself in oblivion. Hari would also diasppear, unknown, not to lose himself but to find and remain himself.

Hari's discovery of a sense of unique and inviolate selfhood was the only way to combat, to overturn Merrick's contempt/envy philosophy and all the other destructive powers bent on his demise. Like Sarah, he was not sure what that personhood meant, he did not know how to fill up this self or how to fulfill this essential core of personhood. But he would protect himself by keeping the vow of silence he made to Daphne. Only through the armor of silence could he refuse to participate in Merrick's defiling "situation." Hari would rely on no one, "no one, for help of any kind. I don't know whether that made me a good Indian. But it seemed like a way of proving the existence of Hari Kumar, and standing by what he was" (p.315). No one had the right to destroy him. Merrick may have had the means, but he did not have the right (p.314).

IV

Hari's participation in Bibighar ended with his interview with Nigel Rowan. It was then he learned of Daphne's death and was released from his vow of silence, a vow never reasonable but the only means by which Hari could retain, protect, and possess his love. He wept silently for her, hardly aware of "this curious emotional expulsion from the deep-set eyes of rivulets that coursed down his cheeks" (p.304): streams which ossified so that it seemed Rowan could lean over and pick them from his cheeks like insect wings (p.305). No one else except Lady Manners had cried for Daphne. Ethel knew that the distance between herself and her niece's lover was insurmount- able. He was lost, just as he and Daphne had always been lost. They were

> lovers who could never be described as star-crossed because they had no stars. For them heaven had drawn an implacable band of dark across its constellations and the dark was lit by nothing except the trust they had had in each other not to tell the truth because the truth had seemed too dangerous to tell (p.305).

There was no God in heaven, no benevolent authority who would look upon their love with favor. There were no stars to guide and inspire them, no light to illumine their way. All the forces of history and society were mustered against them, not only by people who hated them, like Ronald Merrick, but by well-meaning people like Lady Manners, Rowan, and Gopol. They had only each other to cling to in the darkness, defenseless against the unknown spoilers (the rapists) and the known spoilers (Merrick).

Hari told Rowan that he would never have responded to Rowan's questions if he had known Daphne was dead. He would not have bared his soul for the amusement or pacification of a few guilty consciences (p.307). Without Hari's testimony, however, the reader would be ignorant of the immensity of Merrick's evil obsession.

Bibighar is all-pervasive in the second volume. It was, first of all, a point of public interst and gossip in places like Mirat, Ranpur, and Pankot. For Pandit Baba, Bibighar was an opportunity to encourage unrest and rebellion against British rule. Hari's case "should be taken to heart," the teacher admonished Ahmed Kasim (p.113). Whereas Pandit Baba saw the arrests as a political issue, MAK saw the actual rape as an injury done to the niece of a deservedly-respected white governor, an injury "we have a continuing responsibility for" (p.42).

Just as Bibighar affected Indians in different ways, members of the white community also displayed varied reactions. Count Bronowsky recognized Daphne's decision to keep the baby as an action which could be construed by the raj as a "breach of faith," a sign that she preferred to cling to (possibly) her black lover's child than to the code of her own kind. The Count was sorry to see Daphne become an object of contempt rather than of compassion (p.202).

Aunt Fenny's reaction was typical of the raj ladies. She would have been horrified had she met Ethel Manners in the street, but she did not hesitate to ply Ronald Merrick with personal questions just to satisfy her curiosity about the sordid details (p.213). Although Merrick was obviously inferior to the raj in class, he became a figure of interest and admiration (p.196) which would blossom more fully after Teddie's death.

The presence of two figures directly involved with the Bibighar tragedy, Ronald Merrick and Lady Manners, touch Pankot society in a more immediate way. Lady Manners' almost phantom-like appearances puzzled and embarrassed the raj community. There was a complicated tangle of threads which interrelated apparently diverse events. Sarah shopped in the bazaar for her trip to Calcutta to see Ronald Merrick and caught a glimpse of Lady Manners. Teddie's death notice resurrected the story of the stone thrown before his wedding, bringing Bibighar vividly to mind just as Lady Manners' name mysteriously appeared in the Flagstaff house book (p.347,365).[38]

For Susan, Merrick's presence at her wedding introduced a "destructive counter-element of reality" to her illusion of finally fulfilling the raj code and entering the secret garden beyond the wall (p.182). For Sarah, seeing the Nawab at the wedding reception and learning from Ahmed that the gift of Gaffer's poems was well-received called to mind the Lady who suggested them and her niece whose trunk rested mutely in the house boat. Images of the two women rose in her mind "like vapours casting actual shadows" (p.183).

The most important way in which Bibighar becomes

present is the similarity of experiences formerly faced by Hari and Daphne and now encountered by various characters within this second book.[39] Through these parallel experiences the reader repeatedly feels on the verge of witnessing yet another Bibighar, the possibility of which Scott had fore-warned in The Jewel in the Crown. Given similar characters (like Ahmed and Sarah) and Merrick's presence and unflagging obsession, the possibility of Bibighar relived looms darkly on the horizon.

Merrick was the first to observe the similarites between Daphne and Sarah.[40]Neither of them believed in "the line" (p.224). Sarah, like Daphne, did not let the raj code dictate her behavior, and Merrick feared the disgrace of the first interracial affair would be repeated. There were other superficial parallels, such as the way Sarah shaded her eyes, the way she glanced ahead, her gracefulness and less-obvious beauty, her sensitivity (p.223). Merrick was afraid that Sarah would cross the line and join Ahmed, waiting on the other side (p.226). But when Sarah and Ahmed returned from their ride together, Merrick saw that the barriers were up between them, and believed that Sarah abided by the line after all (p.225).

It was one of Merrick's fatal flaws that he judged all behavior according to his own. If there were barriers between Sarah and Ahmed it was not because she chose to adhere to the old racial taboos. Deep down, within herself, Sarah felt far away from Daphne. From the moment Daphne became real on the houseboat at Srinagar, Sarah could not comprehend what it would be like to love a black man. On two separate occasions Sarah had a chance to make Daphne's choice. Her first opportunity came when she was galloping across the plains of Mirat, wondering what it would be like to become close with someone like Ahmed Kasim. For a moment Daphne "was alive for me completely. She flared up out of my darkness..." (p.158). Sarah sharply turned her horse to confront Ahmed playing the role of the perfect black, respect-fully keeping the required number of paces behind. For an awkward moment they faced each other; then with a smile Sarah redirected her horse to the guest house. The gesture remained empty, possibly to be filled at a later time (p.125).

But that time did not come during the Binghams' wedding reception, where Sarah left Ahmed standing alone, reminiscent of Hari's isolation at MacGregor House when Daphne moved away. Sarah saw "Ahmed...standing restricted in the centre of a world she would never enter, did not know and could not miss" (pp.185-86). She felt lucky to have her safe family, her secure world, her privileged life. She felt no common ground between them.[41]

Ahmed impressed Merrick as a man of Hari Kumar's type.[42] He was a handsome, well-educated, Westernized black who spoke only English. "In the taxi I think there was a sort of fantasy in my mind of Hari and Daphne being about to come together again" (p.225). Even though Merrick judged Ahmed "not in the least the usual surly type" (p.152) and recognized that he strictly adhered to the line (p.226), Merrick singled him out. "Glancing from one to the other Sarah thought: No, you mustn't tangle with each other. She felt powerless to stop them" (p.185).

Sarah and Ahmed were not worlds apart. She herself realized that India as they knew it was passing away, and they would be victims of its demise (p.125). But there was more between them than an unknown fate in an uncertain future.

Just as Sarah had to break the news of Teddie's death to Susan, Ahmed had to inform his father of Sayed's traitorous activity in the INA. Neither Sarah nor Ahmed might ever be forgiven for being the ones to impart this message: the India you believed in does not exist (p.486).[43]

There were other substantial similarites which Sarah as yet did not recognize. Not only did Scott develop parallels between Sarah and Daphne and between Ahmed and Hari. Scott also constructed symbolic parallels between the characters so that specific universal themes apply in different degrees to each character. The commonly shared images were the prison, the butterfly in lace, the armor/empty shell, and the scorpion in a ring of fire. There was also the theme of searching: for a home and for a sense and basis of identity. Sarah had not yet discovered the fact, but Ahmed shared all these experiences with her.[44]

Ahmed existed in a limbo of his own, shut out of his father's India but without a country, or at least without a vision of what India should be. To

compensate for his loss and disappointment, Ahmed
girded himself with and cultivated an armor of
lechery and drink to insure his father's continuing
disapproval and attention, which was Ahmed's touch-
stone, his affirmation of identity. It was a false
standard of measuring his personhood, just as Hari's
Englishness was false.

Count Bronowsky recognized Ahmed's rebellious
performance for what it really was--a deliberate
withdrawal from life, from his father, and from
himself (p.94). Ahmed was a prisoner like the raj,
sentenced to solitary confinement (p.89). People and
their concerns seemed remote to him. In this sense
Ahmed lived in a perpetual state of "funny turns" in
which everything and everyone seemed far removed. He
was detached from situations, even from the game of
playing the role of the disappointing son. Although
Ahmed knew the lines perfectly, his performance was
only half-hearted. He did not really believe in it;
there was no life, no spark of inspiration to the
role he played (p.474).

Ahmed could not find an interior source of
illumination. What being an Indian meant and how it
could be achieved was clear to MAK but not to Ahmed.
Just as Hari before him, Ahmed asked how he should go
about being a good Indian. The light of his
inheritance never shone beyond his father's own moral
certainty (pp.89,101,475). He, like Sarah, longed to
find a home and cease living like an exile. But why,
Ahmed wondered, should he look to some dream of the
future when India was there, now. "Shouldn't we stop
squabbling over it and start living in it? What does
it really matter who runs it, or who believes in
Allah, or Christ, or the avatars of Hindu mythology,
or who has a dark face and who has a light?" (p.475)

Just after the Laytons heard about Teddie's
death, Sarah had a dream in which a man no one
recognized made love to her:

>He was there and then not there, then
there again. He had a great, an
insatiable desire for her but it did
not enslave her. He was a happy man
and she was happy with him, not
jealously possessive. He existed
outside the area of claustrophobia,

entered it and left it at random,
without difficulty. He came to her
because she could not go to him. A
climax was never reached by either of
them, but that did not spoil their
pleasure. Disrupted as it was their
loving had assurance. There was
always the promise of a climax
(p.337).

After her encounter with Clark, Sarah interpreted him
as her dream lover. Yet there were several aspects
of her dream which made that impossible. Clark would
not walk into her life again. He only wanted a
pleasurable conquest, not a relationship or commitment. Even as Sarah surrendered to Clark, she had
the fleeting impression of another man, another
attempt to communicate, to embrace. It was "a dim
recollection of an empty gesture that had something
to do with wrenching the reins of a horse and
wheeling to confront imaginable but infinitely remote
possibilities of profound contentment" (p.457).[45] It
is possible that Sarah was simply subconsciously
registering that her sexual encounter with Clark was
empty and inadequate, but given other circumstances,
and perhaps another partner, such an act had tremendous capacities to be made full. But it could also
be that Sarah desired not Clark but Ahmed, and that
Ahmed was the man in her dream, the man who was
unrecognized and invisible to the raj community. If
Ahmed and Sarah were going to find happiness, then
the dream was certainly one of future prophecy. At
the end of The Day of the Scorpion the prospect
indeed seems "imaginable but infinitely remote."

                              V

     Bibighar is an on-going event. Hari Kumar was
innocent but still imprisoned (p.414). There were
the details associated with Merrick's presence in
Mirat: the stone, the insulted Nawab, the suppliant
woman in white. There were the periodic appearances
of Lady Manners floating phantom-like in and out of
Pankot society. There was Sarah's repeatedly feeling
Daphne real and present within herself. And there
were the character parallels between Ahmed and Hari
and between Sarah and Daphne, making the "continuing
nature of the misfortune" a very real possibility

(p.414), particularly since Merrick lurked in the encircling darkness. Bibighar, the situation which "threatens to be more than any conscience can cope with" (p.304), appears to be a never-ending tragedy.

Scott utilizes dreams and images to support this dramatic mood of foreboding and doom. The first image, one which is repeated and enlarged in the fourth volume, is the train journey. India's railroad system was the common means of travel and communication across its vast physical expanses. While viewing the characters traveling along a track, the reader is impressed by the image of a slow, deliberate, single-minded process of events leading to a pre-determined destination. Scott describes the train passing between Mirat the cantonment and Mirat the native city, with all its crossings and curves, as moving between the presiding power and the old glory with a sense of impending disaster (p.137).

There are also the intermittent discussions between Count Bronowsky and Ronald Merrick, and between the Count and the Nawab, about men of passion. These "dark young men of random destiny and private passions" presented difficulties greater than known agitators (p.191).[46] This type harbored deep personal feelings and could strike at any moment. True, they often made passionate mistakes, but their concern guaranteed unrelenting dedication to their goals. As Ahmed observed, if one knew such a man was out to destroy him, like Merrick was out to destroy Hari Kumar, that knowledge increased the chances of success (p.106). Whoever Merrick's next victims were, their dark fate appeared hopeless.

The year 1944 was described as an ill fated-year (p.322). The Japanese crossed the Chindwin River onto Indian soil. Rumors were increasing about Indian officers and enlisted men joining the Japanese against the Crown. Mrs. Mahatma Gandhi died while in prison. And the Layton family problems crescendoed to the embarrassing and puzzling incident of Susan's endangering her own baby's life.

An investigating officer by the name of Morland was sent to trace a story about a two-headed baby born in the hills. Both mother and child had died, but Morland was unable to find the family or the village, although the hill people knew of the rumor and interpreted it as a sign of potential misfortune.

Flowers were placed as offerings before the shrines of ancient Hindu gods.

Then Barbie Batchelor reported her dream in which she found the inhabitants of Pankot retreating from advancing Japanese troops who were already weaving through colored umbrellas on the golf course. Barbie was transported via a tonga drawn by an ass, like the one her Lord road triumphantly into Jerusalem and driven by the Church organist. "Alleluia! Alleluia!" Barbie shouted. The church was no longer there: instead there was a school house as in Muzzafirabad. Barbie ushered children calmly into the school to safety while she herself was stirred by a deep sense of interior peace. Barbie intrepreted this dream to be a message from Edwina Crane, that she was at rest and not tormented in hell for her suicide (p.324).[47]

Sarah dreamed about Teddie's advising her of family responsibility. Then she ran home, over the prostrate form of a woman in a white saree, where her father assured her that he believed she had tried her best. During the dream she was also making love with a mysterious man nobody knew (pp.325,337).

After Susan became dangerously withdrawn like Poppy Browning's daughter, who smothered her baby after her husband was found dead with his Indian mistress in the Quetta earthquake, the dog Panther sensed in her "the invisible demons" of human sorrow (p.364). The beast would wait at her bedroom door for hours on end. The servants from the other side of the wall noticed the birds of prey gathering in the hills (p.364). Minnie, the ayah, made offerings to the hill gods because she was alarmed by Susan's behavior (p.502). Sarah, on two occasions while talking with Susan, felt the touch of a dark premonition on the back of her neck (p.355,369).

An important insight about the present and future came from Lady Manners at the end of Hari Kumar's interview. It was "a vision of the future they were all headed for" (p.317). It was the touch of death. She had what appeared to be a premonition of Indian independence. "The reality of the actual deed would be a monument to all that had been thought for the best" (p.318). It would be surrounded by martial fanfare and political rhetoric. She had believed in it because she believed Indians to be deserving of it. But it would finally happen "in total and unforgivable disaster" (p.317) because it would occur not out of conviction but out of moral failing. That is why the actual deed would "never happen in her heart where it had been enshrined this many a year" (p.317-18).

The Indian chapter of imperial British history would record simply another "transient English experience of outlandish cultures" (p.52). To the people in England who would vote for Indian independence, that brief episode would be closed forever, to the greater glory of Pax Britannia. Yet in India peoples' lives, their foundation and future, would be changed forever just as they had been during the Bingham's wedding ceremony and by the chance quartering of Merrick with Teddie (p.181).

One of the basic questions posed by Paul Scott is whether it was good for England to be in India. It is evident in The Day of the Scorpion that such a question should not be answered in a general, "collective" way. It should be restated as follows: what could India offer Sarah Layton as a person? What did she offer India? The tragedy is that Sarah functioned on the surface of the real India. Her experiences and contributions revolved around life in the cantonment, not in the native quarter. India never felt her presence, and it made no difference to India whether she succeeded in finding her identity there or in England. Until she chose to cross "the so-called bridge" (p.437) to find India, as she did with Jimmy Clark, there would be little point in her being there.

Within the cantonment itself, the raj's iron code of collective conduct and morality impeded her search for identity and clouded her hopes for finding personal happiness in India. Her comment that her fellow exiles would never be happy and should be allowed to come home supports and clarifies Scott's opinion that the British colonization of India was an elaborate misadventure, like the history of Fort Premanager. Yet the reader cannot help wondering whether Scott laments the advent as much as the ultimate failure and departure of his countrymen. The withdrawal from their imperial embrace with India marked a collective and personal loss for the English.

As Sarah and Lady Manners realized, the best a
nation had to offer was what the people contributed
as individuals rather than as cells of their nation.
The raj had only a collective consciousness and made
only a collective contribution, and were thus doomed
to give only their second-best (p.145-46).

Through the symbols of prison, armor, and walls,
Scott builds one of his major themes: the characters, both black and white, suffered from physical,
spiritual, and emotional isolation. Ethel Manners
would weep if her old servant died, but in day-to-day
living showed no affection for him (p.44). MAK
reacted in anger and sorrow (p.36) at the news of
Daphne's rape but could not reach out to her or to
her aunt. Ahmed felt exiled from his father's India
but had no idea where he might be exiled from
(p.494). Sarah scrutinized everything and everyone,
refused to give way to emotions, and could not simply
enjoy life (pp.76,86). Everyone was like Susan, to
different degrees. None of them wanted to be alone
(p.229), and yet in the end all of them were.

There are numerous discussions throughout this
book about love and friendship being possible between
blacks and whites. Because "men are not born
brothers" (p.114), Pandit Baba believed intimacy
neither possible nor desirable. There can be love
only between like and like. Skin color made such a
fundamental difference to the Hindu teacher (as it
did to Ronald Merrick) that only peaceful coexistence
was possible, but never affection or respect. Even
Ahmed doubted whether true friendship could ever by
attained between the English and Indians, but he
attributed the fact to the British's position of
power rather than to their skin color. He found them
emotionally guarded and hypocritical in their
gestures of friendship (p.92). The only such gesture
he valued was the one offered him on the plains of
Mirat by a young women uncertain of her own motives.
Later he retraced the route they took, perhaps
pondering the veiled mysteries of such a gesture made
full and real.

The very possibility of love is ultimately
questioned, along with the existence of God and of
the human soul, the nature of right and wrong, and
the definition of the human essence. To be "fond,"
as Ahmed observed, meant to have some capacity for
self-denial, to be willing to surrender one's own

105

interests for the sake of another. Susan, he judged, did not have that capacity (p.90). Except for MAK in his dedication to a unified India, the India of his hopes and life-work, no one ever discovered or participated in a "great love." Such a love, Sarah realized, was "one more standard of human behaviour that needed that same climate of self-assurance and moral certainty in which to flourish; like all the other flowers of modest, quiet perfection which Susan imagined grew on the other side of the wall, in the secret garden" (p.427).

Love was a lost relic from the mythical Garden where God and man walked together. God is dead, and the Garden is vacant and impossible to enter. Love is overrated, Sarah scornfully remarked later on (p.425); love is an illusion (p.427). Going to bed with Clark may have marked a desire to rebel against the raj's code and Sarah's need to be loved, but it was not an act or expression of love itself.

For Ronald Merrick the myth of "God" was created as an emotional response to a gap in human knowledge (p.395). And Love, if and when it existed, was a threat to true human relationships.[48] Love diluted the "purity of an act" (p.391). It belied "the situation" between blacks and whites and within the white community itself. It only worked against true understanding of the nature of events and of personal action. Merrick could never understand Daphne or accept the possibility that she truly loved a black man. "She was under a kind of spell," Merrick told Count Bronowsky and Sarah (p.202).

As Sarah stood symbolically poised before Clark's naked body, she faced a difficult dilemma. She could rebel against the code and go to bed with Clark, doing her part to end the status quo that encouraged the influence and power of a man like Ronald Merrick. But in doing so she would hasten the night falling on her father's hopes and illusions. She chose to follow a light of sorts, a light she had sensed several times before but had never entered.[49] She did not know where it came from or what it entailed, but if it was light she wanted to share it.

For an authentic source of light and truth she would give up her inheritance. But if Sarah had to choose between that same inheritance and her personal

106

identity she would cling to her selfhood. That was
what Susan meant when she told Sarah: "Whatever you
do and wherever you go you'll always be yourself"
(p.345). Sarah would survive against the flames
because her sense of self, her consciousness of
individuality, was tenacious.

In giving herself to Clark, Sarah "entered her
body's grace" (p.461). Like Daphne, her body was
penetrated and liberated, and she found meaning and
fulfillment in physical intimacy. Perhaps the thin
shell of her regimental skin could be partially
filled by physical intimacy, but sex without love is
only a half-truth. It may not deny Sarah's selfhood
but neither will it complete her. Jimmy Clark only
took her to the "edge of feeling" (p.459).

It is significant that Sarah's act of liberation
occurred in the native quarter of Calcutta "across
the so-called bridge" (p.437). In Mayapore, there
was no bridge connecting the native and white banks
of the river and no bridge spanning the distance
between Bibighar and MacGregor House. Daphne took
her courage in her hands and entered the flood and
let herself be taken with it (The Jewel in the Crown
P.151). Sarah, to use another metaphor, emerged from
the cocoon of her raj shell as a tough little
butterfly. She freely entered a sexual and racial
world which she had never known before. She was one
of Claudine's beautiful butterflies, free at last to
make love in the sunshine even if only for a day.

Sarah is fundamentally akin to Daphne, because
she too would rather throw herself in the river and
drown, having at last been awake and alive, than
stand high and dry on the bank. After being with
Clark, Sarah felt happiness and grace well up inside
(p.504). It is a hopeful note, but the light she has
entered is the light of truth which dims all other
lights, which Daphne and Hari, in their wisdom and
caution, knew was too dangerous to tell. Sarah
stands poised, like Daphne, on the edge of the world.[50]

Tragically, Sarah's fate promises to be as
hopeless as Daphne's, because even if she has rid
herself of the raj's chains she still has Ronald
Merrick looming in the gathering darkness.[51] In The
Jewel in the Crown Scott affirms the powers of human
choice in the "area of dangerous fallibility." The
reader knows that those powers are in the hands of a

man without a conscience. Bibighar, that "total and unforgivable disaster," was a result of Merrick's moral choices. Lady Manners and Sarah felt the burden of this tremendous evil that one man did to another, and realized that Bibighar was not over. This truth, combined with Scott's character parallels, means that Bibighar will go on and on.

Yet the horizon is not entirely bleak. Scott's characters do not believe in nor do they discuss a "moral drift of history" in the second volume as they had in the first, but there are still truths which Scott affirms and offers as anchors of hope. The first of these truths is Hari Kumar's discovery of self, a positive though incomplete realization which is the only meaningful challenge to the raj's collective code. Hari affirms the dignity of the individual, and even in his personal loss and sorrow achieves a stature that the raj, as a group, never did. If there is no "moral drift," then there is no guarantee that this light of truth (e.g., the good) will triumph simply by virtue of being good, but at least one man stood up to Merrick's obsessive game of contempt.

The second truth is that Ahmed Kasim, like Hari Kumar before him, is Scott's reproach and challenge to Merrick's line. Ahmed shared common human experiences with white people, and he suffered and labored like anyone else. Sarah might not know what a human being is. There may be no religious formula, no universal definition of human nature equally acceptable to everyone, but one thing is certain: Ahmed Kasim is as human as anyone, and surely not less of a man than Ronald Merrick. Skin color and environment do not fundamentally determine who a person is.

A third truth is that the individual is of paramount importance and value. Why say we? Sarah asked Susan. You still matter. I matter. "You're a person not a crowd" (p.358). It is who a person is in himself that counts, not any accidental image or qualification imposed from within or outside him. But becoming that person cannot simply be a process of elimination. Selfhood means affirmation, a positive choice with positive dimensions. Otherwise a character like Ronald Merrick must be measured as good as any other whose selfhood is sustained by persecution and rejection.

The fourth truth answers Ahmed's question of why black and white cannot simply accept India as it is, why people cannot simply disregard all differences and live peacefully together in a united India embracing and benefiting from diverse cultures and rich variation. Such a dream is hopeless without the kind of moral certainty the raj enjoyed. But the content of their code and the execution of their sacred mission was sadly lacking. Without a standard of moral order based on reason and/or revelation, the question of right and wrong will be settled by such unguided and undeterred wills as Ronald Merrick's. There is such a thing as a human essence, and if it is parted from reason only the animal is left. To reason is to be human, and to act unreasonably is to act like a beast.

FOOTNOTES TO CHAPTER II

[1]All page references in this chapter, unless
otherwise noted, are from Paul Scott, The Day of the
Scorpion (New York: Avon Books, 1968).

[2]Elizabeth I chartered the British East India
Company in 1600, and thus India was an Elizabethan
rather than Victorian acquisition.

[3]The princely state of Mirat is portrayed as an
almost ideal world. Scott refers to it as a small and
insignificant rose in a desert of dead Moghul
ambitions (p.33). Under the guidance of the Russian
emigré Dmitri Bronowsky, Mirat became "modern" though
still ruled autocratically by the Muslim Nawab. The
Nawab himself, rather than the state, was the
crowning triumph of Count Bronowsky's labors. In many
ways the Nawab personified England's own code,
believing it was his duty to protect and his
privilege to rule (p.163). He turned from a life of
voluptuous despotism to one of austere personal
devotion to his religion and his mission: to rule
Mirat with detachment and benevolence (p.162). The
Nawab's degree of personal austerity made even the
Laytons seem like pleasure-seeking exploiters. Count
Bronowsky's ultimate goal was to see the Nawab's
daughter Shiraz married to Ahmed Kasim, and prudently
move Mirat into a more democratic structure of
government. He could undercut British influence by
making Mirat stable and secure while maintaining good
working relations with the English. The Count was
sensitive to the potential danger of the Hindu
majority rising up against the ruling Muslim minority, and encouraged the Nawab to promote higher forms
of education and political opportunities for the
Hindu population.

[4]Rose Cottage, Mabel's home, was built before
this style became fashionable (p.328).

[5]The hill station of Pankot, built on three
hillsides and the conjoint valley, was "thoroughly
English" in climate and topography. There the English
could retire comfortably, serene with the sense of
duty well done (pp.56-57).

[6]MAK's own Muslim ancestor, Mir Ali, married a Hindu princess (p.31).

[7]In The Jewel in the Crown the stranger, in his correspondence with Robin White, refers to Mary Tudor's losing Calais as a parallel to England's giving up India. Losing Calais in war with France turned out to be of tremendous economic benefit to England. Calais had become more and more expensive to defend and maintain, and had ceased to be an important trading center as the world market shifted to Antwerp.

[8]Scott examines faces with great care and artistry. Fenny had "private marks of public dis-approval" from years of regrets and accusation (pp.144,157). When relaxed her mouth drooped to its habitual hard line. She was fleshy, as Millie would be. Yet Millie's face gave the impression of under-lying steeliness, and showed "signs of effort-in-achievement" (p.154). Millie would not grow old gracefully. Sarah had the enduring Layton face, sculpted to the bone. She would have a predatory look in old age like Mabel. Her face was so obviously itself that make-up could not substantially improve it (p.148).

[9]When John Layton came to Chillingborough he felt the same distance between himself and his family he left behind in India. When his mother came to visit him after several years of separation, she seemed unreal to him, as if his real mother was still back in India (p.58). John was not beguiled by English life on the island, and his years of education strengthened his desire to serve India (p.61).

[10]In childhood, Scott observes, a person harbors "magical, misty...more vivid impressions" (p.71). Everything serves as a background for a game, which the child recognizes as such. In the attic, amid cobwebs and old chests, the child holds his treasures to help pass long days indoors when he is thrown back on his own frail resources because he is afraid to go outside and wet his feet and catch a chill (pp.71-72). In this sense Susan never grew out of her childhood. She had an aptitude for deliberate perfor-mance, and until Teddie's death she played the game

adamantly--Susan playing Susan. Her talent, which attracted so many, was her ability to pretend she was in the center of an untroubled world. Teddie, too, played as if life were a game, as an amateur in love with the myth. Both Susan and Teddie tried to hold off the chilly outside, the threatening elements, the scorching heat of the ring of fire, the "convulsive flicker of an ancient terror" (p.360).

Sarah, too, nurtured her own set of childhood illusions. She regarded her family as a source of security, a "circle of safety" (p.157,230). "How lucky we are, she thought. How very very lucky" (p.186). After traveling all night from Pankot to Calcutta, Sarah arrived tired and over-excited, "Like a child. She was aware of Aunt Fenny stooping to unlace her shoes for her...Weightless, her legs lifted easily on to the bed. Curtains were drawn. Comforted by all this evidence of family devotion and the softness of the pillow under her head, she fell asleep" (pp.377-78). While driving with Uncle Arthur and Jimmy Clark after visiting Ronald Merrick, Sarah cleared a view for herself in one of the misted windows of the car "and felt like a child intent on observing, from a position of safety and comfort, an alien and dangerous magic" (p.420).

At first Sarah resented Clark's presence, which threatened to infiltrate this familial circle of safety all the way to undisturbed, silent Pankot, and farther still to "the still centre of her father's patience and yearning for release and a quiet passage through the night" (p.421). At Mira's, while she applied her makeup in Jimmy Clark's bathroom, Sarah "felt in need of some show of kindness, such as Aunt Fenny had made, taking her shoes off, making her rest" (p.452). Perhaps the greatest contribution Clark made to Sarah's personal growth was to take her "across the so-called bridge," to show her that life beyond the family, reality beyond the illusion of safety, could in fact be "unfriendly, vast, and dangerous" (p.72) but could also be fulfilling and comforting. Unaware of the significance of his gesture, Clark "touched her right ankle, gently lifted and eased the shoe from her foot and then the shoe from the other foot" (p.459). In the darkness of Clark's bedroom, Scott creates an image of safety and prospect of magic, outside the "geometric pattern of light and the circle of safety" (p.230). The winds of change have touched everything--things are being replaced, and images, proven and assumed, now give way to new ones. The final, ultimate refutation of

112

the illusion of this familial "circle of safety"
occurs when Susan endangers the life of her new-born,
placing him in a circle of flames. Minnie the ayah
threw a sheet on the flames, "entered the circle and
picked the child up and carried it to safety"
(p.504). On the final page, the circle of the family
became the antithesis of safety and security.

There is what Scott calls mystery and magic,
which are not bad things, especially for the young,
who are more open to them (p.475). Significantly,
Ronald Merrick was not sensitive to mystery. He
believed things would not seem problematic if men had
enough information and did not let their emotions
interfere (p.395). The raj in general would agree
with Merrick, not being a people who accepted
mysteries if they thought there were explanations to
be had (p.501). But Merrick differed from the raj in
that he refused to play the game (p.387), even though
life in India seemed like a play. He was in love with
the myth because the myth distinguished people, made
ordinary men seem larger than life. But he could not
warm his hands at the hearth of Man-Bap's dying fire
because he refused to be like a child and believe. He
could not accept, as Count Bronowsky told Sarah, that
mysteries "warm the powers of perception and in
themselves can be quite beautiful" (p.475). While
gazing at the Count with his nocturnal eye, Sarah
felt pierced "as if by a singularity of purpose and
intent. But that was a mystery too. Perhaps it was
beautiful. She did not know. In a few minutes the
chance to know would have gone, would have joined the
sad jumble of all the other limited chances...she
felt everyone was given" (p.475).

The cycle of youth, vitality, and old age
reflects the wholeness, the complete circle of life
as prescribed by the figure of dancing Siva: creation, preservation, and destruction. But in India
this cycle is disturbed, as evidenced by the image of
MacGregor garden. There, in intense sunlight and
sunlit shadows, the cycle of life is accelerated
because there is no autumn: "leaves coming into the
tenderest flesh, superbly in their prime, crisping to
old age" (The Jewel in the Crown, p.74). Such a
climate caused Lydia Muir to conclude that India was
an unnatural place, especially for white women (p.78)
who did not transplant well. The hothouse-like heat
brought them on too quickly so that they faded fast.
Often only an artificial husk remained of a once
young, fresh, and vibrant girl (p.139). Missionary
life in India had dried out Barbie Batchelor--a case

in point (p.336).

The scorpion, too, was sensitive to the heat and usually hid under stones during the day. The raj found themselves trapped, out in the open, like the black insect Sarah remembered encircled by ring of fire--not only on a literal level, but a symbolic level as well. They were no longer sheltered by the carapace of their history and lay exposed in their tender skins (p.415). Something in the English out of their natural environment died, Sarah believed. They lost the ability to act as individuals, to believe in and depend upon their personal rather than collective worth (p.146). The result for Susan was to feel "out in the open. Like when you lift a stone and there's something underneath running in circles" (p.355).

In India the toll of heat, alienation, and extinction-through-exile were heavy. Of the older generation of Laytons, Scott conjures an image of bitter and disappointed people who doggedly insisted on still playing the game but who had become soured by years of snobbery, isolation, and callousness: Fenny, who spoke too loudly and whose mouth curved downward once still; Millie, who each day counted the hours before her first drink and held life in abeyance. The magic was gone but they still abided by the game. "We don't really believe in it anymore. Not really believe...and our not believing seems like a betrayal...so we can't any longer look each other in the eye and feel good...so we hate each other, but daren't speak about it, and hate whatever lies nearest to hand, the country, the people in it, our own changing history that we are a part of" (p.358).

The image of Lady Manners, who no longer played the game, is one of a frail old woman stalked by a sinister and threatening presence, which she knew as death (pp.317,319). Repeatedly, Scott describes her as seeking and finding with her hand the assurance of pleats and buttons just below her throat (pp.52,233,235,242,296,318,359) as if she were clutching a cross that wasn't there (p.503). Sarah had once said to her, "What a lot you know" as if it were a state of grace (p.50). Lady Manners was not, as Sarah first thought, undisturbed by the issue of the meaning and value of life. For her, and for Sarah, the years of belief were over and the years of disbelief had begun (p.358), so that this terrible kind of knowing was not really knowing but "bowing my head, as you are bowing yours, under the weight of it" (p.503).

Only Mohammed Ali Kasim, who played the old

man's game of politics honorably--according to the rules (p.494)--remained young. Although his most recent years of imprisonment had aged his body, MAK's youthful longing for and commitment to a unified India had never been corrupted. His dream shone "like something new and untried and full of promise" even in his old man's body (p.495). He had come full circle, as he explained to Ahmed: he was severely limited and prey to all kinds of quaint illusions and expectations--like a child. Every man hung on to the memories of his different stages of growth, in the hope of seeing something whole (p.467). The price paid for never experiencing the disillusionment of adulthood, never abandoning the notion of what made life worth living (p.494) was high: he wore his Congress cap straight and firm, "like a crown of thorns" (p.495). Yet the time for MAK's dream of a united India had passed. The prospect of power was too sweet a prospect for either of the major religious sects to demur in the name of unity. This inevitable passing away was celebrated by MAK's poet ancestor (See Gaffur's poem, p.137).

[11]Jimmy Clark believed that Chillingborough was a font of liberal, imperial wisdom, and as such cultivated in future administrators very old-fashioned attitudes about the English function and position in India (p.445).

[12]Merrick spoke bitterly of Teddie's naive and antiquated loyalty to the regiment and to the mythical code which Teddie valued above all else. Sarah wondered if Merrick's criticism manifested a longing to participate in the legend (p.411). Although his contempt for Teddie was genuine, Merrick envied him because he "belonged."

[13]Ethel Manners interpreted Hari Kumar's interview in the same way: a charade, a game of pretend rather than an exercise in justice (p.320).

[14]An obvious example was Merrick's reaction to the stone-throwing incident, a reflective smile which belied the impression he conveyed to Sarah of a lonely, persecuted victim who sought someone to witness and share his burden (pp.220-21). Another example occurred when Merrick's doll-like blue eyes kept closing in the hospital as if he were fatigued

115

while his voice was quite strong. It was part of the total effect he wanted to make (p.387).

[15]In this respect Sarah was like the woman in purdah who wore Chanel No. 5. Her clothing was a sign of conforming to her social and collective responsibilities; her perfume a sign of secret inclinations (p.347). Sarah conformed in a public way but rebelled and affirmed herself in a private way. She was a person of conflicting signals and confusing gestures. So too was Ethel Manners, who would not impose her or Parvati's presence openly on raj society, but did so subtly, as when she published the birth notice and signed the book at Flagstaff House (p.365). Susan also sent out conflicting signals. As a child she apparently adjusted to the "uprooting" between India and England very well but complained to her parents that she was unhappy (p.75). During her courtship she expected Teddie's affection in public but rejected his gestures in private (p.91). Susan acted like a queen bee, incapable of lifting a finger on her own behalf and depending on the busy workers even to draw breath (p.90). But she was adamant about her plans to marry and ruthless about completing the task no matter what the difficulty. The raj community considered her flawless (p.128). Susan was loved and pampered and apparently secure in her beauty, but she never found that secret garden she appeared to inhabit. She would continually step in and out of conversations to affirm the impact of her personality, and to demand the constant attention she craved (p.143).

[16]Baksh falling at Teddie's feet recalled the image of Aunt Shalini groveling at Merrick's feet, begging mercy for Hari Kumar. Both gestures were tragically pathetic because neither Teddie nor Merrick had the power to save the penitents from their fate. Neither could (or would, in Merrick's case) grant forgiveness.

[17]On the contrary, Sarah observed a definite change in the wedding party's bearing--a heightened sense of self and a pronounced air of calm dignity. "It entered and stirred them like the divine breath of a God who had bent his brow to call forth sterner angels" (p.173).

[18]The INA phenomenon was also a blow to MAK's

116

image of India. If Sayed had broken his sacred oath as a commissioned officer, then he had betrayed India as well as the British (pp.488-89). That such an act could ever be considered "patriotic" would mark an end to the India MAK had served and hoped for all his life.

There is the obvious historical parallel between the INA's of World War II and the sepoy mutiny of 1857, when British-trained natives turned upon their own officers in a bloody and violent attempt to regain control of their country.

[19] It irritated Sarah the way raj members never talked about "it," the unspoken and sacred code. For her it was a way of hiding their prejudices and being able to live with them.

[20] Sarah believed Susan's life was irresponsible though she followed the code scrupulously. It was irresponsible because it was founded on a notion of responsibility from a vanished age. And because it was irresponsible, it was mirthless (p.145).

[21] See also The Towers of Silence, p.207.

[22] Clark was a hedonist in a style antithetical to the raj's code of duty, mission and responsibility. Sarah could never adapt to his life style and be happy, but Clark was correct about her. She was tough and intelligent but lacked joy. She needed to be happy and enjoy life (p.457).

[23] Scott uses the phrase "state of grace" to describe the fulfillment of human capacities, the attainment of a condition of equilibrium and realization of some degree of interior peace. Daphne, when pregnant, was described in this way. When Sarah first spoke with Ethel Manners, she exclaimed, "What a lot you know," as if it were a state of grace (p.51).

[24] Sarah was not perfectly consistent, feeling that a certain code of behavior should still be followed. A thin layer of Christian sentiment still shaped her attitudes about how people should try to be unselfish and charitable (p.83). Susan also judged events from a sentimentally christian point of view.

She regarded Merrick's action of saving Teddie as a Christian act (p.362).

[25]This particularly difficult passage recalls Kipling's poem, The Day's Work, in which the labor of the raj is likened to a shepherd's leading his flock. Kipling's parallel to the Good Shepherd parable is unmistakable. Lady Manners does not display the same certainty about the raj shepherds' being guided and illumined by God's presence. She sees the shepherds' driving their flocks in a dark plain without divine light. These flocks are invisible, implying that the raj's self-image of shepherd is illusory. Such shepherds have only the expectation, not the guarantee, of God's forgiveness.

[26]Sarah appears to think of her baptism gown as another relic of her personal/collective past, part of the "accumulation of unwanted years" (p.504). As with all such remnants, Sarah regarded the gown with conflicting emotions. It was a symbol of an antiquated and meaningless observance, a decayed relic of a former flowering which had to be pruned away to ensure her own vigor. She shed the symbol of her baptism just as she shed (with relief) her bridesmaid dress, symbol of dogged attempts "to ensure the inheritance and keep it pukka" (p.139). Such an enterprise was doomed just as Sarah's baptism was doomed. Instead of the life and grace of the Christian God flooding and illuminating her depths, "certain spectres had come like unbidden guests" (p.450), as in a fairy tale gone wrong. She had cast off the beliefs, affections, and expectations of childhood but the spectres refused to let her fill up the empty shell with anything else (p.450). The shell of her regimental skin was unalterable, preserved like the baptism gown.
Yet the soft, still supple yellowed lace with a story behind it was far preferable to what Susan wore: "something modern," anonymous and forgotten, which was either lost or did not last (p.359). On her baptism day, in that butterfly gown, Sarah must have looked beautiful (p.371). It helped give "a certain set to her bones, a toughness to her skin" (p.86), as did all of her past. It helped to make her the person that she was, a person who had inherited the conflicting attitudes of the Muirs and Laytons which made her an instrument of resistance and at the same time of acceptance (p.86). It was not simply an

example of an artificial shell, a sapless and unnatural husk. As in the garden at Mac Gregor House, new life came from the old: "In the shadows there are dark blue veils, the indigo dreams of plants fallen asleep, and odours of sweet and necessary decay, numerous places layered with the cast-off fruit of other years softened into compost, feeding the living roots that lie under the garden massively, in hungry immobility" (The Jewel in the Crown, P.74). For all Sarah's denials of the existence of a god, she "could not bear the thought of this man [Merrick] clinging through a god-relationship to the family she loved" (p.415). To Sarah, the ritual of baptism was an answer no longer adequate. It belonged to days that were different, when things were simpler (The Jewel in the Crown, p.32). Yet the questions, the litany of human needs, the "flicker of an ancient terror" still stalked her steps, and she could find no substitute with which to fill her shell and satisfy her longing, and the hunger of her "living roots."

27Susan's action is one of the most difficult to explain. In describing the event, Scott includes numerous threads from plot, themes, and images in one circular symbol and motion, completing and uniting many ideas. In The Towers of Silence Susan's actions were seen as expressing a strong element of mockery, since there was little danger to the child in the wet grass (The Towers of Silence, p.291-292). Edward was dressed in Sarah's baptism gown, Sarah whom Susan admired for having an adamant sense of selfhood, and Sarah who burned the relics of her English stage of childhood just as Mahmoud burned the "accumulation of unwanted years" (p.504). Susan herself was metaphor- ically surrounded by the threatening flames and menacing trials of a hostile environment. Scott mentions that she was a "Scorpio." There is a strong element of an Abraham/Isaac sacrifice of appeasement, an offering not to God but to the bad spirits which Minnie believed surrounded the bungalow. Flames enclosed the sacrifice (The Towers of Silence, p.293). But Minnie also wondered if this was an alien, religious ritual or an act of divine interven- tion. "Little prisoner, shall I free you?" (p.502) Susan asked her child. In this baptism by fire, Susan herself may have been playing God by recreating conditions which for her made up life: the circle of flames next to a symbolically insurmountable wall guarding the secret garden. Her action can be seen as an initiation into the reality of the raj's closing days.

[28]The ring of fire is used by Scott as a substantial sign of the raj's metaphysical condition. It also suggests several other images. The Lord Siva, god of destruction and regeneration, dances in a petrified ring of fire, with his left leg held in the air and his right leg poised to spring into action (The Jewel in the Crown p.410). Edward may be a Siva figure laying in the center of the circle, gazing at the sky and working his legs and arms (The Towers of Silence, p.293). Susan had been frightened by the prospect of only having herself to give to the child. Now, in this alarming gesture, she might give him an opportunity for rebirth through destruction, as the god Siva symbolized. The names of Edwina, Teddie and Edward all derive from the same root, meaning "a rich guard" (A Division of the Spoils, p.523). They all represented, in some way, the best of the raj code and witnessed its demise. First Edwina (representing old age and the fourth stage of Hindu spiritual development), then Teddie (representing the fullness of manhood and the second stage) and Edward (representing youth and the first stage), all faced the same fate. Susan, in her madness, may have been assisting Edward through the dying process in order to be reborn, a parody of the baptismal ritual. It is significant that Minnie, the Hindu ayah converted to the Muslim religion, saved Edward from the flames. All of the ideas and images mentioned here only trace the circumference of the circle; they do not in themselves exhaust or isolate the deep, rich mystery of the center of the circle.

[29]Since there is no absolute, rational or spiritual standard of morality, Merrick could only see himself as "socially" rather than "morally" objectionable.

[30]Merrick did not despise the INA's cowardly actions. He despised the cowards, not as soldiers but as men. He was not concerned with INA treachery as a moral question, but only as a racial question.

[31]Merrick would not "call them by name" like God. He refused to call Sarah by her first name. His conversation with her was not coupled with the

blessing and ablution of her name (pp.226,417,452).

[32]This contrasts with Sr. Ludmila's belief that what distinguishes human beings is their ability to laugh and to weep (The Jewel in the Crown, P.129).

[33]There is a possibility that Merrick, even at this point, subconsciously wanted to be punished for Bibighar and for his other acts of "cruelty and perversions" (p.115). He told Sarah that people ought to be held responsible, accountable for their actions, that one should not be able to get away with murder even if one were part of the establishment (p.223). Count Bronowsky cheekily observed that compulsively tidy people (like himself and Merrick) were subconsciously trying to wipe the slate clean and give themselves another chance (p.188). Merrick's interior torture, stemming from self-hatred, might be surfacing at this point in the Quartet, although it does not become fully evident until Vol. IV.

[34]It is not too early to refer to Merrick as a devil-type. County Bronowsky uses the description about Merrick while talking with Ahmed Kasim. "Courage, monami...le diable est mort" (p.481).

[35]Merrick understood Hari's despair of having to live a life of an "inferior" after identifying himself as an Englishman. Part of Merrick's contempt for Hari stemmed from Hari's inability to face up to his setback, his not dealing with his humiliation and pain courageously (p.208). Merrick had suffered such humiliation in England. It must have given him a great deal of pleasure to placate his envy by creating the kind of situation with Hari that had been imposed upon himself.

[36]Merrick's homosexual tendencies were hinted at during his conversation with Count Bronowsky, whose sexual preferences were well-known. "There's the other thing about us--I mean about our tidiness" (p.188), the Count prattled on, but his meaning went beyond his words. When the two re-entered the Bingham's wedding reception, the Count intimately leaned toward Merrick and asked about an attractive young officer across the room. Merrick hesitated to answer, as if he were uncertain of the meaning or the intention of the question, but his blush betrayed his

121

true reaction (p.211).

[37]Scott wrote the interview in the same way. It was a very prolonged, powerful scene weaving together a graphic account of Merrick's obscenity, his disdain for Daphne, and his consuming contempt of and cruelty toward Hari--with the pathos of Hari's despair, loss and ultimate dignity. Scott, too, is extracting everything possible from the scene.

[38]On her return trip by rail from Calcutta to Pankot, Sarah had a vivid dream of Clark's awakening and enclosing her body once again. When her fellow travelers woke her at the Ranpur station, Sarah experienced "a strange, unbelievable, soundless splintering; an extraordinary convolution of time and space" (p.460). Such a convolution was a common one for the adult Sarah Layton, replacing the "funny turns" of her childhood. Instead of feeling remote from herself and her environment, she found other people's experiences filling up and converging in her own consciousness. While riding with Ahmed in Mirat, Daphne "flared up out of my darkness [Sarah relates] as a white girl in love with an Indian. And then went out because--in that disguise--she is not part of what I comprehend" (p.158). And yet Daphne was a part of Sarah's experience, just as was the suppliant woman in white, who came to mind while Sarah spoke with Ronald Merrick, shopped in the market place, and dreamed of Teddie and her father. Numerous images fused: converging strands of circumstances met and intermingled so that the presence of Lady Manners and Daphne, of the suppliant woman in white and the Poppy Browning's daughter defied their prosaic environments of time and space, just as did the woman in burkah wearing Chanel #5 who could be pictured in Pankot just as easily as in Ranpur (p.347). These "extraordinary convolutions of time and space" wherein the characters defy their environment modify Sarah's speculations about the chemical, fated aspect of human experience. While riding with Ahmed, Sarah felt the "light and mysterious pleasure that existed for creatures who broke free of their environment" (p.121). But at other times, as during her sister's wedding reception or when she met Count Bronowsky on the platform in Ranpur, she had impressions "of them all as dolls dressed and positioned for a play" (p.178), a "sense of charade, of puppet-show; of dolls manipulated to a point just

short of climax" (p.464). Other characters, too, felt the confining perimeters of a course of events not of their own making: MAK, who was carried forward by circumstances which seemed to stand still while he was in prison (p.492); Ahmed, who strove to preserve a sense of detachment from issues and situations not of his own making (p.483); Ronald Merrick, who felt a sweet indifference of man's environment to his problems, an indifference that amounted to contempt (p.395); and Hari Kumar, who was surrounded by others bent on his destruction, and who wondered whether the only act of free choice left to him was to do the job for them (p.314).

Sarah regarded the world, in moments of dejection, as a chemical accident, a mine of raw material (p.421). She felt like a tough little butterfly trapped in occasions and conditions of despair (p.429) or a clinical speciman captured and cosseted for some kind of experiment (pp.421,423). Ahmed, too, fell victim to such fatalistic attitudes. He expected friendly Englishmen to take advantage of him, or to pull away before intimacy was attained, at "a point just short of climax," as Sarah would say. In this light he anticipated his scheduled morning ride with the elder Layton sister: "It is like being a student of chemistry, knowing a formula, waiting to see it proved in a laboratory test" (p.93).

In The Day of the Scorpion there is a strong, undeniable element of fate, but simultaneously, an adamant belief in the role and power of human free choice. Even Merrick understood that "no act is performed without a decision being made to perform it" (p.391). The reader is left with the paradoxical image of Sarah, imagining herself to be Susan, "leaning her head against the bars that separated her from the window pane. She closed her eyes as perhaps Susan was doing, even now, and after a while felt the quietness of her own happiness and grace welling up inside her; and smiled, ignoring the rain that seemed to be falling on her face" (p.504).

[39]There is the minor parallel between Daphne's seeking a home for her fatherless child and Susan's asking Sarah to take care of her baby.

[40]In fact, it is probable that Merrick "noticed" Sarah for the same reason he chose Daphne. He was quick to join Ahmed and Sarah as they spoke together at the reception.

[41]There was also the apparent similarity between Daphne's and Sarah's affairs, both defiant acts against the raj code. The similarity was only superficial because Daphne's choice to become intimate with Hari was not motivated by her desire to reject the code or even to find herself, as was Sarah's choice. Daphne's action was fundamentally positive: To co-mingle with the person of Hari Kumar.

[42]This is not surprising because Merrick recognized and understood only "types" and never individual persons. See p.208.

[43]No matter what he suffered in prison, MAK faced a harsher trial and deeper humiliation once released from Premanager. As a man unjustly imprisoned, he was a hero, a martyr. Prison was a public badge of political honor and personal integrity (p.490). Major Tippitt had told MAK that the Fort was a refuge from life's turmoils and disappointments, and his advice proved true. Upon his conditional release MAK was notified by Ahmed that all he must do was reside in Mirat and meet with Sayed. MAK could not forgive Sayed's action because the INA phenomenon threatened his dream of a united India as surely as did Mr. Jinnah's designs for a separate Muslim state. "What are we living in, a jungle?" MAK asked Ahmed during their discussion about the INA's (p.488). If a man's oath was not sacred, then there was nothing "civilized" about India. MAK had only one life to live and one notion of what made it worth living (p.494). If that notion was wrong, his entire life would be wasted. MAK's love for India was a great love, a love never to be fully realized but never corrupted. He had to condemn his son to save his country (p.495). He wore his Congress cap squarely pressed down upon his head "like a crown of thorns" (p.495).

[44]The structure of The Day of the Scorpion emphasizes this theme of reoccurrence. Scott continually interrupts his narrative to insert an incident from the past. After describing MAK's arrest and Lady Manners' leaving her moorings on the lake, Scott expands a lengthy account of John's, Susan's, and Sarah's background in England. After the wedding party arrives at the Nawab's guest house, Scott

124

digresses into an analysis of the English male's collective response, repeats the description of the arrival, and then expands on the ride which Sarah and Ahmed shared, which he had introduced many pages earlier. The most important trip into the past was the interview between Rowan and Hari in Kandipat prison, when an event of the past becomes all-absorbing. After Teddie's death, as Sarah walked to the veranda at Rose Cottage, she realized that the "situation was familiar. It had all happened before--people on a veranda and herself returning to join them. How many cycles had they lived through then, how many times had the news of Teddie's death been broken? How many times had Susan been taken indoors..." (p.335).

[45] The empty gesture of wheeling her horse around is simply one in a series of such gestures. The silences between Sarah and her mother, which characterized their relationship, were filled with "gestures unoffered" (p.148). Lady Manners regretted not having the courage to make a gesture which would be seen by others as out of character (p.46). After Sarah caught Susan's wedding bouquet on the train platform, Susan continued to watch Sarah, "waiting perhaps for some particular word or gesture but there was no word or gesture to find..." (p.217).

[46] The Count's viewpoint was obviously shaped by his own experience in St. Petersburg when he was the target of an assassination attempt.

[47] On her last day at Rose Cottage, after talking with Ronald Merrick, Barbie rode in a horse-drawn tonga which was over-loaded with her trunk full of relics. It had begun to rain and Barbie spied colored umbrellas on the golf course as the tonga slowly made its way down the hill. People were running for cover under colored umbrellas. "Why! It is my dream!" (p.391) Barbie thanked God for the blessing of it and felt young again, when in fact her hair was not long and black and flying free but grey and lank, and twisted in the shawl of captive butterflies (p.390). The lace blew across the face of the tonga-wallah as well as across her own like a "monstrous membrane." Lightning flashed across the sky, and the tired old nag bolted down the hill. Barbie tried to help the old man by pulling on the reins of the "four horses," the steeds from the

apocalypse. It is the end of time, the end of
Barbie's sane existence, and the end of the British.
The demise is announced by the presence of the
colored umbrellas which did not signify that the
Japanese had invaded, as in the dream, but that the
British had come to an end of themselves as they
were. For Barbie it did not matter. She had
triumphed, she had been through hell and "come out
again by God's Mercy" (p.392). She did not mind
being a captive butterfly as long as the God of love
had captured her and not the prince of despair and
darkness. [All page references in this note are from
The Towers of Silence.]

[48]Without ever preaching, Scott has successfully
established an abiding causal link between a world
without God and a world where love is scarce or even
impossible. The metaphysical assumptions and consequences of these first two volumes are pervasive and
insistent and are developed through events, dialogue,
and symbols. The reader cannot help but recall the
first two verses of St. John's Gospel in relation to
the theme of silence in The Jewel in the Crown:
          In the beginning was the Word;
          the Word was with God
          and the Word was God.
Without God there is no Word, and silence takes on
metaphysical dimensions as does Scott's light imagery
in the second volume. Verses 3 and 4 in St. John's
Gospel read:
          Whatever came to be in Him found life,
          life for the light of man.
          The light shines on in the darkness,
          and the darkness knew him not.
In the Quartet darkness thus means not only moral
evil but a world devoid of God, a world devoid of
meaning, purpose, and intelligibility. Men are
reduced to the level of insect-like butterflies and
scorpions in a sometimes beautiful but always hostile
world.

[49]The first time occurred in England when Sarah
burned her childhood relics: "She could feel the
heat on her bones, the heat on her skin. Within them
remained the nub, the hard core of herself which the
flames did not come near nor illuminate" (p.86). The
second time occurred as she undressed after Susan's
wedding (p.214).

[50]In The Jewel in the Crown it seemed to Daphne as she ran in the dark from Bibighar to MacGregor House after the attack that "if I ran long enough I would run clear off the rim of the world" (p.436). In The Day of the Scorpion Ethel Manners remembered that phrase from Daphne's journal as she listened to Hari's testimony. "Well--she had gone. Yes, eventually she had gone clear off the rim of the world..."(p.307).

[51]It was true, as MAK's father advised, that the important Englishmen are the unseen ones in England who make policy (p.66). But what good are liberal, humanitarian policies in the hands of men like Merrick? In an immediate sense, they are the important and influential ones.

CHAPTER III

THE TOWERS OF SILENCE

In The Towers of Silence Scott introduces a new
image, one which helps explain the structure of his
Raj Quartet. He depicts raj society as a vast sea.
In developing this image Scott describes the childhood of Susan Layton as so calm compared to adult
waters that barnacles had to be symbolically scraped
away (p.35).[1] But as the Edwardian sun sets and the
golden age of moral certainty wanes, the sea begins
to churn and convulse, increasing the sense of
imminent danger (p.32). Mabel Layton, as an unwill-
ing representative of the lost golden age, was like a
buoy marking a sunken ship full of lost treasure
never to be recovered because the waters were
becoming more and more treacherous (p.32).

Those elements which disturbed the sea of raj
society were 1) changes in the moral climate of
England (the headland) which made Indian independence
a foregone conclusion, 2) the humiliating course of
the war against the Japanese, 3) the INA phenomenon,
and 4) an apparently insignificant disturbance in the
equally insignificant native town of Mayapore:
Bibighar. Scott traces the impact of Bibighar, as if
it were a stone thrown into the sea producing
ever-widening, encircling waves like rings of influence to even remote distances. In the first volume
of the Quartet Scott described the disturbance
itself, the moment of actual impact. In The Day of
the Scorpion Scott explores the circle of immediate
effect--upon Daphne's aunt and child and Ronald
Merrick, and that part of raj society which came into
contact with them. Now, in The Towers of Silence
Scott develops the influence of Bibighar within an
ever widening circle: the raj community in Pankot.

Scott retains his symbolic style in The Towers
of Silence while implementing the cyclic narrative
pattern which he explored in volume one. The plot
does not move forward from its development in The Day
of the Scorpion. Rather, the author goes back over
the same ground, digging deeper into his characters
and enlarging the scope and application of his
imagery.

129

Being similar to England in topography, climate, and vegetation, Pankot was an ideal posting and retirement sight for the military members of the raj community.   To Barbie Batchelor, newly arrived from Ranpur and the flat, hot Indian plains, Pankot looked like paradise itself.   "Praise God!" she cried on first seeing the panoramic view Aziz presented with a sweep of his arm (p.17).   A "celestial range of sunlit peaks" (p.373) crowned tree-covered mountain-sides and their converging valley.   A holy silence lay on the lush, green vegetation which proffered a rich and private pasture to God's privileged flock (p.18).   Pankot seemed like Paradise and Barbie soon loved it.   "In coming here she had been afforded a glimpse of something life had denied her but which she was not unfitted for, having prayed for it once in a different form: tranquility of mind and nature" (p.28).

The vital, divine spark to the raj Eden was its military tradition.   The roots of these sacred customs extended beyond the town itself into the hidden mountain villages where generations of Indians celebrated, revered, and participated in the finest regiment: the Pankot Rifles.   Within these villages lay the magic of the valley, because therein were found the roots which nurtured the blossoms of the military tradition and made Pankot an idyllic place, a chosen land (p.39).   The virtues of paradise did not emanate from its tender green, ethereal mists or rolling hills (p.38).   Pankot's pride, prejudice, and lore were rooted in the Rifles (p.38).   To command them, as did John Layton, was to bear a Crown. Millie shared that Crown with her husband and thus personified and enjoyed the highest military connection and most privileged and responsible position (pp.38-39).

Because of its military inspiration the community of Pankot treasured and abided by the raj code with dedication and discipline.   The purpose of the white man's presence in India could be neatly reduced to their regimental principles: leadership, service, and loyalty--those elements for which Teddie Bingham gave his life.   Millie observed that "what Teddie tried to do was worth the whole bloody war put together" (p.262).

Isobel Rankin voiced the community's definition
of good: those virtuous blooms of trustworthiness
which flowered from courage, honesty, loyalty, and
common sense (p.61). Such virtues could be achieved
by black and white alike.[2] In fact, the history of
East-meets-West was inspiringly adorned with numerous
examples of that holy and shining loyalty natives
showed to any man or woman whose salt had been eaten
(pp.154,260).

Anything but disloyalty could be forgiven
(p.39). Disloyalty struck at the root of the
military tradition which was based on trust between
officers and their men. It was this very trust which
Millie attempted to reaffirm in traveling along the
mountainsides of Pankot, visiting the families of
enlisted men who served and were captured with John
in Africa, and who everyone suspected would be
separated from their officers in prison camps (p.43).[3]

The military community knew that the chain of
trust could not exist apart from the chain of
command. A sense of and reverence for authority was
absolutely essential (p.62). Everyone from Isobel
Rankin down to Barbie Batchelor believed in the good
will and inherent wisdom of established authority
(p.9). Any attempt, whether peaceful (like the
all-India Congress voting to adopt Mr. Gandhi's plan
of non-violent non-cooperation) or violent (such as
the 1919 and 1942 riots) was viewed as an action of
the most despicable nature. To the Pankot community
the sides of the British-Indian coin were not love
and hate, as Edwina Crane believed. Nor were they
contempt and envy, as Ronald Merrick insisted. The
great dimensions of life in India were trust and
disloyalty.

As Edwina Crane observed, the raj's sense of
sacred mission and privilege derived initially from
their Christian tradition. The English saw God as
the ultimate authority figure who had delegated to
them his rights and power (The Jewel in the Crown,
p.34). The raj's place as sovereign rulers was as
certain as God's presence in heaven. But after
decades of the raj's ruling by divine right, God
dropped out of the game while the raj still regarded
its authority as absolute and unquestionable. After
having initially formed God into their own image (an

131

Authority figure), they in practice deified their own code and their own truth. They made gods of themselves and served their own ends and interests rather than God's. The raj code became a religion of its own.

As Barbie came to realize, the white man's interest became severed from the authentic Christian enterprise. The raj were not in India to serve and discover God in the poor stinking blacks (p.80). They did not strive, above all else, to cultivate joyfully the blossom of a personal relationship with a Trinitarian godhead. Even Barbie admitted that she came to India for the satisfaction of leading a rewarding life. To save even one heathen child would be a salutory achievement (pp.10-11). She served to feel good, not to do good.

The Pankot Mess was "like a temple" in which this spirit of idolatrous worship was symbolically concentrated (p.38). The hoard of dust-covered silver and the shredded and faded flags were the holy relics of the divine presence. Marble busts, like beasts, guarded the room with glaring eyes (p.199). The Mess was where absolute certainty was enshrined (p.200), and outside the new acolytes (Pankot Rifle recruits) drilled and paid homage (p.262).

As she walked down the long regimental trophy room, Barbie noticed a large portrait of a long since dead commander on a horse. Within that picture was concentrated the mystery of the governing genius of the temple (p.200). It hung like a crucifix for all to adore, like a sign of their salvation.

Since the raj code exemplified the good and the holy, its relics became a half-way house for supplication. Barbie found the picture of Queen Victoria a surrogate for God, a more immediate source of inspiration than her crucifix (p.75). The picture of the Queen receiving India while surrounded by approving angels eclipsed the form of Christ crucified as "a half-way house of intercession" (p.75), this "picture that pointed the reality of a Christian act..." (p.76).

But somewhere between Mabel's generation (the golden age of certainty) and Millie's, doubt entered Paradise. Even on a sunny day "it lay upon the valley, on invisible mist, a barrier to the clearer echoes of the conscience" (p.262). There were a few ardent believers left, like Teddie, but even his sacrifice was not appreciated by the military authorities as it should have been (p.263).

The angels no longer hovered above the throne as depicted in Barbie's picture. "The layers of authoritarian support above one's head thinned and those of hostile spirits thickened" (p.262). Barbie had imagined flames from Edwina's burnt-out car rising to heaven where approving angels welcomed it (p.75), an acceptable offering like Abel's sacrifice. But the rites of the temple, like Teddie's death and Millie's visitations, were no longer propitiatory sacrifices. They did not merit godly favor, and their smoke settled low along the land like a mist in the valley: Cain's rejected offering. The god had left the temple and no one knew where or how or why (p.262). As Nicky Paynton expressed it: "The bloody rot's set in" (p.255).

Just as Millie Layton exemplified the finest traditions of both family and regiment, she also became a symbol of the collective pressures which Pankot's white community faced (p.44). Millie met life with eyes hooded, with the corners of her mouth drooped in displeasure, with a posture expressing boredom. She used languor like a protective cloak, and her drinking emphasized every gesture of "studied effort..." (pp.40,43).

She found it difficult to live within her means, but it was not expected of an officer's family to subsist on military pay. The vulgarity of unpaid debts and the inconvenience of having to live in shabby military housing settled like a layer of dust, clouding the once clear and distinct reason for the raj being there at all, and symbolically tarnishing the illuminating gleam of shining silver in the temple (p.45).

Anything that broke through the mist of doubt, that fought through the layer of dust to let clear conviction shine brightly once again, was welcomed with desperate relief (p.45). General Dyer, General Reid, and Ronald Merrick were men of action who issued "a challenge to dark and perhaps superior forces..." (p.45). Despite these highlights the general impression was that "the game that had never been a game was very likely up" (p.44).

All forms of violent challenge to British authority were seen by the raj as involving an element of scornful rejection (p.82). But the INA phenomenon especially "blighted the tendrils of affection which entwined and supported the crumbling pillars of the edifice" (p.82).[4] The actual data concerning the INA probelm was kept confidential, but rumors nevertheless spread within the raj community. The essential facts as outlined in Ronald Merrick's lecture were these: Sudhas Chandra Bose, an Indian Congress renegade, formed the first INA battalion in Germany in 1942. The endeavor was basically a failure because he could not recruit enough officers, but shortly after, a Captain Mohan Singh was captured in Malaya and volunteered to organize Indian POW's to fight with the Japanese against the British in Malaya and Burma. Singh's command grew to over 10,000 Indians, and in August 1942 a handful of INA recruits stole into the country to meet with and seek Congress's support. The clandestine enterprise was betrayed by one of the INA's who disclosed important information which before could only be guessed. In December of 1942 Singh was arrested by the Japanese for refusing to fight in any theatre but India. Soon after, Bose traveled to Tokyo to direct the free India movement.

As a military threat the INA was negligible. The troops were poorly equipped and treated with contempt by the Japanese who exploited and betrayed them in battle. Even the powerful personality of Sudhas Chandra Bose could not create the illusion of common purpose. There were too many different motives for joining the INA forces: physical torture, fear, confusion, misplaced sense of patrio-tism and duty, or the possibility of escaping back to the regular Indian army. No matter what their motives, the INA's would suffer the contempt of their fellow Indians who had remained loyal to the white man's salt (pp.134-144).

In terms of moral and psychological impact, the INA problem led to overwhelming consequences. It signified the monstrous evil: disloyalty to the Crown, to the raj, to India and to Man-Bap. It meant the raj could not trust those they had "served" and ruled. "It's a bloody bore because you end up distrusting everybody," Nicky Paynton complained (p.319). If thousands of British-trained blacks had betrayed India and the Crown, then moral collapse

134

appeared imminent (p.262). Teddie realized that
nothing was sacred, that nobody could be relied upon.
The thin layer of civilization which the raj had
tried to cultivate never took root. They were all
living in a "bloody jungle" (p.148). Teddie regarded
INA's as "beyond the pale," on the other side of the
line between right and wrong (p.156).

As Merrick knew, myth-breaking was tricky business. Because he held the honor of the Indian Army
in his hands, he had to convey the impression that
the illusion was still intact, or even that he had
personally restored it (p.155). He was quite content
to let Teddie go on believing that "the line" was an
objective, absolute truth drawn for and not by men
(p.156).

The INA problem was only a symptom but not the
cause of the moral decline and estrangement between
whites and blacks. Whatever good, whatever service
the raj could have provided had been lost, sacrificed
on the idolatrous altar to white supremacy. The
charade was over, as Barbie realized while attending
the Bighams' wedding reception held at the Mess. The
word was "dead." "The edifice had crumbled and the
facade fooled nobody" (p.229). Even the table of
wedding presents, which should have been
sacramental-like miniature monuments to the enduring
and revitalizing rites of the code, was instead like
a funeral bier displaying the remains (p.195).[5]

The mist of doubt, the sense of doom and
finality tainted the white community's judgment and
values. The horror and brutality of British violence
against their subjects was completely overlooked or
minimized by most members of the raj. They believed
heroes like General Reid and Ronald Merrick were
cashiered like General Dyer to placate the natives.
Thanks to the disloyalty of Edwina Crane and Daphne
Manners, the real criminals of Bibighar would never
answer for their sins. The white community regarded
the men who tried to quell the riots and punish the
culprits as the real Bibighar martyrs who were
sacrificed by the government to regain India's
confidence (p.82). As rumors circulated about
alleged torture and defilement of the six Hindus
arrested by Merrick and of the coutless blacks killed
in the August riots, "that melancholy shadow was
burnt away by fires of irony which, lighting faces,
gave them the glowing look of belonging to people who

found themselves existing on a plane somewhere between that of the martyr and the bully" (p.82).

Without absolute moral certainty--which was lost somewhere in a past golden age or buried beneath the dust-covered silver, the ragged flags, and the neglected and lifeless traditional forms--everything seemed confused, disoriented, turned upside-down. Major questions like the INA's and Bibighar, or smaller community concerns such as the reorganization of the Pankot military station or Nicky Paynton's selling all her belongings and pulling up her shallow roots to leave without a backward glance or Mabel Layton disassociating herself from functions and cares of the collective "us" all added to the sense of imminent danger. The raj sea was disturbed by mighty waves which crashed against the shores in ever-rising tides.

England had always been viewed as the bastion, the headland standing fast. But the war had shattered this belief because "home" now faced its own over-whelming flood and could not support India with its former level of concern and attention (p.32). Previously, moral support from England had been guaranteed. Now this support was questionable because the moral climate in England had changed. Independence for India was a foregone conclusion, but in India (according to Isobel Rankin) certain prin-ciples and values still applied (p.61). The raj would have to carry on bereft of direction, support, or blessings from England and from God.

"The rot" which Nicky Paynton observed but assumed to be outside cantonment life was in fact attacking the raj from within. The insufficiencies of the raj's collective psychology were laid bare in Pankot's everyday life. The raj ladies fancied themselves as socially and culturally superior to types from the lower classes like Ronald Merrick and Barbie Batchelor, and yet they led vacuous lives with their committee meetings, bridge games, and club socials. Barbie's background may have been "vulgar," but she came from stock which loved life and knew how to enjoy it. Lower-middle-class life in England had been without privileges but was less grim, less solemnly important than raj life. Barbie's memories of childhood, especially those of her father, had a relaxed, magical, happy quality despite financial hardships.

Millie Layton spent hours riding with Kevin Coley among the mountain villages visiting women who knew far more than Millie about what made life endurable and worthwhile. Her visits were more arrogant, Barbie judged, than compassionate (p.245). Millie made sacrifices for the regiment just as Teddie did. But both gestures were obsolete (p.258).

Nicky Paynton's short, marginal entry was especially pathetic. She treated her husband's death as a totally private affair, giving no appropriate testimony to her loss through words or tears. Her stoic demeanor was extreme even by raj standards. She discarded the relics of her life in India as casually as Barbie fiercely preserved hers. Although India had taken her husband and separated her from her children, Nicky felt no ties, neither love nor hate, loyalty nor resentment (p.311).[6]

The women of Pankot took almost sadistic delight in their anticipation of the trials waiting frail, beautiful young girls like Susan Layton. Her gaiety was touchingly flowerlike, and the older women anticipated the day when she would be plucked in the fullness of her beauty and carried off to fade and wilt under the heat and hardships of adult life in India (p.35). It was as if they mentally tossed Susan into the ring of fire, like a scorpion, to see how long it would be before the flower succumbed to the flames.

It was assumed that Susan Layton, or any other member of her family and class, would face the destructive forces with pride and fatalistic nobility. Barbie recalled holding a pin cushion for her mother. She coupled this image with her impression of the stoic, sacrificial air the raj community conveyed:

> Hold it higher, her mother said, so she held the porcupine higher and counted pins going into place where the neck and shoulders had to be altered. Altared. Her mother was sticking in the pins too deep. Little beads of blood appeared like drops of red sweat on the white satin. The bride continued to smile like the Spartan boy with the stolen

fox under his shirt. Observe, her
mother said, the advantages of a
strict upbringing in a family of rank
(p.93).

The code decreed that Susan (the bride) or Nicky or
Millie would all face the flames with unfailing
determination to the death, if need be, without any
vulgar display of suffering, cowardice, or doubt. It
was a great deal to expect from people who no longer
believed in the Spartan code or the Spartan gods.

Barbie suffered from Pankot's social snobbery.
She fancied herself capable of conducting herself as
any other woman of genteel breeding, but Millie's
vulgar behavior and accusation that Barbie was born
with the soul of a parlor-maid (p.242) caused the
retired missionary to reflect on the Apostle spoons
Millie refused to have in her home: "I wouldn't give
tuppence for your chances, least of all if you tried
to get into that place where the silver is and asked
permission to sit at that table and break your bread
and drink your wine" (p.298). Even the Apostles were
the wrong type of whites in India, too crude, too
earthy. Their type and their sacramental rituals
would not be approved.[7]

From her experiences in Pankot's white community
Barbie came to the realization that the entire
enterprise was a sham. The British had never become
"bone of India's bone." They were only visitors,
never becoming one with India or with its people.
The raj had no purpose God would recognize or bless.
They only wanted to make the sky as cloudless for
themselves as possible. God had not followed them
there (pp.245,283).

Millie Layton sensed that the game was up, but
she did not lament the passing of the golden age
(p.44-45). She slanted a different way from the Muir
and Layton headstones, yet her life too, was a
monument to the code. Despite her drinking problem,
her need for pretending certain events never happened, and her habit of pretending that "everything
in the garden is lovely" (p.324), Millie stood out
like a figure of stone, refusing to let changing
circumstances influence her vision or judgment
(p.262). In the stormy sea, Millie chose to go down
with the ship.

138

Millie was not as honest, or as courageous, or perhaps not as desperate as Mabel Layton who knew that the edifice of the temple was hollow and meaningless. Mabel could not see the raj way of life as the guarantee, the foundation of virtuous blossoms like pride, loyalty, and honor (p.261). From her life as a gardener Mabel knew that for a rose or a person to flourish, one had to nurture individuality, coax roots to dig deeply, and cultivate with fingers occupied by years of patient custom and love (p.224).

All the edifice needed, Mabel and later Barbie came to understand, was to be toppled by a political or supernatural disaster, a symbolic Quetta earthquake. Such a disaster might prove an end to the Raj's earthly ambitions (as in the case of Kevin Coley) or even to their sanity (as with the daughter of Poppy Browning), but that was preferable to the pathetic waste and impotent attempts to breathe life into the skeletal remains.

> The charade was finished. Mabel had guessed the word years ago but had refrained from saying it. The word was 'dead'. Dead. Dead. It didn't matter now who said it; the edifice had crumbled and the facade fooled nobody. One could only pray for a wind to blow it all away or for an earthquake such as Captain Coley's wife had died in (p.229).

But Mabel could not find a replacement for the code in her life. She had withdrawn inside herself to such a degree that she was a stone figure like Millie, a rock (p.95). She would let no one in, not even poor Barbie who regarded Mabel as her final opportunity to earn God's blessing. "It was a curious relationship, like one between two people who hadn't yet met but who would love each other when they did" (p.95). Barbie did not blame Mabel for her coldness. Mabel brought no consolation, but she did not pretend to as others did. She knew, so Barbie believed, that to bring consolation to anyone was impossible (p.245).

Barbie flooded Mabel's ears with words just as she flooded God's, but neither responded, neither would make an inviting gesture, neither would afford her the safe harbor of an embrace. Barbie's secret

sorrow, once emanating from feelings of being
isolated from God, now centered around Mabel. "I'm
rather like a wave dashing against a rock, the sounds
I make are just like that. There is Mabel, there is
the rock, there is God. They are the same to all
intents and purposes" (p.95).

Barbie became enclosed in and surrounded by
towers of silence. It was a logical conclusion of
the raj code, the Spartan-like standards of the
ruling class. Mabel and Millie, Susan and Sarah,
even Nicky Paynton and the rest of the women were
emotionally isolated, inaccessible and unreadable.
Each was housed in a separate tower like a minaret of
a Parsees temple surrounded by birds of prey drawn to
death. People were so isolated that they repeatedly
misinterpreted acts of despair (such as Edwina
Crane's holding the dead Indian's hand or Millie and
Kevin Coley's coupling) for acts of love, and judged
acts of love (like Daphne's keeping her baby or
Aziz's disappearing after Mabel's death) for acts of
treachery. For these towers of silence everything
was remote--God, each other, and all of India.

II

The reader is torn between being angry with and
pitying Millie Layton. She admitted she was not a
good mother. She intentionally ruined Sarah's
chances of marriage to Dicky Beauvais, although she
would have welcomed Dicky into the family on Susan's
behalf (pp.326-333). When Susan was unable to nurse
her baby, Millie seemed relieved that the young
mother would not become too physically involved with
the child (p.247). To family and friends she was a
tower of silence, forever cold, withdrawn, determined. But she was also frightened. Her attempts to
pretend "everything in the garden is lovely" (p.324)
were exercises in survival just as was Susan's search
for the acceptable life through marriage. Millie's
need for the myth was not a personal, desperate
life-and-death struggle like Susan's. It was not a
heart-rending, metaphysical journey like Sarah's.
The end for the raj was fast approaching, but Millie
would not scramble to safety. Such action was too
vulgar, too common (p.287). "Her languor was not
that of someone superiorly regretting the passing of
the golden age" (p.45). She personified the noble

140

heritage of the Muir family, yet ironically slanted in contrast to those headstones in St. John's cemetery: "contrast in deductions and expectations from identical premises and identical investment" (pp. 45-46).

Besides her "slightly drunken tilt" (p.45), the only indication of Millie's deep needs and pressures was her relationship with Kevin Coley, the man with a face like an insignificant medieval martyr (p.193). When Barbie stumbled upon their rendezvous in the hot and dark interior of Coley's bungalow she heard whimpering sounds which seemed to come from some kind of creature relieved to be finally set free. She followed the creature's sounds through the subterranean light to the bedroom where the naked creature coupled with another "in a human parody of divine creation" (p.307). Their desperation rather than their nakedness alarmed her. It appeared to Barbie that Millie was driven by despair, not love or passion, as if she knew her world and her kind were doomed. Her pathetic coupling was "a bitter hopeless expression of the will...for the species to survive" (p.308).

When Fenny told Millie that Susan's dog Panther was dying, her sister's cynical response was "lucky dog" (p.322). Life had become a burden, a prison sentence, and the end, in whatever form it finally came, would be a relief. If Millie had been a praying woman like Barbie, she would have petitioned God to disabuse her of a "growing and irritating belief...that she had been abandoned to cope alone" (p.46). But the knowledge that she was alone and under attack from every quarter did not force Millie to break out of her tower and seek solace and help. It caused her to strengthen and fortify her own defenses.

It is no accident that Millie Layton was a pillar of the raj community. She radiated an image of stone "splendidly upright, and revealing her true distinction through her refusal to compromise either her upbringing or position" (p.262). She personified and perpetuated the code and in so doing became an occasion of despair for Barbie Batchelor. She refused to keep Barbie's gift of Apostle spoons, refused to honor Mabel's wish to be buried in Ranpur, and refused to let Barbie house her trunk of relics in the mali's shed at Rose Cottage. The cumulative

141

effect on Barbie was so demoralizing that the vision of Millie's face became interchangeable with the face of the devil who regarded her, chin in hand, thoughtful and patient (pp.270, 390-91).

Millie's treatment of Sarah's pregnancy was also despicable. She placed the blame entirely on her sister Fenny and commissioned her to take Sarah to Calcutta and "get the bloody thing aborted" (p.325) because she had washed her hands of all responsibility and concern. For Millie "it hasn't happened" (p.326). Her attitude about Sarah and her baby was identical to her attitude about Sarah and Panther, who had come out to die. Both conditions were unpleasant, vulgar situations for which Sarah (so Millie believed) was responsible. Sarah should not be "allowed just to opt out" (p.328) by letting the thing live.

There was also Millie's deliberate desecration of the garden at Rose Cottage. She erased all evidence of any person's being there, transforming it into a stark monument to the perpetual presence of raj rule. As Barbie realized, "it's easier to beseech against a background of roses (p.384).[8]

Although the thought would have insulted Millie, her abandoned condition made her a kindred spirit to Barbie Batchelor. Barbie had grown up as an only child in England's poorer middle class. Her father had "champagne tastes and beer income" (p.19). He sang vulgar songs about cheap love and played pranks on spinsters during parlor games. His drinking and gambling forced her mother to supplement their income as a dressmaker. Barbie's drunken father was trampled to death and her mother killed herself out of heartless love and heartless pride by trying to keep up appearances (.98).

Her childhood memories were a mixture of magic both light and dark: of waking up on Christmas morning and of hearing her parents quarreling at night (p.211). She had no regrest, except that she talked too much and acted impulsively. It was not a spur-of-the -moment decision to become a missionary and serve heathens in India. Because her mother opposed the decision, Barbie postponed her departure until her mother died (p.342).

All alone in the world, Barbie left for India.

At least God would have her (p.206). She anticipated the satisfaction of bringing heathen children to God (p.11). But to her enduring disappointment, the mission authorities were not as zealous as she was about conversions. The schools were contaminated by secular attitudes and aims which masqueraded as religious tolerance (p.12). In support of England's "divide and rule" policy, the missions encouraged both the Hindu and Muslim religions, emphasizing their superior education rather than religious affiliation. Barbie acquiesced to the warning that over-zealous behavior might alienate their heathen brethren and bowed to the wisdom of mission authorities (p.11).

One of her earliest assignments was to take Edwina Crane's place at the mission school in Muzzafirabad. Barbie's stay was not successful. She remembered taking away all the children's blue crayons because one of the little girls had colored Christ's face blue like Krishna's. Barbie could make no impression of her own, because her students measured her behavior by Edwina's heroic performance. She left the school with a small replica of Edwina's picture of Queen Victoria and a deep respect for her predecessor. "God is truly with her" (p.26). Barbie thought Edwina knew the secret of Christian life: that through her Jesus worked amid "suffering, sweating, stinking, violent humanity" (p.80).

Barbie proved to be a reliable workhorse and looked forward to retirement and having time to deal with a personal problem, her "secret sorrow." Esteem from her colleagues, students, and their parents was a satisfying reward for her years of service, but she had always held her supernatural mission above any earthly accomplishments. She believed firmly in "God, in Christ the Redeemer, and in the existence of Heaven" (p.10). But during her final years of teaching, Barbie found her faith weakening. She still believed that God existed, but could no longer feel His presence. Perhaps He no longer believed in her. He turned his face from her as if her life-long labors displeased Him, as if she were a great sinner instead of a missionary of the light (p.12). God no longer answered her prayers, that devotional machine she once worked to perfection (p.31). Tenaciously Barbie bombarded Him with words, but He was deaf to her pleas--a Tower of Silence.

Barbie admitted to Sarah that she always felt a little ashamed for coming to work among the heathens, as if she were unclean by association. She mentally made herself small, inconspicuous, to get through the mesh of people's disapproval. Now there was no way to become large so that God would look across the vast spaces and notice her again.

> One may carry the Word, yes, but the
> Word without the act is an abstrac-
> tion. The Word gets through the mesh
> but the act doesn't. So God does not
> follow. Perhaps He is deaf. Why
> not? What use are Words to Him?
> (p.342)

Abandoned, Barbie's prayers rose up, and meeting a cold reception (again like Cain's sacrifice) showered back down. "But she pressed on, head bowed, in the hailstorm" (p.31).[9] Barbie's prayers did not heal her waning faith in God, just as Millie's drinking did not bolster her lagging faith in the raj code (p.46). Both were abandoned to face the ring of fire alone.

Secretly fearing a lonely old age, Barbie answered Mabel's ad to share Rose Cottage. Her most pressing concern was how to transport her luggage. She could not allow the tide of retirement to leave her high and dry on the beach without it (p.14). Her possessions were like sacramental signs of her sacred labors. They explained her; they were the skeleton, the bones of her history, her holy relics (pp.14,279). No one else appreciated her trunk, her writing table, and her row of shoes, but Barbie would not allow herself to be separated from them.

Barbie's belongings made her more real, as if they bestowed existence and identity. Without them she felt naked, like a bundle of unfleshed bones without a shadow (p.15).[10] There were even times when Barbie believed the souvenirs of her missionary endeavors spoke more eloquently to God of her years of labor than did the state of her soul or her prayers. She would kneel on the rush mat before the trunk as at an altar, as at her life (p.272).[11] It contained, more truly than her fallible memory, evidence of all her endeavors. The relics were all God ever need notice. Barbie regarded her posses- sions as more herself than her body and soul. She clung protectively to the suitcases and boxes she

transported by tonga from Rose Cottage to her new
home with Clarissa Peplow, as if they were "crammed
with the numbered pieces of the fallen tower that had
been her friend" (p.257). They were, in fact, the
only real things left from her life with Mabel.

The book of Emerson's essays supported and
expanded Barbie's feelings about her own past. Just
as Barbie believed herself explained by the relics of
her past, Emerson regarded all of humanity to be
explained by its history: "Man is explicable by
nothing less than all of his history..." (p.76).
This meant that modern man, whether raj or Indian,
must look to every and all aspects of the past
belonging to all peoples before he could adequately
understand himself.

Emerson also applied the universal to the
particular: "If the whole of history is just one
man...it is all to be explained by individual
experience. There is a relation between the hours of
our life and the centuries of time" (p.77).[12] Barbie
was quick to see the philosophical implications. In
her experiences "lay an explanation not only of
history but of the lives of other living people,
therefore an explanation of the things that had
happened to Edwina and to Miss Manners" (p.77). As
Barbie was later to explain to Sarah, without her
trunk "none of us is explained because if it is my
history then it is yours too and was Mabel's"
(p.279-80). Barbie's past illumined and explained
Edwina's attack and her guarding Mr. Chaudhuri's
body. Barbie's life explained why and how Daphne
Manners could love a black man, fall victim to
ruffians, and choose to have a baby fathered by any
one of six natives. Furthermore, Barbie was as much
a victim as Daphne, who was first pictured as a
fragile figure in white and later as a large, awkward
girl. Barbie, too, sat on the roadside in the rain
holding the dead Indian's hand. Every man was as
heroic as the bravest, every man as blessed as the
most loving and faithful.

According to Emerson, Barbie could relate and
contribue to any other person's experiences, whether
he be above or below her station in life, whether he
be living in the present or in the past. There could
be no age, no event in all history which did not act
as an explanation of her own life. "He should see
that he can live all history in his own person,"

Emerson says (p.94). The past tends to abbreviate and to yield its own virtue to the individual in a most wonderful manner (p.94). If Emerson was correct, no matter how humble, how narrow the perimeters of Barbie's life had been, she could tap the rich treasures every man toiled to possess: wisdom, love, selfless heroism. She would immediately comprehend the emotional anguish of being attacked by six black men in Bibighar, because that would be as much her experience as Daphne's. All mankind would be truly one. Teddie's death and Edwina's gesture would hallow Barbie's own labors. If one man counted in the eyes of God, all men counted.

Suddenly the world opened up for Barbie. Her personal horizons extended to the tragedy of Poppy Browning, a brave woman among the stubble of reaped human experience (p.256). Edwina's gesture of holding Mr. Chaudhuri's hand, when viewed as an act of love, summed up Barbie's as well as Edwina's life of service in India. Once Barbie realized the gesture to be one of despair, she felt her own doubts and distress laid bare (pp.73,98).

As Barbie's despair increased she found her history a burden rather than a consolation. The weight of her trunk pressed her downwards, as on the hill leaving Rose Cottage for the final time (p.390).[13] She wondered if she would be better off if her past blew away like dandelion seeds or dry leaves, even if her religious principles departed with it (p.186). Emerson's message that "nothing can bring you peace but the triumph of principles" greatly alarmed her (p.202). Without her history she had no principles. But her past was a failure and as such would never win God's approval. Emerson's words "impinged on her own like a shadow of a hunched bird of prey patiently observing below it in the ritual of survival. The bird should have been an angel" (p.77).

Barbie's mistake was regarding her past as more important, her relics as more expressive of her value and accomplishments than the state and dignity of her soul. The importance of history, for Emerson, was to help explain and enrich the lives of individual men. To enslave men to the mistakes and rituals of the past, to attempt to freeze the past and impose it upon the present, was the crime of "society." "Society is a wave. The wave moves onward, but the water of which it is composed does not. The same

146

particle does not rise from the valley to the ridge. Its unity is only phenomenal. The persons who make up a nation today, next year die, and their experience with them" (p.202).[14] Barbie experienced the evils of raj society, how it conspired against her individuality and dignity and attempted to dictate her behavior and determine her duty.[15] What Barbie had yet to learn was that she was not doomed by her past mistakes and that her sins were not written in stone, on the tablets. Neither was she doomed by the evils and abuses of the raj's past and present behavior even though "the whole or history is one man."

That the raj was doomed is an unarguable fact, as Scott present it. His death imagery, from the very beginning of The Towers of Silence, crescendos to a climax in the last pages. The raj community in Pankot was caught between a new world and an old (p.278) as the Edwardian sun was setting. Their time was rapidly drawing to a close.

The first indication that there was something amiss in paradise occurred early on in Barbie's days at Rose Cottage. During her probationary period, while writing to Edwina, Barbie felt a nausea, a sickness that had haunted her several times in Ranpur and which dogged her even to Pankot. "But I'm not ill. There's illness in the room but it isn't _my_ illness" (p.24). She advised the emanation to leave and search for the Lord.[16]

But the spirit continued to plague her. The next visitation came after Edwina's suicide. The room was "rank with nausea, fetid and foul" (p.99) filled with a presence so intense that Barbie retched into the bowl. It was the Devil, the fallen angel, the lord of despair. "There was in its foulness a sense of exquisite patience and desire" (p.99). Edwina's despair had been the work of the Devil, and now he hunted for Barbie.

While talking with Sarah at Rose Cottage after Mabel's death, Barbie felt a "disturbance, another quick displacement of air, but this time a faint whiff of the malign breath, of the emanation" (p.279). Only a few days later Minnie the ayah felt the unappeased black spirits gather around the grace and favor bungalow where Susan would attempt to "free" her baby, the little prisoner (p.291).

Barbie next met the Devil in the form of Ronald Merrick. Before she even identified him she sensed a "noxious emanation that lay like an almost visible miasma around the plants along the balustrade which had grown dense and begun to trail tendrils" (p.375). She fought down the sickness inside herself and addressed the stranger, remembering Sarah's thorough dislike for the man but determined to approach him without pre-judging him.

The last visitation was at the moment of her death. On August 6, 1945, Barbie felt the final nausea enter the room (p.397). The sickness was not simply despair. Despair itself was merely a foreshadowing of death, of the lonely expanse of hell, which, though it be densely populated, was filled with isolated, hungry souls entombed in their towers of silence.

As the sickness stalked her, Barbie began seeing things in terms of another death image: the vultures drawn to the dying body of the raj. Her first such impression came with the nausea which she assumed had remained in Ranpur. When she commanded the sickness to leave and search for the Lord, she sensed an "ungainly winged departure as of a heavy carrion bird" (p.99).

When Susan's dog Panther lay dying, the sound of Millie's uncontrolled laughter drove the beast to snap at the sound as if it were "small predatory birds or maddening insects" (p.329). The old tonga wallah Barbie recruited to transport her trunk from Rose Cottage to the rectory "was an enclosed dilapidated man with a curved nose and predatory sleeping eyes, a starved bird with folded wings" (p.373).

The final bird image was manifested in the asylum in Ranpur, Ranpur facing west. Every evening Barbie witnessed the death of the day, the symbolic sinking of the Edwardian sun. She gazed reflectively upon her birds, the vultures of the Parsees which picked the bones clean.[17] The vultures circled the Towers of Silence, where the Parsees made their last earthly journey. Barbie was very proud of her birds (pp.393-94).

Scott also utilized bones and skeleton imagery to emphasize the closing days of the raj. When Barbie went to the garden seeking Mabel, expecting to be asked to leave Rose Cottage, her impressions of the afternoon were vivid: "The house was soundless and the world outside the window was full of bones" (p.27). When Mabel left Susan's wedding reception at the Pankot Mess, her excuse was that she felt unwell and did not want to be a "skeleton at the feast" (p.261). Barbie's trunk was stored in the mali's shed after being sewn up in sacking, as if encased in a shroud (p.281), and carried in a funeral cortège to the shed.

During her visit with Ronald Merrick at Rose Cottage, he spoke of starting a new life as Barbie faced the death of her former life (p.373). Barbie watched Merrick's cigarette burn to ashes in the tray which came from Benares on the banks of the Ganges. She envisioned the ashes of bodies floating down the sacred river to the unimaginable sea. Behind the ashes flowed her trunk containing the relics of her life, and with them the picture of Queen Victoria depicting Man-Bap. In the rear floated Ronald Merrick's arm (pp.384-85). They were offerings to the ancient god of fire, a foreign, threatening being who encircled them all and would soon devour everyone.

At the time of her death, as Barbie drifted between her own personality and Edwina's, she found that she could not remember who her blond visitor was. The birds had picked her memory clean. She would not speak. The birds had picked the words clean as well. While trying to sleep, she blew the dandelion pods to the bone. She was "sure in the Lord and the resurrection and the spade" (p.396).

The fourth image of death was the jackal packs. They hunted in the hills surrounding Pankot, and often their cries reached Barbie's bedroom in Rose Cottage as on the night that Queen Victoria's picture, reflecting no light, seemed to dim and then be extinguished. "I have gone out," Barbie thought as the jackal cries reached her ears. "Thou hast gone out, He she or it has gone out" (p.93). Soon it seemed to Barbie that the cries of the jackals were almost indistinguishable from the cries of the Unknown Indian, that figure left out of the Man-Bap picture, who was homeless and suffering like the dead teacher laying on the roadside in the rain, and like Daphne's lover thrown into prison and forgotten, like the little children Barbie never really loved. The cries of man and the cries of beasts were scarcely distinguishable (p.78).

After Susan placed her angel in a ring of fire, she became enclosed in her own madness, "touched by the special holiness" (p.294). Her melancholy cries blended with the cries of the pack. Susan, too, was a lost victim like the Unknown Indian. The cries

> could be heard all night but faded out as morning came leaving a profound, an ominous, silence and stillness that seemed to divide the races, brown-skinned from pale-skinned, and to mark every movement of the latter with a furtiveness of which they themselves were aware if their aloof preoccupied expressons were any guide (p.294).

Susan's puzzling behavior alarmed the raj community. It emphasized the feeling of hostile spirits in place of approving angels hovering overhead. Their safe, disciplined world was suddenly unintelligible and inhospitable. The creatures of the night were drawing closer, sensing imminent death.

The raj had not succeeded in civilizing the heathen world. The forces of dark magic were awaking from a long slumber, and the animals and plants of the jungle were closing in right through Barbie's window at the rectory (p.265). Barbie no longer imagined the body of the Unknown Indian laying half-way up Club Road. "All the bodies were buried but the jackal packs had multiplied; men ran with them on all fours, ravenous for bones" (p.373).

The end was drawing near, the end of Barbie's happy life at Rose Cottage and the end of the raj. The English honored their past but did not live it, perverting their own high principles and hastening the reign of the savage. The hunters and scavengers had multiplied. They could afford to wait. Soon there would be a feast for all. Death filled the world and nature was violated, perverted: "men ran with them on all fours," while the jungle crept in. Sin had entered Paradise.

Paul Scott's complicated garden imagery makes use of blossoms to symbolize each precious, unique individual. Mabel explained: "No flower is quite like another of the same species. On a single bush one is constantly surprised by the remarkable character shown by each individual rose" (p.207).

Barbie associated Parvati with a rose, both God's creatures, because she suspected that Lady Manners was the one who recommended the book of Gaffur's poems to Sarah (p.175). Susan's beauty and gaiety were regarded as especially flower-like. When her time came to marry she would be plucked and carried off, and her bloom would quickly fade (pp.35-36). Poppy Browning was envisioned as hardy like the flower, "brave among the stubble of the reaped field of human experience" (p.256). Even Barbie was depicted as a flower. She chose a heliotrope material for Susan's wedding (and inadvertantly for the moment of her death). The heliotrope was a plant which turned its flowers to the sun, and symbolized Barbie's search for light and for God. [18]

Scott also uses the flower image to symbolize the triumphant expressions of virtue, such as trustworthiness, which the raj believed blossomed from the nurturing elements of courage, honesty, loyalty, and common sense (p.61). Rose Cottage, once a metaphoric paradise for the flowering of virtue, became merely a piece of property after Mabel's death. Millie did not consider the garden as an appropriate setting for her own virtue (pp.263,377).

Trust, the highest virtue (according to the raj) involved a growth process. It had an organic nature which took years of cultivation to flourish. Any violent challenge to British authority destroyed that trust and "blighted the tendrils of affection which entwined and supported the crumbling pillars of the edifice" (p.82). Those green tendrils would no longer support the temple. "The bloody rot's set in" (p.255).

Barbie's vision of Pankot as a lush, green paradise (pp.18,28,38) was enhanced by the beauty of the garden at Rose Cottage. it was the heart, the core of Barbie's Eden.[19] Scott intends this garden to be not only a symbol of the lost garden of Paradise but also a metaphor of how the British should have accepted India:

> Each bud was merely a convoluted statement about itself and about the austerity of the vegetable kingdom which was content with the rhythm of the seasons and did not aspire beyond the natural flow of its sap and the firm grip of its root. The bushes from which these roses came had been of English stock but they had traveled well and accepted what was offered. They had not wished to adopt the solid or put a veil across the heat of the sun or spread the rainfall more evenly throughout the year. They had flourished (p.282-283).

Following the example of the roses, the raj should have asked for no privileges, no rewards other than to couple with India, to respond to its unique virtues, to dig deeply into the soil and blossom from native nourishment: bone of India's bone. Eventually the raj would have lost its former identity, like the English bushes, and become a native garden, successfully transplanted and uniquely resplendent. But the raj never became "of the country," and whatever roots they sprouted were shallow and temporary e.g., Nicky Paynton. They were only visitors. "That is why God has not followed us here" (p.283), Barbie reflected. He had bestowed many blessings upon them, but they did not return or multiply His gifts.

Another garden metaphor involved the question of how the British should have honorably withdrawn from India when the inevitable time came. Isobel Rankin believed that such an action could be done honorably if the raj discharged all its duties beforehand (p.62). Such a passing would have been like Mabel's death. When she felt herself arrested by a hand "more grandly and fearfully informed" (p.224) while leaning over one of her roses, she withdrew to the veranda, leaving the blossoms to their freedom and perfection and not violating them with her passing (p.223).

The actual withdrawal of the British from India could be likened to the death of Panther, who plowed through the garden in a circular and then random pattern, oblivious of the chaos and destruction he left behind (p.329). But even this atrocity, this animal behavior, would be preferable to Millie's calculated and willful desecration of the garden. The fact that she found the garden to be an inappropriate setting to her virtue indexed how fraudulant, how decayed raj virtue had become (p.263).

Another image Scott relates to the garden is the image of the jungle. Without care and discipline the vegetable kingdom soon encroached on the borders and monuments of civilization as at Rose Cottage after Mabel's death. The plants along the balustrade had "grown dense and begun to trail tendrils" (p.375). Sometimes this lush, uncontrolled development gave the impression of rare beauty to what was actually ugly, like Kevin Coley's bungalow: "...the revelation of what was ordinary and ugly stunned her for an instant into acceptance of it as rare and beautiful" (p.306). This "Eden" of sorts appeared unoccupied. But the jungle could also be a threat, such as the vegetation which crept uninvited through Barbie's window at the rectory. In contrast to Mabel's beautiful and sweet-smelling roses, these groping tendrils had tough skin and foul-smelling sap (p.265).[20] If the vegetable kingdom grew at will, without direction or design, it would choke out more delicate blooms of virtue and finally threaten all civilized behavior. This was the "bloody jungle" Teddie believed threatened the regimental code if Merrick's lecture about the INA's were true (p.148).

The new tennis court at Rose Cottage emphasized the garden's vulnerability. It was wide open to the destructive as well as creative energy of the human mind and will (p.279).[21] The garden, whether it be understood as the blossoming of human virtue, the flourishing of a nation on foreign soil, the growth of each unique human person, or the site of earthly and/or spiritual paradise, was a product of choice, of deliberate and constant care motivated by love.

Mabel was the archetype of the gardener image.[22] She said of her garden: "It often strikes me as something the gods once loved but forgot should die young and that there's only me left to love it. I'm not here forever and I'm not sure I love it enough" (pp.30-31). What angered Mabel most about the raj and their tradition was its unchanging quality. As she surveyed the silver and flags in the trophy room she told Barbie, "I can't even be angry. But someone ought to be" (p.201). There had been no changes in forty years. Human history and achievement should not be written in stone.[23] It could not be considered so absolute, so sacred, so inviolate that it remain unchanged or concretized.

This was the evil perpetrated by "society" upon the individual, according to Emerson. A man "should see that he can live all history in his own person" yet "not suffer himself to be bullied by kings or empires, but know that he is greater than all the geography and all the governments of the world" (p.94).[24] No law or political movement, no code or long-standing collective posture or prejudice should stand before the inviolate dignity of the individual or else the person is consumed by "society" and all that is left are towers of silence: hard, crusty shells and stone monuments. Such monuments smell of death. They are only broken temples and graven images.

As Barbie knew, if someone came and demanded that she empty herself or her past, the "logical end to the idea was total evacuation of room, body and soul, and of oneself dead but erect, like a monument marking some kind of historical occasion" (p.177). There had to be a balance between being informed, developed, and filled by history (both one's own and other people's experiences) and having the past imposed upon a person in such a way as to deny growth and freedom of the individual. On the surface Barbie seems faced with a dilemma: if history controlled her she would lose her personhood. If she denied her ties to history she would lose the "story" of herself. Either way only an empty shell would be left (pp.186,279).

Scott's balanced solution is found in Mabel's conduct and beliefs. "Her days are spent in celebration of the natural cycle of seed, growth, flower, decay, seed" (p.207). Or as the Christian message affirms, there could be no life without death. There was an appropriate time for the raj to flower. But its .time of growth and fullness had passed. They were in their final autumnal days and

the air was filled with the sweet smell of decay.
The British would never grow by hanging on to the
past like grim death (The Towers of Silence, p.16).
They had to die to themselves, let go of their
petrified past, or they would never again blossom as
individuals or as a nation.

At the end of her life Barbie found the true
value of her past: "One keeps up if one can and
cherishes those possessions which mark one's progress
through this world of joy and sorrow" (p.392). Some
of her relics "were blessed by the good intentions
that created them" (p.396), but they were not
synonymous with herself or her value as a person.
She gave meaning to her past and to her belongings,
not they to her.

Scott's lesson is that the raj should have
relinquished their strangle-hold on India as long as
they refused to co-mingle with India and insisted on
inhabiting their towers of silence. The passing of
the British would not be lamented:

> You oughtn't to say, Gaffur,
>   That God created roses,
> No matter how heavenly they smell.
>   You have to think of the time when you're both
>   dead and smell nasty
> And people are only intersted in your successors (p.174).

IV

Sarah Layton, one of Scott's major characters in
the second volume, fades into the background in The
Towers of Silence. Barbie Batchelor took her place
as the moral guide, and very little information is
added about Sarah that was not already revealed. The
reader knew that Sarah had been born into "grace"
(p.174), a state stemming not only from her privileged and dedicated family tradition but from her
sense of selfhood, of unshakeable identity. Her
actions still lacked spontaneity and joy. The look
of happiness apparent on her face while she held
new-born Edward soon faded, and the only remnant of
her night spent with Jimmy Clark was a saucy sort of
nerve...and her pregnancy. Nothing was revealed of

her feelings about the abortion.   Her only veiled
comment was on a post card to Barbie: "I'm better
too, fit as they say for human consumption again
(p.362). Sarah may have had more "guts" (p.254) than
most of the raj, but she lacked the courage to love,
the courage of Daphne Manners.   Sarah succumbed to
the social pressures which conspired to make her
"little" by aborting her baby (p.341).

The last vision the reader has of Sarah is of a
young, unhappy, unfulfilled woman who regretted being
away from "the sort of people we really are," people
like Clark whom she and Susan had just begun to meet
before returning to India (p.277).   Barbie wondered
if the "real" Sarah was the person she might have
been if she had not returned to India (p.279).   That
sense of doubt and regret is what impresses the
reader about Sarah, that and her judgment of Ronald
Merrick.   She believed adamantly that for Merrick to
function without a conscience was far worse than him
admitting he was wrong about Bibighar and having to
live with the guilt of his wrong-doing (p.340).   To
Sarah, it was better to realize a mistake and suffer
the consequences, even to the point of absolute
despair like Edwina Crane, than to refuse to see the
truth.

Scott expands the reader's knowledge of many of
the characters who, like Teddie Bingham, appeared
marginally in The Day of the Scorpion. In this third
book it becomes evident that there was more to Teddie
than cheerful vacuity (p.100), or a driving urge to
realize a collective ideal.   He was still portrayed
as thick-skinned, just short of insensitivity
(p.103), which enabled him to court Susan unabashedly
only days after breaking off with Sarah.

Teddie's life was dictated by the rules of his
class (p.109).   He pursued Sarah and later Susan not
as people but as embodiments of an ideal (p.106).
Sarah knew that love had nothing to do with Teddie's
kissing her in the car, and that both of them were
bored.   In a small way, kissing Sarah, like using
vulgar language, was breaking out of the pattern for
Teddie--a baby step out of the armor (pp.107,111).
But the code triumphed in the end, boring and empty
though it was, because Teddie could not face the
truth: that his entire life had been boring and
empty because it was structured to mirror the code.
It was a monument to "society," but it was not a

reflection of Teddie as a person, thriving and
blossoming like a rose. To be honest like Sarah not
only threatened his ego but opened up a frightening
world, a world outside the code, a world devoid of
certainty and direction (p.109).

Teddie regarded his own life as a series of long
gaps linked by a few significant events. The first
notable gap in Teddie's military life was the year
between his war experience in Burma and his arrival
in Pankot (p.101). No one, not even Tony Bishop, was
sure of the details. The only obvious result was a
coarsening of language, although such a tendency was
never manifested in the Mess or in a lady's presence.
One of the most interesting gaps in Teddie's history
was information about his sexual exploits (p.105).
And there was also a (characteristic) "little gap"
between his courting Sarah and "turning up a couple
of days later to take up with Susan" (p.109).

> Perhaps the gap in this case repre-
> sented a dark night of Teddie's soul
> (a whiff of that pungent odour?),[25] a
> battle between a disturbing new
> instinct, only half felt, and an old
> safe and happy one which was familiar
> and reliable and inevitably the
> victor. In that case the spoils were
> Teddie, not Susan (p.109).

Only when he confided to Merrick about the
insignificant details of his mediocre life did Teddie
feel his past was important; at least it merited
Merrick's undivided attention (p.158). The one thing
his past accomplished was strictly to mold Teddie's
tastes, opinions and values to the raj code.[26]

Teddie lamented the vulgarity of modern English
life which blighted India (p.146) and did not approve
of undirected, undisciplined bursts of activity
(which characterized Americans) or of guerrilla
warfare. The military life was intrinsically a
gentleman's occupation demanding a stable relationship between an officer and his men and meriting the
privileges of an officer's life (p.123). Such things
were impossible to sustain in hit-and-run fiascos
carried out in the jungle. Despite the fact that he
sometimes felt confined and controlled and had to ask
permission for everything, Teddie believed his future
was secure and his contribution significant.

Once Teddie decided it was time that he marry, he plunged into a state of constant sexual arousal which Susan's presence heightened but did not cause. Both Teddie and Susan were possessed by a sense of urgency--to abide by the rules (to marry and reproduce their own kind) while the rules still existed (p.109). At times Teddie felt that his wedding really mattered only to himself and Susan, and that what was significant to them was unimportant in the wider scheme of things (p.158). During their engagement, Teddie was afraid that his plaguing bad luck would prevail and that Susan was a tantalizing taste of what he would miss. He hoped that she was compensation for his previous lack (p.118).

Susan's "trim little body was protected by some sort of absolute statement about its virginity this side of the altar" (p.116), but hers was a different kind of statement than Teddie's constant state of erection (p.117). Teddie wanted to believe that Susan was made for a life of simple loving (p.117), but when he touched her she was so tense her whole body was like a skull (p.117).[27] He could not penetrate her self-contained shell. On their wedding night her fingers on his shoulders conveyed a reluctance "which he supposed was a degree better than distaste" (p.166). In bed she lay in rumpled sheets pretending to sleep and appeared to Teddie as if she were a discarded victim--not by him but by herself (p.166).

Teddie discovered a joy in coupling, a legitimate, endorsed, blessed joy "with nothing murky or restricting perched on its shoulder" (p.167). The tragedy of their brief relationship was that Susan did not join him in this small, private area of freedom within the stockade (p.167). All too soon the light that was Teddie Bingham was extinguished. He limped into the story from Burma as onto the margin of a page, into temporary safety, Susan's arms, a moment of truth, and then fiery oblivion (p.46). Scott comments that Teddie surely would have been cheerful about the course of his life (p.46). He had been loyal to the end. His was a death he could have (so to speak) been able to live with.

Susan's fate was not as salutory as Teddie's according to raj standards. The women of Pankot found her melancholy withdrawal inexplicable. Susan had the support of the entire community, and she had her child as an immediate and insistent reminder of her duty (p.290). She was such a bright, refreshing personality, so determined to do the right thing. Then, with one startling, alarming gesture, Susan destroyed years of effort. Her neighbors could not decifer her conduct, and wondered if she, by recreating a childhood prank, was mocking them all (p.291). General Rankin was the one who realized the significance of Susan's action. She had made a statement about life:

> a statement which reduced you...to the size of an insect; an insect entirely surrounded by the destructive element, so that twist, turn, attack or defend yourself as you might you were doomed; not by the forces ranged against you but by the inadequacy of your own armour. And if for armour you read conduct, ideas, principles, the code by which you lived, then the sense to be read into Susan's otherwise meaningless little charade was to say the least of it thought-provoking (p.296).

By enacting a memory from her childhood, Susan had depicted the dignity of man as far below that of a composite substance enjoying a spiritual as well as physical nature. As a being of inferior stature in the world order, man could neither assume nor deserve constant and dedicated attention from God. Man was all alone against his enemies, and from the time of birth found himself threatened by a ring of fire. His deadliest enemy was the weakness of his own armor. For Susan it was the raj code, for Barbie it was her past as a missionary, for Merrick it was his "line." Every man staged his own defense; every man would fail.

With the help of Dr. Samuels, Susan re-emerged into Pankot social life in time for Nicky Paynton's farewell party. To the other women Susan appeared to have no "secret life," no more illusions or misconceptions. "She was looking at the world as it was" (p.351). She mingled freely at the party, going out of her way to contribute, to offer herself as if she were publicly affirming her commitment to the code (p.352). Just when it appeared that Susan may have conquered her self-centeredness and insecurity, she suddenly dropped her cocktail glass--a foreboding prophecy that she still was not whole.

Just as Susan withdrew emotionally from the community, Mabel Layton isolated herself physically. For Pankot, Mabel symbolized the spirit of a lost age along with those Edwardian attributes of certainty, self-assurance, and total conviction (p.193). Since she had lost two husbands to India and her stepson was a prisoner of war somewhere in Germany, it was natural to think of Mabel as "representing something" (p.30). Often visitors would come to Rose Cottage to make sure everyone was representing it together (p.30). The raj did not condemn Mabel's silence and isolation because they assumed her silence was from one "who knew events could speak for themselves and would do so" (p.258), and they were sure they all would agree on the message.

As guardian of a golden age Mabel was like "a bleak point of reference, as it were a marker-buoy above a sunken ship full of treasure that could never be salvaged; a reminder and a warning to shipping still afloat in waters that got more treacherous every year" (p.32). What the raj community did not realize was that Mabel saw the flood coming but did not regret it (p.33). Like Noah she closed herself up in her ark and let rampaging forces destroy the sinful world around her.[28]

Mabel's advertisement for a roommate surprised everyone. If it was a maneuver to keep Millie out of Rose Cottage, it was only partially successful. During the day the bungalow filled with family, friends, and suitors, yet this activity strangely emphasized Mabel's isolation (p.36). She hid her real feelings so well that no one suspected her hostility toward the sacred regimental tradition. She asked nothing from anyone, helped pay Millie's debts, and gave to Indian charities. She suffered the sentence of life with great patience (p.207). Only in sleep did the past press around her. People and places surfaced from out of the past, names which would be forever lost with her death.[29]

Mabel welcomed Barbie into her life at Rose Cottage because she believed that the retired teacher would appreciate her garden, although she worried that sharing her life would be too dull. "...I'd

160

hate you to think it had to be appreciated in my way and no one else's," Mabel told her (p.30). Barbie felt guilty for encroaching on Millie's territory and bustled around the Cottage fetching and serving with more than her usual display of misdirected energy. But she earned nothing except Millie's disdain.

Barbie quickly fell in love with Pankot, with Rose Cottage, and with the Layton girls. Because her attachments did not extend to the flesh (p.74), Barbie was incapable of imagining physical contact with Mr. Maybrick or loving a black man. People said that Daphne must have been hypnotized. Perhaps Barbie herself had been mesmerized by God years and years ago (p.79).

The attacks on Edwina and Daphne caused a stir in Pankot society, but the effect on Barbie went deeper than her casual relationship with Edwina justified. Edwina's gesture of holding the dead Indian's hand in the rain captured Barbie's imagination and spurred her hope. If Emerson were right, then Barbie shared in Edwina's heroic gesture and could draw God's attention to herself as surely as Edwina must have done. "Right from the beginning Edwina had been close to God and therefore to herself. Not teaching but loving" (p.74), so Barbie believed. Edwina appeared to achieve an apotheosis, and Barbie desired one of her own: "nothing in the least grandiose...but...quiet with a still-centre to it that exemplifies not my release from earthly life although it might do that too but from its muddiness and uncertainty" (p.74). She desired to act out of love, humility, and singularity. She desired to attain Daphne's wholeness of purpose. But for now she had to share in Edwina's apotheosis. "In her mind she too guarded the body" (p.73).

Her image of Edwina's dead Indian soon mingled with her image of Daphne's lost lover to produce a single personality: the Unknown Indian (p.78). He was the figure missing from the Queen Victoria picture and from the eager ministries of Barbie's life. For a time she thought of him lying along Club Road and heard his howls blending with the jackals' cries at night.

Daphne was at first pictured as a languid figure in white, a victim of the most heinous crime. Later, the Pankot women were informed that she was really

large and awkward, even plain, and had refused to
identify her assailants. Barbie preferred the more
accurate description, which made Daphne easier to
identify with (pp.79-80). The violence surrounding
Edwina and Daphne brought one truth, one elusive goal
to Barbie's attention: love. She saw Edwina and
Daphne holding the hand of Indians as the same
gesture Queen Victoria made when bending to accept
the jewel for her crown. This gesture also reminded
Barbie of Mabel's kneeling to prune her beloved
roses, and of herself teaching her little heathen
children (pp.75, 77-78).

Until the truth of Edwina's gesture became
clear, Barbie entertained the prospect of welcoming
her to Rose Cottage for a period of recuperation.
"And I shall be large again and shapely with intent,
so close to Edwina that God will remember and no
longer mark me absent from the roll" (p.75). But
after Edwina's suicide, Barbie finally understood
that gesture in the rain as one of despair rather
than love.[30] Edwina felt that her life in India had
come to nothing; the body she guarded was the remains
of her hopes, ambitions, and illusions (p.98).
Barbie realized that she herself had done nothing to
destroy the division between whites and blacks, and
wondered if she had ever really loved her children
(pp.203,208). Her life of service had never been
performed out of love and humility, had never had a
wholeness of purpose (p.74).

What was true of Barbie as an individual was
even more true of the raj community which professed
allegiance to Man-Bap, that balance of hardness and
sentimentality which became an excuse for whites to
serve only themselves (p.275).

After this apotheosis of self-knowledge,
Barbie's life quickly disintegrated. She had seen
Mabel as a vehicle for salvation, a person placed in
her life by God Himself. Believing that Mabel had
not entered a state of tranquility and could not do
so alone, she prayed to "bring light to the darkness
that lies on the soul of Mabel Layton" (p.31). As
with Edwina, Barbie had set before her mind a
situation of conditional redemption--a proposition
for God. If she could help Edwina or Mabel find
peace, then she would finally earn God's attention
and approval. Barbie also yearned for an affectionate relationship with Mabel. She wanted to rest in

the safe harbor of Mabel's embrace, like a child
(p.212). But Mabel was a rock like God, against which
Barbie repeatedly dashed herself.

Later Barbie would look to Lady Manners as one
blessed by God, and sought her attention in order to
obtain His (p.271). But this was no magic formula
either. What Barbie came to think of as her only
solution was a program of silence: to retreat
deliberately into a silent tower of her own.[31]

Barbie had not only continually talked to God,
to her neighbors, and to Mabel, but also to herself
(p.70). But while with Sarah after the Binghams'
wedding, she entered the realm of imaginary silence,
where she spoke without being aware of it. Such a
state, Barbie hoped, could be used to create contact
between herself and God (p.186).[32] Words were no use
to Him (p.342); they piled up and toppled down like
towers of bricks, like towers of Babel. The avenue
of escape from the state of isolation was blocked by
the toppling towers of words (pp.191,196). Barbie
wanted to be talked to, above all else. She had to
learn to keep quiet, to listen, and to wait (p.280).

During Susan's wedding reception in Pankot,
Barbie entered an area of "blessed privacy" where the
words she actually spoke were different from the
words she voiced within herself (p.196). It was a
small part of herself, a tiny state of freedom much
like Teddie's short honeymoon, or his use of vulgar
speech.

After her illness Barbie's voice, once something
she was proud of, became a source of humiliation
(p.334). It was "a hoarse, grating sound alternating
between a crackling whisper and an uneven cry"
(p.362) like the voice of death. After she met the
devil in the person of Ronald Merrick, Barbie gave up
speaking altogether, observing a vow of silence to be
ready for God's call.

When Millie refused to bury Mabel's body in
Ranpur, Barbie realized that the family did not care
at all about Mabel's wishes. She witnessed a
manifestation of the raj's sin of collectivity
(p.245). From then on she became a rebel, like Mabel
before her, like Sarah and like Ahmed. She resolved
to donate the rejected Apostle spoons to the Mess,
matching Millie's vulgarity with a greater vulgarity

of her own."   ...Bugger the lot of you" (p.300). It
was a small way in which Barbie, as a representative
of the common man, could defy the class snobbery and
insensitivity of the raj.   When Clarissa Peplow
returned the spoons to her house guest, Barbie
responded: "Blessed are the insulted and the shat
upon...for they shall inherit the kingdom of Heaven,
which is currently under offer with vacant
possession" (p.296). Her veiled critiscism of the
spiritual condition of the raj was lost on
self-righteous Clarissa, but the comment was significant. Barbie, who at the beginning of the volume
bowed to established authority, would never have
thought or voiced such an opinion until she had
undergone a process of disillusionment much like
Edwina's.

Barbie is an important character because she
senses truths which helped cause her madness. But
she also had a personality trait which was her
strength and her weakness. It was a sensitivity to,
an ability to see beyond sensual phenomenon to the
hidden meaning of things. Such a talent manifested
itself as a habit of interpreting reality metaphorically. She envisioned the body of Edwina's Unknown
Indian halfway up Club Road. Later she expected it
actually to be there and was surprised to find it had
been removed (p.78). After moving into the rectory
Barbie noticed that her shoes aligned beneath the
curtain looked like a line of old people eavesdrop-
ping (p.265). She came to think of them as really
being there, shrunken, malevolent spirits like the
creeper waiting at her window (p.366). Barbie came
to believe the metaphor was real and not just a
vehicle of interpretation.

Barbie instinctively sensed, before she read his
essays, the truths she found in Emerson. Emerson's
ideas were the articulation of Barbie's perceptions
of and sensitivity to the unity of human experience.[33]

From the time Barbie answered Mabel's ad, she
was preoccupied with her trunk. She regarded it as
her shadow (pp.14-15), the altar of her life even
before she read in Emerson that "man is explicable by
nothing less than all of his history..." (p.76).
After the criminal attacks on Edwina and Daphne,
Barbie read: "If the whole of history is one
man...it is all to be explained from individual
experience. There is a relation between the hours of

our life and the centuries of time" (p.77).   With
Emerson's help Barbie realized that without her trunk
not only she but Edwina, Sarah, and all of them could
not be explained (p.279).   Unless men tapped into,
gave heed to, and permitted themselves to be touched
and enriched by others' experiences, they were mere
bodies, monuments of stone, lonely towers of silence
(p.279).

Her own sensitivity combined with Emerson's
thoughts helped Barbie understand not only her own
experiences but Edwina's and Daphne's.   Her insight
of the Unknown Indian was one which even Mabel and
Sarah, in their reflective wisdom, did not unearth.

The truth of Emerson's words are vindicated by
Barbie's own experiences.   "He should see that he can
live all history in his own person," she read, and
then smelled something burning, "a faint odour as if
something singed" (p.94).   It was the day Edwina
burned herself out of despair in the raj myth.
Barbie, afraid of the heater in Mabel's room, checked
to make sure her friend was safe, and heard her
mumble: "Gillian Waller" (Jallianwallah).

After the wedding reception at the Mess when
Barbie witnessed the dust-covered silver, the ragged
and faded flags, the spirit of the regiment petrified
and unchanged, she read the "Society is a wave"
passage from Emerson's essay on "Self-Reliance," a
reminder of the evil of a past revered and imposed
upon individuals, like the conspiracy Barbie's
poet-father warned her about: "There is a conspiracy
among us to make us little" (p.341).   The individual
"is greater than all the geography and all the
governments of the world" (p.94), Emerson reminded
Barbie, but this knowledge could not bring her peace.
"Nothing can bring you peace but yourself.   Nothing
can bring you peace but the triumph of principles"
(p.202).   But Barbie had not found interior peace.
She had forgotten what her principles were, and began
to doubt whether she ever really loved or served
anyone (p.203).

Barbie functions as one of Scott's most reliable
and "graceful" of moral guides.   She did not succumb
to the raj's social and moral blackmail as Sarah did.
She did not let them make her small, although they
tried to deny and starve her individual personhood.
She was able to face the truth about evils of the raj

165

more courageously then Edwina because she did not depend on some impersonal "moral drift of history" to right the wrong.[34] She would do so herself by becoming her own glorious, unique rose. She adoped the little boy Ashok, and entrusted the keys of her trunk to Aziz, Mabel's faithful servant (p.273).[35]

Barbie foresaw the future, which was death. When she demanded a spade from Clarissa Peplow, she could have wanted to rebury Mabel, or to bury them all. Do not pity her, Scott admonishes the reader, she had a good life (p.396).

In The Towers of Silence Scott again develops character parallels involving universal symbols depicting the human condition. He fully defines the meaning of the scorpion in a ring of fire and explores his new "tower" image. Scott seems to believe, with Emerson, that "the whole of history is one man..." and that there is a relation between the experiences of individuals, a relation so accurate, so binding, that the explanation for one is the explanation for all. Such an idea, if true, could become the philosophical basis for Scott's parallel development of characters. It also enables Scott to associate artistically events and characters which the reader may otherwise not see as related. These artistic associations differ from logical ones (such as the thrown stone linked to Teddie's death) because they do not spring from the events themselves but are designed by the creative talents of the author to enhance meaning and broaden awareness.

The artistic association of Mr. Chaudhuri and Hari as the Unknown Indian binds Daphne and Edwina more closely than any previous historical connection. When Scott brings Barbie into the association with Edwina (because of their prior relationship) and hence with Daphne to the extent that the three figures are sometimes confused by the raj community (p.66), the author unleashes the full impact of Bibighar upon Pankot. This impact extended even to Teddie's engagement, when it was marked by the fatal connection of being announced the same day as Daphne's death and Parvati's birth (p.100).

The vision of Edwina holding the dead Indian's hand reminded Barbie of Queen Victoria bending with extended hand, which in turn suggested Mabel ministering to her roses (p.77). She associated the open-mouthed cry of the Unknown Indian (p.81) with the howling of the jackal pack, the same melancholy cry which escaped from Susan when she learned of Teddie's death, the same mute sound which formed her own mouth in a fixed position to cry out (p.202), like Mabel's soundless cry of horror at the moment of death sealed upon her corpse (p.238).

Barbie associated Parvati with a beautiful rose because Lady Manners had been the one to suggest Gaffur's book of poems to Sarah during their brief visit (p.175).[36] She reflected on the names of people in Mabel's past: Ghulam Mohammed who was gone like Poppy Browning's daughter, and Bob Buckland, the uncle of Dicky Beauvais--all gone with Mabel to the grave (p.202); Mabel who cried out soundlessly like the Unknown Indian and the girl in white who ran from something unimaginable which might even have been love (p.304). They were all gone.

Everything seems to be connected, as Barbie observed: Lady Manners, Daphne, Captain Merrick, even Apostle spoons. Through Scott's creative artistry different people and events are associated, and their own meaning thereby enhanced. By using this tool Scott illustrates the tremendous penetration of Bibighar into a wide circle of people, like creeping tendrils of the jungle.

V

Scott utilized light imagery in a more consistent way in The Towers of Silence than in the previous volume. The difference between light and darkness is more defined. There are not the infinite shades of grey as found in The Day of the Scorpion.

Natural sources of light are celebrated as good, as illuminating. "Romeo," says Emerson, quoting Shakespeare, "if dead, should be cut up into little stars to make the heavens fine" (p.203). "...I like the sunshine," Mabel told Barbie (p.214), who in turn chose heliotrope material for Susan's wedding: a flower that turns to the sun.

But the light, as Barbie observed, was fading fast (p.281). Dark forces were massing against the raj (p.45), and even within the protected confines of

Barbie's room at Rose Cottage the light could not illuminate Queen Victoria's picture. "I have gone out, Thou hast gone out, He she or it has gone out (p.93). Light signified what was real, true, alive and present. Darkness denied all of these elements within a person and the larger world. Darkness surrounded the loveless, degrading parody of the creative act which Barbie witnessed at Kevin Coley's cottage (p.307). It was the evil done to the black man in the name of religion; it was the cold, empty bitterness which captured Mabel's soul (p.31).

There was the light of the golden age, the condition of absolute moral certainty captured in the gleaming silver of the regimental Mess, Pankot's temple of military sacramentals. Any action, such as Teddie's noble death, which magnified that shining light, was one of the highest goods in the days of doubt when mist hid the sun and confusion clouded the issues (pp.45,200,262).

Daphne stood in shafts of sunlight which were alive with particles of dust (p.80). Her rape momentarily renewed the determined spirit of the raj, who viewed any attack on one of their own as an attack upon them all. For a short time it appeared that Daphne's personal tragedy would rekindle that gleaming vitality. But doubts and suspicians began to surround her name after she refused to identify her assailants and in so doing proved disloyal to the community. Thus dust mixed with sunlight in the image Pankot held of Daphne, and soon she would fade from laurel-dappled sunlight (her mythical fate) into the oblivion from which she was dragged (p.68).

The same confusing patches of light and shade surrounded the mental image of the suppliant woman in white (p.181). The patches of light revealed nothing but "were like mysterious glowing areas attempting to burn their way out of an imprisoning mass of darkness" (p.181). She symbolized the conflicting elements of Bibighar, elements composed of reputed acts of heroism for the sake of the code, and the rumors of brutality and injustice which, as fires of irony, lit the faces of those involved, giving them "the glowing look of belonging to people who found themselves existing on a plane somewhere between that of the martyr and the bully" (p.82).

Important again in this volume is shadow symbolism. It is used in one sense to depict an evil presence, a negation of life such as the shadow of death which leaned over Mabel while she ministered to her roses (p.223). Aziz saw "the sunlight and the shadow and in his heart interpreted them correctly" (p.214). The shadow of Emerson's words impinged upon Barbie like a hunched bird of prey (p.77). There is the kind of shadow produced by the interaction between a person and a strong source of light. Susan trailed her wedding after her like a "diaphanous shadow" (p.178). Barbie hoped she would attract God's attention by her good deeds, evidence of which was packed away in her trunk. Without the relics of her past she feared the light of the divine gaze would not fall upon her. Without her trunk she could cast no shadow of her own (pp.15,280).

Barbie interpreted the job offer at Dibrapur as a divine invitation, an opportunity to atone for her mistakes of the past. "She shut her eyes and in the dim room turned her face to the enormous white sky and the scorching over-breath of the sun that baked the earth and the body to a holy exhaustion" (pp.368-69). God's attention is likened to the scorching, draining Indian sun which demanded and laid claim to her energy and life's-blood. Later, when Merrick imparted Edwina's last message of despair to her, God made His presence known in another form: "An invisible lightning struck the verandah. The purity of its colorless fire etched shadows on his face. The cross glowed on her breast and then seemed to burn out" (p.386).

Barbie died on August 6, 1945, the day the first atomic weapon was used on Hiroshima. The description of her corpse might depict any one of the Japanese victims, as if she participated in that experience.[37] "They found her thus, eternally alert, in sudden sunshine, her shadow burnt into the wall behind her as if by some distant but terrible fire" (p.397).[38] The reader must examine the pages immediately preceding her death in order to determine whether Barbie's shadow measured and signified the triumph of the burning fires of hell and the exquisite desire of the prince of darkness, or whether the "distant but terrible fire" was the burning love and overwhelming desire of God in the heaven she finally found.

Barbie's test of faith had been a long, bitter temptation. She had to struggle with the cross of

despair through her years of hailstorms[39] and dark
nights. In the midst of that despair which plagued
her, the same despair that shaped her parents' lives
and the despair that drove Edwina to take her life,
Barbie recognized the face of the devil. The devil
was a real presence to her, a fallen angel, whose own
despair was of the heaven he had lost forever and the
face of God he would never see. The devil's passion
for souls was as great as God's, but all he had to
offer was the darkness of his own despair. The devil
was despair as surely as God was love (p.98).

Edwina's suicide forced Barbie to face her own
despair. If there was no saving love in Edwina's
past ministries, there could be none in hers. "After
many years of believing I knew what love is I now
suspect I do not which means I do not know and have
never known what God is either" (p.203). Just when
Barbie needed Him the most, God withdrew from her
even further. She questioned her existence and her
right to it (p.203). Perhaps God had fled the entire
universe, abandoned all men as He abandoned her. "Is
the Universe an unprincipled design? Does God weep
somewhere beyond it crying to its prisoners to free
themselves and to come to Him? If it is all
explained by chemistry, that chemistry is majestic.
It can only lead to the most magnificent explosion,[40]
to which God will hearken while we burn and disintegrate and scatter into pieces" (p.207). The image
suggests the Parsees' action of casting the ashes of
their dead into the sacred river.

To the little black boy Ashok Barbie said: "You
are my little Unknown Hindu...and you are a brown
butterfly. Me, I am white, But we are the prisoners
of the good God" (p.364).

After Mabel's death Barbie felt compelled to
view the body, to know whether or not she rested in
peace. The sight was Barbie's first authentic vision
of hell: "The mouth was open too and from it a wail
of pain and terror was emitting" (p.238). And later,
when Barbie faced removing her belongings bit by bit
from Rose Cottage, she saw the face of the devil,
"chin in hand, regarding her with that compassion and
patience, that exquisite desire" (p.270). When she
left the cottage forever, she entered an arena of
defeat from which she could see no exit. "...Already
she felt the onset of the last, the grand despair..."
(p.270). As God became more and more remote and

seemingly unresponsive, the devil stalked poor Barbie relentlessly. It was he who desired her soul, not God. She would meet the devil face-to-face in the form of Ronald Merrick on her last visit to Rose Cottage.

On the surface, Merrick's character development in The Towers of Silence revealed a knowledgeable, dedicated, perhaps even gifted man who had courageously overcome life-long barriers to serve his country in India. Certain information concerning Bibighar is reiterated: that Merrick still held Hari in contempt and felt no pangs of doubt that he was guilty and that he quit feeling fond of Daphne when he realized which way she had "jumped" (p.384).

Sarah sensed something terribly wrong about Merrick: he had no conscience. He would never admit he had ruined an innocent man's life out of personal hatred under the cloak of the white man's justice (pp.184,340).

Scott states that Merrick represented Teddie's death (p.127). Literally that was of course true, as depicted in The Day of the Scorpion. From the stone incident to the INA debacle in which Teddie was killed, Merrick was the storm center which drew in and devoured Teddie Bingham. Even Teddie's face was changed by the scar from the stone: Merrick's wound which Teddie bore (p.166).[41]

But Merrick also was the vehicle for Teddie's spiritual death. He was a self-professed myth-breaker. He turned down better jobs to enter the INA field (p.130) because it suited him. He delighted in being an occasion of scandal and despair for others. After Teddie heard Merrick's lecture, he returned to his hut only to find a discarded woman's bicycle and cabalistic markings. Instinctively, he connected the markings with the pain in his bowels, and the lecture with the growing sense that his entire life had been disrupted (p.148). In talking with Merrick he felt drawn out, enlarged, as if exposed to new territory and new possibilities (p.156).[42] After Teddie got pleasantly drunk over dinner, Merrick led him through the maze of covered walks back to their hut. "Teddie was satisfactorily several over the eight but still on his feet. He protested when Merrick helped him take off his shoes. He did not remember getting into bed" (p.162).

Merrick, by taking off Teddie's shoes, symbolically entered into his life just as Clark entered into Sarah's (The Day of the Scorpion, P.459).   By performing an act of comfort usually provided by another (in this case, Hosein), Merrick became a symbol of the changing tide of circumstances in Teddie's life.   Through Merrick's influence, Teddie left the regiment's circle of safety just as Sarah left her family's circle of safety through Clark. Symbolically Merrick was the serpent in Teddie's Eden, offering the fruits of the knowledge of evil.[43]

When Barbie saw this devil incarnate, she sensed a "noxious emanation that lay like an almost visible miasma around the plants along the balustrade" (p.375).[44] As they chatted and drank coffee together Merrick watched her, chin-in-hand, just as the devil had done a few days before.   Merrick was deliberate in his words and his actions, conscious of the black child nearby who watched him with mingled wonder and disgust.   Merrick described his life as newly begin-ning, having to relearn skills like mounting a horse or pouring a cup of coffee (p.379).[45]   It was a sacrilegious parody of Christ's resurrected but still wounded body.   Then he addressed Barbie: "I hope you don't interpret this elegant monstrosity as payment deferred for having made a tragic mistake" (p.383). It was significant that Merrick anticipated such an interpretation, but he would not be bothered if people believed it.   As Barbie reminded him, he was famous because of Bibighar.   If his wounds kept Bibighar alive, then they were a means to eternal life.

As they spoke, Barbie had a vision of Hari Kumar's aunt, the suppliant woman in white, between their feet abasing herself (p.384).   She asked him about the other woman in white, the widow of India who burned herself.   It was Merrick who imparted Edwina's final message of despair to Barbie: "There is no God.   Not even on the road from Dibrapur" (p.386).   Barbie felt invisible lightning strike the veranda and etch shadows upon Merrick's face (p.386).[46]   "He looked desolated as if Edwina's discovery were a knowledge he had been born with and could not bear because he had been born as well with a tribal memory of a time when God leaned.   His weight upon the world" (p.386).   He looked as if he needed consolation, and Barbie (by his design) felt drawn to him.

172

The truth was that Merrick did not regret the loss of God's presence because the world which bore the weight of God would not tolerate Merrick's behavior, his "situations" or his "line." But, as Emerson would have it, when people of the past or present believe that there was or was not a God, that experience is part of Merrick's experience also. It was part of his "tribal memory," his historical heritage. Whether he recognized or lamented the fact, he existed as an abandoned orphan, a once child-of-god left to cope alone, like Barbie and like Millie (p.46).

Scott makes several references to this childhood image.[47] In choosing Teddie, Susan picked out the toy she liked the best (p.108). When Susan placed Edward in a ring of fire she shattered her image as a child might destroy his own edifice of bricks (p.291). When Barbie saw Kevin Coley for the first time after discovering him and Millie together in bed, she appreciated that narrow area of courage which enabled him to face her. He impressed her as having kept a box of bricks somewhere in his background (p.372), whereas Merrick seemed like a boy without bricks (p.389).[48]

Even Teddie Bingham recognized the element of mystery in life, but this element aroused "an old instinct to dislike on sight anyone about whom there was a faint mystery, a difference..." (p.131). He pondered what foreign bacteria would send his imagination out of control and cause an ordinary bed to appear lit by St. Elmo's fire: half-ship, half-catafalque (p.121). "Something odd had been happening ever since he arrived in Mirat" (p.161).

As a child Barbie accepted magic as a "normal part of life. Everything seems rooted in it, everything conspires in magic terms" (p.211). Often she found magic strange, incomprehensible, and threatening, like the icy hand of the demon spirit that touched her low down on the back of her neck--the invisible, malicious party guest (p.174). There were the twenty stairs in her childhood home: "She sang the first line of the vulgar song over and over going up the stairs but still under her breath because the stairs frightened her" (p.93). She experienced the same fear when she faced the door at the end of the hallway in the regimental Mess. It seemed as far away, "as unattainable as the landing at the top of the frightening stairs in the gloomy little house in Camberwell" (p.199). But there was good magic also, the magic of Christmas mornings when her parents always had some small gift for her.[49] "I adored Christmas mornings. I always woke while it was still dark and worked my toes up and down to feel the stocking's weight and listen to the rustle and crackle" (p.211). Even as an adult Barbie would imagine herself the nocturnal visitor who rode a sleigh and left "a lingering glittering frosty scent of her own magical intrusion" (p.337). Always open to the mystery of life, to the conviction that there was meaning and purpose beyond her own powers to grasp or design, Barbie never outgrew her sensitivity to this childhood magic. She perceived a mystical element surrounding Susan's wedding (p.168). The book of Gaffur poems (p.172), the recounted story about the suppliant woman in white who fell at Merrick's feet (p.181), and Mabel's long-awaited presence in the regimental Mess (p.193). Barbie was still fascinated, like a child, by the prospect of viewing someone else's possessions: "for these had a magic quality of touch-me-not that belonged in fairy tales and in such tales dispensation was possible but not inevitable and every invitation to come nearer was a sugared gift" (p.186).[50]

To deal with the chaos and misfortune of adult life, one had to remain a child in some respects. There would always be an element of an unknown, inexplicable, uncontrolled destiny; sometimes labelled fate, sometimes Providence. Whether men believed themselves to be chemical accidents or children of God, their capacities to understand themselves and their universe was fallible and limited. Men, whether young or old, lived like children. Some sensed the magical, game-like quality of life--they had a set of bricks. Merrick refused to play the game. He never gave himself over to magic, and therefore could never trust, never believe, never surrender his life or destiny to anything except his own will and his small, twisted feelings of contempt and envy. People could choose to create or build with their lives, or like Merrick and MacGregor, to destroy what others struggled to achieve. But for everyone, life was the mystery at the top of the stairs (p.219). There was that element in life of the unknown, the experience of present trials, the possibility of at least future happiness, and the long steps in between.

This was Barbie's vision as she rode in the over-loaded tonga away from Rose Cottage: the "toy-like happy danger of human life on earth, which was an apotheosis of a kind" (p.392). It had begun to rain, and the drops on her face were like the water from the carafe Millie had thrown at her (p.390). Barbie saw Millie's face appear before her, then "thought she smelt burning" (p.391). It could have been the smoldering brakes of the tonga or the odor of hell from where the lord of despair desired her. Millie's face slowly changed into the face of the man (the devil in the form of Ronald Merrick)[51] who regarded her, chin in hand "thoughtful and patient, so purposeful in his desire for her soul that he had thrown away Edwina's" (p.391).

As the tonga made the precarious journey down the hill, the storm worsened and a "rogue element of electric mischief"[52] shattered the silence "like a child bursting a blow-up paper bag containing flashes of paper fire" (p.391). Barbie spied colored umbrellas on the golf course, just as she had seen in her dream that convinced her Edwina was not damned. "Why! It is my dream!" (p.391) Barbie felt like a child again, a child of God and a believer in his magic because He was present in this blessing, the actualization of her dream;[53]present in the "brightest amalgam of blue and yellow light ever seen in the region: an alert such as even the combined rifles of Pankot and its tribal hills could not have achieved by sustained fusillade" (p.391). Barbie knew that "God had shone his light on her at last by casting first the shadow of the prince of darkness across her feet" (p.392).

The force of the wind blew the lace butterfly shawl in the face of the tonga-wallah and her own. "He tore at the monstrous membrane that blinded him and which blinded Barbie too like a great light followed by a giant explosion, a display of pyrotechnics that put the old November Crystal Palace shows to shame" (p.392). The intensity and dimensions of the divine presence, manifested in this barrage of lightning, eclipsed any known display. Barbie was free and young again, happy to be a prisoner of God. God had exorcized the devil of despair from inside her, and the devil seemed to enter the old tonga horse. Barbie tried to help the old man resist the gadarene[54]pull of the apocalyptical four horses. It was the end of time, the coming of the Lord to rescue her. Barbie fell endlessly like Lucifer but without his pride and to a different destination. "My eyeballs melt, my shadow is as hot as a cinder--I have been through Hell and come out again by God's Mercy" (p.392).

Barbie had not been defeated by raj society. Her principles ultimately triumphed over her society which fancied itself a Christian people but which never coupled His actions to the spirit of the Christian message. The Words got through the mesh of God's approval but the actions did not. "One may carry the Word, yes, but the Word without the act is an abstraction" (p.342). This "Christian" people only preached the Word, they did not live it, and so practically speaking God was dead, snuffed out in the hearts of these towers of silence.

The raj found Daphne's love for Hari and her choice to keep his child offensive to the code in the same way the raj regarded Indian independence as imprudent and undesirable. Perceiving Indians as politically equal and essentially equal in dignity was something the raj never achieved. Until white society could not only visualize Jesus working against the background of "suffering, sweating, stinking, violent humanity" (p.80) but could also understand Jesus to be those people, they would never know God and therefore never know real love. The raj's own members as well as the native population were deprived. They were left only with an Eden of a kind, like Kevin Coley's bungalow which was really ordinary and ugly, and wherein a man and woman could only engage in a "parody of divine creation" (p.307). Or they are left with Pankot, no longer a paradise because sin had entered and men ran in packs on all fours (p.373).

Barbie's one authentic experience of earthly love was a remote rumor--the ill-fated love between Daphne Manners and Hari Kumar. Barbie wanted to give her Apostle spoons to Lady Manners because she was the trustee of their baby, that incomparable rose.[55] Nowhere else in raj society did Barbie find a love like theirs, not between Kevin Coley and Millie, not between Millie and her daughters or between Poppy Browning and hers, not between Sarah and her never-to-be-born child, not between Edwina and God.

Without the immeasurable font of divine life to transform and actualize human love, there can be no access to people, no hope of maintaining a love relationship. Without God the nurturer, the cultivator, there can be no lasting union between individuals, or between English and Indians, rose and soul.

The raj, like Ronald Merrick, should have been haunted by Bibighar and by all their other hypocritical deeds (p.185). That is why Edward's baptism was surrounded by a furtive and forbidden air (p.274). The baptismal party was not only shocked and confused by Susan's gesture, they were fearful that God would discover their profane act, their parody of sacramental magic. The truth of Rev. Peplow's sermon at Teddie's funeral was ironic: "Except the Lord build the house: their labour is but lost that build it. Except the Lord keep the city: the watchman waketh but in vain" (p.284). The raj were doomed, their days numbered because they had denied their own heritage and forsaken their source of vitality and virtue. There is no garden, no Eden. All that remains is to witness the flood (like Mabel the Noah figure) and to note which of the water particles rise and which fall with the waves of change.

Just as it would be better for Merrick to admit his wrong-doing and live with the guilt (p.184), it would be better for the raj to acknowledge the truth. If the result is grief and guilt it would be preferable to living a lie and remaining unloved. The ideal solution would be appreciating people as Barbie believed Sarah appreciated her: seeing down to the "terrific thing were really is in me, the joy I would find in God[56]and which she would find in life, which comes to much the same thing" (p.175).

FOOTNOTES TO CHAPTER III

¹All page references in this chapter, unless otherwide noted, are from Paul Scott, The Towers of Silence (New York: Avon Books, 1971).

²Isobel in fact "liked" any Indian who could be trusted to preserve what the British and blacks had built together, a sentiment which proved (she believed) that she harbored no personal prejudice against natives.

³This was one reason why Millie resented Barbie's presence in Rose Cottage, because it appeared to be a sign that Mabel distrusted Millie and so schemed to deny her right of possession.

⁴This image recalls Sarah's words in The Day of the Scorpion about "the crumbling carapace of our history" (p.415). Scott expands this image in The Towers of Silence to incorporate a religious aspect and to develop his garden image.

⁵It is significant that Barbie's Apostle spoons were not allowed to mark the grave or adorn the remains. They were witnesses of the Most Sublime Love but remained unwanted and homeless.

⁶Nicky's callous announcement of her departure during a gathering at Rose Cottage contrasts sharply with the dog Panther's withdrawal, collapse, and death because of Susan's absence. Ironically, Panther's reaction seems more "human."

⁷There was also the anti-semetic feeling toward the psychologist Samuels, the "trick cyclist wallah..." (p.350) The raj community felt defensive in his presence, suspecting that he might blame them for Susan's breakdown. (p.358)

⁸There is also a symbolic parallel between the devil's presence ("the nausea, fetid and foul"), which made Barbie's skin "freeze and harden as warmth went out of her blood" (p.99), and Millie's presence. Millie made the devotional machine come to life by

178

dousing Barbie with a carafe of water (p.243), like
the hailstorm, the air of frosty particles which had
once received Barbie's prayers and was once so warm
(p.31). When Barbie entered Kevin Coley's bungalow
where Millie and Kevin were engaged in "a human
parody of divine creation" her "flesh tightened,
attacked by frosty particles of fear" (p.307). It
was like being back again "in the chill corridor
approaching other doors that gave a view through oval
windows" (p.307), where Mabel's dead body lay, and
where Barbie caught her "first authentic vision of
what hell was like" (p.239).

[9]In light of this thematic parallel to Millie it
was appropriate that Millie made the hailstorm
materialize for Barbie by dowsing her with a carafe
of water. "The devotional machine had come to life in
the shape of Mildred and a handy jug" (p.243).
Millie would have been pleased to know she was a
god-figure. In this very tangible, literal way a
member of the raj played god. But this similarity of
function also emphasized Millie's scandalous role as
an occasion of despair for Barbie--a disturbing
reminder of God's silence.

[10]Even Susan appreciated "things that have
stories to them" (p.213). The history of Sarah's
baptism gown, which Barbie told her, made not only
the gown, but Mabel seem more real to Susan.

[11]The relics of Barbie's life were not acceptable
offerings because angels no longer looked with favor
on the English. In like manner, Millie rejected
Barbie's gift of Apostle spoons because nothing had
gone right since the offering was made. For the
spoons to be laid to rest finally in the Officers'
Mess was like a sentence of death.

[12]In the Complete Essays and Other Writings of
Ralph Waldo Emerson,(ed. Brooks Atkinson [New York:-
Random House, 1940], Emerson also speaks of "one mind
common to all men" (p.123) and states that "of the
universal mind each individual man is one more
incarnation" (p.124). "It is the universal nature
which gives worth to particular men and things"
(p.124). "Who hath access to this universal mind is
a party to all that is or can be done, for this is
the only and sovereign agent" (p.123). "Of the works

of this mind history is the record" (p.123-from Emerson's essay on "History"). The reader might conclude from these passages that there is an absolute, existing humanity, or mind, which exists outside and beyond any and all individual men. It is presumably this mind which unifies all human experiences.

[13]The complete reference reads: "Barbie could feel the weight of the trunk at her back: her years pressing on her, pushing her forward, pushing her downward. She pressed her feet hard against the curved footboard but her legs had little strength" (p.390). The passage is significantly similar to the description of Sarah's reaction while she sat with Ronald Merrick in the hospital in Calcutta: "When he began speaking she wondered whether the way in was being widened; salted, like the way in to a danger-ous, derelict mine. She found herself exerting pressure on the ground with the soles of her feet and on her chair with the small of her back" (The Day of the Scorpion, p.386. See also the following descrip-tion of the same reaction, P.414). Sarah felt as if she were being drawn into Merrick, "felt the pressure of his willing her to enter and explore the myster-ious area of his obsession" (The Day of the Scorpion p.412). While Sarah was falling into Merrick, so to speak, Barbie felt herself "falling endlessly like Lucifer" (p.392), hopefully to a different destin-ation.

[14]It is unfortunate that his passage on Society is quoted in isolation, because this wave image gives the impression that society moves ever onward while men and their experiences remain stationary. If there is a "relation between the hours of our life and the centuries of time" (p.77), then it is the experience that is enduring and timeless. Later on in the essay on "Self-reliance," Emerson states that "society never advances. It recedes as fast on one side as it gains on the other" (Complete Essays and Other Writings. p.166).

[15]If Barbie had gone further on in Emerson's essay on "Self-Reliance" she would have read: "Your genuine action will explain itself and will explain your other genuine actions. your conformity explains nothing" (p.153). Roses make no apology, "they are for what they are," simply a rose, perfect in every

moment of its existence (p.157).

[16]Barbie was sensitive to a reality beyond the mundane and so acted as a prophet for her people. She herself did not welcome the inconvenience of being a visionary, and was relieved to see the absence of a stigmata (p.25).

[17]The Parsees, originally fire-worshippers who followed Zoroaster, fled before the Moslem advance from Persia to India in the seventh century. They laid out the bodies of their dead for vultures to pick clean, then cremated the bones and threw the ashes into the sacred Ganges River.

[18]In A Division of the Spoils Scott observes that Susan's name means white lily (p.523).

[19]Sarah believed that roses came to symbolize the flowering of Barbie's state of happiness at Rose Cottage (A Division of the Spoils, p.134).

[20]In The Jewel in the Crown the inquisitive stranger celebrated his return to India after an eighteen-year absence by absorbing the smells surrounding him. "It is not only the smell of habitation. It is the smell, perhaps, of centuries of the land's experience of its people" (The Jewel in the Crown, pp.193-94). The intense Indian heat brought out the essential fragrance of the land like "the warmth of a woman's skin releasing the hidden but astonishing formula of an unusual perfume" (The Jewel in the Crown, p.101).

In The Towers of Silence Scott continues to explore the world of odors, associating them this time not so much with the exterior, material world but with an interior and hidden secret world. The smells in Teddie's world consisted of the scent of Susan's hair (p.165), the pungent odor of "voluntary or involuntary nocturnal emissions" (p.105), and of night-scented Susan, "a warm aromatic combination of breasts and thighs" (p.167). Barbie was especially sensitive to smells. When she crouched behind the pillar in St. John's church expecting to see Mabel's ghost, she was "fearfully alert for the sweet odour of the ghost, the compound of flowers and formal-dehyde that must attach to the newly dead" (p.270).

181

As she imagined her trunk floating down the sacred river along with Merrick's amputated arm, she smelled the air "heavy with the scent of jasmine, decayed fish, human and animal ordure" (p.385). In her memories of childhood Christmases, Barbie remembered sitting up and sniffing "very cautiously to smell the magic. I mean of someone having been there who drove across frosty rooftops and had so many chimneys to attend to but never forgot mine" (p.211). While she sat on the balcony of her hospital room, her lap covered with a red blanket, Barbie imagined herself as the someone who left "a lingering glittering frosty scent of her own magical intrusion" (p.337). The scent of roses was all-pervasive at Rose Cottage and became the scent of Barbie's own happiness, just as the creeper's foul-smelling sap was a sign of Barbie's loss and emptiness. Different smells not only indicate the imaginative or sensitive attributes of the observer, but signify the true nature and intent of the object. When Teddie found the bicycle and cabalistic markings "he sniffed the air for the lingering scent of an ill-wisher, wondering whether he would be able to isolate such a smell from all the others to which he had become used" (p.147). This is why, to Sr. Ludmila, Ronald Merrick "looked right but he did not smell right...To me, who had been about in the world, he smelt all wrong" (The Jewel in the Crown, (p.134). This is why the devil, lord of despair, was an illness, an emanation fetid and foul. And this is why the magical, frosty memories of Barbie's childhood Santa had its own pleasing scent, along with all the good and happy experiences of her life.

21 The destruction of Mabel's native roses by Millie in her design to make Rose Cottage more raj-like (see A Division of the Spoils, pp.139-40) metaphorically describes the white man's wanton destruction and utter disregard of the beauty and riches of the Indian culture.

22 Mr. Maybrick had once been a planter. Barbie imagined him showing the coolies how to pick only the tender leaves. "As he shows them God sings through his fingers" (p.75). Growing things was a divine, creative task.

23 This image was used in reference to Daphne Manners: her name would be "written the tablets"

(p.68).

24Emerson's belief in the dignity and development
of the individual person is of paramount importance
in his body of thought. He writes: "stand before
each of the tablets and say, "Here is one of my
coverings. Under this fantastic, or odious, or
graceful mask did my Proteus nature hide itself"
(p.94). Emerson does not mean to infer that the human
person is a low creature on a par with amoebic or
bacterial life forms. He writes this to remedy "the
defect of our too great nearness to ourselves"
(p.94). By seeing our vices mirrored by others
living in the past, we are able to distance ourselves
from our own actions and attain some degree of
perspective. The passage quoted by Paul Scott concludes: "As crabs, goats, scorpions, the balance and
the waterpot lose their meanness when hung as signs
in the zodiac, so I can see my own vices without heat
in the distant persons of Solomon, Alcibiades, and
Catiline" (from Emerson's essay on "History" in The
Complete Essays and Other Writings of Ralph Waldo
Emerson, p.124).

25This passage may not only refer to the pungent
odor of "voluntary or involuntary nocturnal emission"
(p.105) but perhaps also to the odor "fetid and foul"
which stalked Barbie: the devil, lord of despair.

26In speaking with Merrick the night they
acquainted themselves in the bar, Teddie was impressed with how much history he actually had,
whereas Merrick was a "mystery that attracted him"
(p.158). Even compared to Teddie, Merrick had a
vacuous history. Little is known about Merrick that
he does not choose to reveal. The most personal and
accurate information about him is revelaed by Hari
Kumar because of the intimacy of their relationship.
Only Merrick's victims come to substantive knowledge
about his real nature, his interior self. Yet even
that type of knowledge is not adequate. The reader is
never let loose into the workings of Merrick's soul,
into his mind and heart. Scott never opens that door,
and one reason must be that Merrick has no history
and therefore symbolically has no interior life. He
is like the vacuous "monument marking some kind of
historical occasion, "just the mere body Barbie was
afraid of becoming without her history and her trunk
(pp.177,279). Merrick, the man without a history and

183

Teddie, the man enslaved by his history, signify the horns of Barbie's dilemma.

Barbie's trunk is described in the following way: "The once black paint was scored and scratched with the scars of travel and rough handling; and the name, painted in white roman capital--BARBARA BATCHELOR--had faded into grey anonymity of a kind from which a good report might be educed by someone who did not know her; a chance discoverer of a later age" (p.272). Merrick's trunk was "just as old and a battered as Teddie's" but there was no indication where it had come from." The rank of captain was freshly painted in, however, and a band of new black paint obliterated something that had been written underneath the surname" (p.123).

Even the trunk hinted of the mystery surrounding the man. It had traveled "from somewhere else" (p.123), advertised Merrick's rank but disclosed no other information. Merrick did not value his trunk as Barbie valued hers. His contained no relics of his vacuous past.

[27] This is reminiscent of Sarah's tension with Jimmy Clark (The Day of the Scorpion, p.449), which disappeared when Sarah crossed the "so-called bridge." Susan never did.

[28] This image is reinforced later by Barbie's impression, as she took her long walks, or being a dove sent out to check the flood level (p.73).

[29] Barbie misinterpreted Mabel's dream-mumblings as "Gillian Waller" when in fact the word was "Jallinwallah," the site in Amritsar of General Dyer's slaughter of black innocents in 1919 (see p.317).

[30] When she first heard about Edwina's attack and interpreted her gesture of holding Mr. Chaudhuri's hand as expressing her altruistic, devoted life of service, Barbie hung the Queen Victoria picture in her room at Rose Cottage, the picture which symbolized Edwina's act of heroism at Muzzafirabad (p.73). On the evening of the day Edwina killed herself Barbie's picture "had gone out," symbolically anticipating Barbie's own despair in the Man-Bap myth after realizing the truth of Edwina's gesture.

[31]Scott's "towers of silence" image functions on at least three different levels. On the literal level it refers to the towers of the Parsees, where bodies of their dead were brought to be picked clean by vultures before being cremated and the ashes thrown into the sacred Ganges River. It also functions as a symbolic expression of the Spartan-like, stone facade members of the raj conveyed in public, an emotional veil which caused Barbie to think of Mabel as a rock, like God. Mabel is a particularly appropriate example since she had a "gift for stillness" (p.257). There were the towers of words which toppled like towers of Babel (pp.191,196). Barbie believed her imaginary silences would not destroy contact but create it (p.186). But on the outside Barbie too becomes a tower of silence.

It is interesting to note that, as Barbie became more and more withdrawn after Mabel's death, Sarah began to talk more and more after her encounter with Clark, events which occurred at the same time. "She's always had guts. Suddenly she has nerve," Nicky Paynton observed (p.254). Yet neither Sarah (who spoke more) nor Barbie (who spoke less) disclosed their true feelings or thoughts.

[32]Emerson says: "Silence is a solvent that destroys personality, and gives us leave to be great and universal" (essay on "Intellect," The Complete Essays p.302).

[33]Emerson says: "You have first an instinct, then an opinion, then a knowledge, as the plant has root, bud, and fruit...it shall ripen into truth" (essay on "Intellect," The Complete Essays pp.294-95).

[34]She had recognized early on in her career as a missionary that the mission schools were lukewarm in their labors to bring heathen children into the fold (p.12) and interfered with Barbie's own zealous attempts at conversion.

[35]Barbie begins to place the key in her purse but continues to hold it, just as Sarah held the key to Clark's bedroom door (The Day of the Scorpion p.458). Lady Manners also held a key to the tin box which entombed Daphne's diary (The Day of the Scorpion, p.44). Barbie, Sarah, and Ethel are the most reflective of Scott's characters in these two middle

volumes, and all three held a key. Emerson says: "The key to every man is his thought" (essay on "Circles," The Complete Essays p.280).

[36] In trying to recite the poem, Barbie, too, entered into the "connexion between a poet and a prince and an imprisoned politician" (p.175).

[37] The bomb may be understood as another instance of nature abused and perverted, like the spreading of the jungle, like Millie's tennis court, like men running on all fours--the antithesis rather than the measure of civilizaton.

Emerson says: "He should see that he can live all history in his own person" (p.94). If Emerson's theory of history is to be believed, Barbie actually did experience the bombing of Hiroshima. Her dreams and imaginings intensified as August 6, 1945 approached. "If it is all explained by chemistry, that chemistry is majestic. It can only lead to the most magnificent explosion, to which God will harken while we burn and disintegrate and scatter into pieces" (p.207). After seeing Merrick at Rose Cottage, Barbie got her trunk and her dream became reality. "The tonga gathered momentum. The old man began to apply the brake" (p.390). "Barbie could feel the weight of her trunk at her back: her years pressing on her, pushing her downwards" (p.390)."On the downhill sweep the equipage gathered speed, out of control of the crazed horse" (p.392). The reader can almost feel the momentum of man and his history pressing forward into the atomic age and the destruction of Hiroshima.

The tonga-wallah "tore at the monstrous membrane that blinded him and which blinded Barbie too like a great light followed by a giant explosion, a display of pyrotechnics that put the old November Crystal Palace to shame" (p.392). "My eyeballs melt, my shadow is as hot as cinder" (p.392). This is an accurate description of the bombing of Hiroshima and of what happened to the victims.

On August 6th, Barbie took a seat at the barred windows of her hospital room. She could not see the birds. "But imagined their feathers sheened by emerald and indigo light" (p.397). "And felt the final nausea enter the room" (p.397). "Emerald and indigo light" of these large birds are the same colors as the lights on bombers.

In A Division of the Spoils Sarah mentions that she is afraid that the birds might take some predatory advantage and turn into Barbie's birds of ominous intentions, the same kind of intentious harbored by the B-29's. In her dying hours Barbie may have transcended the physical and become part of "one mind common to all men" (p.123).

[38]Merrick's face in the harsh sunlight appeared "hardened, burnt by experiences..." (The Day of the Scorpion, p.181) as if he, too, was exposed to a terrible fire.

[39]The first thematic reference for this phenomenon reads: "The prayers hardened in the upper air, once so warm, now so frosty, and tinkled down. But she pressed on, head bowed, in the hailstorm" (p.31). Barbie's secret sorrow was not so much a crisis of faith but a crisis of feeling: "She believed in God as firmly as ever but she no longer felt that He believed in her or listened to her" (p.12). Because of the sensation of a cold reception, this feeling of being rejected and abandoned, Barbie associated the "enclosed winter" of the morgue with "a season of frost" (p.238). God and now Mabel had left her. But in her childhood the sensation of frost had a good smell, the magical association of Christmas--being loved by her parents and remembered by someone "having been there who drove across frosty rooftops and had so many chimneys to attend to but never forgot mine" (p.211). When she imagined herself as Santa Barbie she saw herself "leaving a lingering glittering frosty scent of her own magical intrustion" (p.337). God may indeed have intruded His magic into Barbie's life, only she did not recognize Him in His frosty disguise, and thus despaired in the magic of her own prayers to conjure His attention. To convince Barbie of His presence God had to manifest Himself visibly, even dramatically, in "the brightest amalgam of blue and yellow light ever seen in the region" (p.391).

[40]To imagine what existed before the universe was created, Barbie mentally tried to "draw in the billions of light years of space and stars and darkness, compress and compress until all existence, all space, all void is the size of a speck of dust. And then blow it out" (p.207). It was this very action, this blowing down to nothing, to the bone, which Barbie performed with her dandelion clocks (pp.27,92). "To blow them to the bone was the one

sure way she now had of sleeping, sure in the Lord
and the resurrection and the spade" (p.396). Her
blowing exercises for sleeping prefigured her own
death. Scott observes that sleep is the drug of each
day's little death (p.95) and that there is no
visible difference between sleep and death (p.224).
Soon she would die, blown out by God. When Sarah
visited Barbie in the hospital and bent down to kiss
her cheek, Barbie "felt the girl's head close to her
own again and breath coming against her cheek as
though she were an old yellow candle being blown out
very gently" (p.344). Barbie's death would signify
God's own way of transmitting prana to her just as
Barbie tried to transmit to Susan. (Prana: "The
goodness in the air. You breathe it in. And out.
Like smelling roses. Like blowing dandelions,"
p.336). The goodness of others could be absorbed as
easily as taking a breath, or inhaling a fragrance.
The goodness within could be transmitted outward in
the same way. With such a breath Sr. Ludmila
exercied "microcosmic power" years before: "To translate, to reduce, to cause to vanish with the breath
alone the sugary fruits in their nest of laced-edged
paper. To know that they are there, and yet not
there. This is a magic of the soul" (The Jewel in the
Crown, p.282).

[41] It was almost as if fate were reluctant to
bring them together, the way Teddie and Merrick kept
missing each other, "as if Merrick knew and kept
giving Teddie a chance to pack his bags and go before
a meeting actually took place (p.128).

[42] Teddie thought that "this was dangerous because
if you were enlarged there was more of you and the
world was still exactly the same size. It didn't get
bigger to make room for you" (p.156). Merrick's
effect upon Teddie contrasts sharply with Hari
Kumar's effect on Daphne Manners: "I felt that
Mayapore had got bigger, and so had made me
smaller..."(The Jewel in the Crown, p.404). She felt
this way because her association with Hari, "...the
one thing that was beginning to make me feel like a
person again--was hedged about, restricted, pressed
in on...diminished by everything that loomed from
outside, but not diminished from the inside..." (The
Jewel in the Crown, p.405).

[43] There was also Teddie's curious "dream" about

seeing a Pathan in a long robe standing in the middle of the room. Scott is hinting about another dark, inexplicable side of Merrick which Scott will develop further in the last book.

[44]Teddie sensed something about Merrick that smelled of death, but he was not receptive like Barbie to "thinking in imaginative terms" (p.121). During his first few nights in Mirat, in a violent storm, Teddie thought Merrick's empty bed "seemed lit by St. Elmo's fire; it rode the night rock-firm, half-ship, half-catafalque" (p.121). Teddie remembered that same funeral image when he witnessed Merrick's face shut down like a machine waiting "for someone to come and disconnect him" (p.161) after Teddie asked him if a bicycle had any special significance for him.

The catafalque reference recurs in A Division of the Spoils when Guy Perron stays in a bungalow once occupied by Ronald Merrick. At first Perron could smell damp and "sensed the presence of hidden fungus, a sweet, heavy smell which...immediately depressed him" (A Division of the Spoils, p.510). Later, the sweet smell turned foul, and Merrick's bed "looked like a catafalque" (A Division of the Spoils, p.521). Perron was sensitive to whatever impressed Sr. Ludmila years before. She had said that Merrick "looked right but did not smell right. To me, who had been about in the world, he smelt all wrong" (The Jewel in the Crown, p.134). Perron would finally associate the smell not only with Merrick's diseased and rotting interior but with the "archer's wound" (A Division of the Spoils, p.572), the evil done by Merrick to Hari Kumar as "Philoctetes."

[45]Another meaning of this statement relates to Merrick's being accepted into the raj as one of their own kind, being "reborn," coming to life in that way because of his heroic action.

[46]Throughout The Towers of Silence there are violent electrical storms, which Teddie referred to as the electric beast (pp.120,121,164). Barbie, like Sarah, (The Day of the Scorpion, P.421) felt that nature often fell short of reflecting the interior secret dimensions of reality: "Nothing in nature confirmed as real the restlessness of the surrounding air" (p.307). And yet there is a tie between these

189

exterior electric beasts and the interior workings of
the characters. At the moment of Mabel's death "one
wave scarcely distinguishable from any of the others
puts out the faltering spark" (p.224). The wicked lie
about Barbie's sexual preferences aroused anger and
"the electric surge of intelligence that awakened a
desolate withered capacity for needing affection in
return for giving it" (p.268). While sitting with
Sarah she tried to explain how everything depended
now on the "pumping of her old heart and the strange
electrical impulses of her brain which switches from
one picture of her life to another, encapsulating
time and space, events, personalities" (p.340). Both
interior and exterior reality are "charged," alive
like the electric beast...except Ronald Merrick. When
Teddie asked Merrick if a bicycle had any special
significance for him, there was an "electrifying"
change. "The tingling sensation communicated itself
to Teddie. For a moment Merrick looked as if he had
been made by a machine and was waiting for someone to
come and disconnect him so that he could collapse
back into his component parts because there was no
possibility of his being galvanized by the vital
fundamental spark" (p.161).

Just as Scott has interiorized the "charged"
nature of reality, he uncovers another hidden aspect
of the secret self. Barbie felt estranged from God
which Edwina, too, must have felt: "...the ever
increasing tenuousness of the connexion, the separation in space as God inexplicably turned His face
from humble service He no longer found acceptable but
was too kind to actually refuse" (p.99). Barbie felt
this same estrangement in space from her youth: "She
felt distrubed and then...lost in an immense area of
experince, the whole area that separated her childhood and young womanhood. She thought of it as an
area because the separation seemed to be in space,
not in time" (p.93). After hearing about the
malicious gossip about her, Barbie "wanted to put
immense distance between herself and her life"
(p.270). But such a distance already seemed to
exist. There were times when Barbie felt estranged
from her present self. There were foreign elements
she did not recognize. "My life, she thought, has
become extraordinarily complicated. There is more
than one of me..." (p.79). After entering into the
realm of imaginary silences and detaching herself
from the sound of her own voice, Barbie was "left in
a state of immobility or suspended animation,
surrounded by what she could only describe as a vivid

sense of herself new and unused" (p.186). After her prolonged illness "Her wasted body filled her with revulsion; in the room it alone lacked the security of shape and form and definition. It was like something the bed had invented, got tired of, and left half-finished to fend for itself" (p.334). When she saw Rose Cottage for the last time, "She felt no pang. All this had been in another life. It seemed strange that it still existed" (p.373). Even in her dreams Barbie experienced a secret, other self: "My short grey hair flew black and long and I was filled with joyful longings and expectations. I was not myself" (p.205).

As a child Barbie accepted magic as a normal part of life (p.211), magic both light and dark. There was the lingering glittering frosy magic of Christmas and the demon-spirit of the party with a "thrilling kind of malice" (p.174). "I expected to find toads hopping on the staircase and misshapen things falling out of cupboards" (p.211). What she actually discovered on the stairway of twenty steps was her own fear. And she came to recognize that the demon spirit did not have an existence of its own but thrived inside a person she loved:"...I used to watch him [her father] hard. I imagined the poet in him as an unborn twin, one that could be cruel to him as well as kind. Like the demon spirit of a party. After he said that about there being a conspiracy among us to make us little I thought of the demon spirit or poet as a giant bottled up inside him and turned into a dwarf by a spell which only liquor could break" (p.341). Barbie's reflections are meant to be understood as more than fanciful imaginings. Good and evil, like lightning (the electric beast), are in each of the characters. Prana, the goodness in the air, is transmitted and communicated from within each person who acts as a host for that goodness. When Sarah thought of Merrick as the dark, arcane side of the raj, the evil observed is as much a statement about the raj and about herself, as it was about Ronald Merrick.

[47]There is also the parent-child aspect of England's attitude toward India. The entire Man-Bap, father/mother relationship sprang from a sense of superiority. The civilized white man shouldered the responsibility of guiding and correcting the heathen, undeveloped blacks. For Man-Bap to work, the natives had to trust the raj implicitly, like children trusting their parents (p.320). The code of being

true to the white man's salt (p.260) ironically reversed the role of dependence. The British needed the Indians for their survival. The old chaukidar slept across the threshold like a tired shepherd guarding his flock (p.93), just as the old woman in a nameless village fed curds to an ailing Robin White years before "as she would have fed her own son" (The Jewel in the Crown, p.348).

[48] "Poor boy," she said to him (p.389), just as she addressed the nausea which visited her at Rose Cottage, "Poor creature..." (p.99).

[49] Sr. Ludmila also treasured her own Christmas memories. "The magic of Christmas was still in the streets....Our cozy reflections in the windows of the shops, my mother leaning down to whisper a promise or a fancy to me, her gloved finger on the pane, pointing out a box of crystallized fruits lying in a nest of lace-edged paper" (The Jewel in the Crown, p.130). Ludmila, too, believed in magic and in God.

[50] This "sugared gift" recalls the "barley sugars and sugared almonds still to be eaten" during Sr. Ludmila's memorable first day of the new century (The Jewel in the Crown, p.132). The image conveys feelings of warmth and safety, such feelings which Colin Lindsey and Hari Kumar must have shared together, toasting their hands at the grate. "Such microcosmic power. To translate, to reduce, to cause to vanish with the breath alone the sugary fruits in their nest of lace-edged paper. To know that they are there, and yet not there. This is a magic of the soul" (The Jewel in the Crown, p.282). Barbie's sugared gift" materialized when she found the butter-flies in lace folded in the top of her trunk.

[51] There was the striking scene when Barbie gave her Queen Victoria picture to Merrick, insisting that he could "carry" it in his dead hand, just as Barbie could "carry" a dress made of the heliotrope material. He had lost his arm and his handsome features because of Teddie's belief in Man-Bap and the regiment (pp.380,387). She told him what was missing in the picture: the Unknown Indian, reminding him that it should be understood as depicting love rather than loyalty, representing unfulfilled hopes rather than accomplishments. Symbolically, the

picture became too heavy for Merrick. He could not support the weight of it, the challenge. Barbie said, "let me relieve you of its weight..." (p.388).

[52]It was "winter lightning"--suggesting the electrical, charged magic as well as the magic of glittering frost.

[53]Barbie believed that her dream had been a form of communication from God, "Which means I am not abandoned" (p.205). For the dream to materialize was therefore a certain sign of her salvation.

[54]Gadarene means rushing precipitiously forward. It derives from the biblical town of Gadara, also called Gerasa, where Christ exorcized demons from a man. The demons entered into a herd of swine which rushed over the cliff and drowned. See accounts in Matthew 8: 28-32, Mark 5: 1-10, and Luke 8: 26-32.

[55]The mystery of the missing spoons (p.343) became a symbol and a reminder of the unholy love between Kevin Coley and Millie, and thus the spoons no longer signified the Sublimest Love.

[56]Sarah believed that Barbie found peace, "the peace of absorption in a wholly demanding God, a God of love and wrath..." She was not "unanchored, unweighted, withershins, attempting to communicate with the doomed world of inquiry and compromise". (A Division of the Spoils, p.392). At the end of a long spiritual pilgrimage Barbie had defeated her doubts. Her principles had triumphed.

194

CHAPTER IV

A DIVISION OF THE SPOILS

In A Division of the Spoils[1] Paul Scott introduces one of his most reliable of moral guides, Guy
Perron. As a student of history, Perron's reflections
give the reader added perspective needed to arrive at
the truth about the raj's contributions to and impact
on Indian life. Throughout this final volume, Scott
refrains from making judgments about his characters.
Yet it is clear that there is a truth to be
uncovered, a final valid conclusion about what
history should ultimately say about the British in
India.

Paul Scott uncovers these elements of truth in
the experiences of his diverse characters. There is
some justification to Sayed Kasim's choice to join
the INA; there is some value to Millie Layton's
formula for survival; there is some virtue in
Britain's occupation of Indian soil; just as there is
some accuracy in Leonard Purvis' bitter rejection of
his country's presence in India. As Nigel Rowan
pointed out about the 1942 riots, nothing can be
accurately understood out of context (p.280). Somewhere, in all the grey shades of truth, is Scott's
final message. He does not ultimately trust it to the
raj nor to Sarah Layton. He leaves it in the hands of
Guy Perron, who labored to an objective viewpoint by
detaching himself from the prejudices of his class,
from the prejudices of his ignorant and indifferent
countrymen at home, and from the attitudes of the
transient English and the black natives in India.
Besides historical knowledge and detachment one more
element was necessary to bring Perron to the truth:
the virtue of compassion, which he developed by
taking Bibighar to heart.

Unlike the two middle, highly symbolic books,
this fourth volume is journalistic in style like The
Jewel in the Crown. Scott utilizes and completes the
symbolic framework developed in The Day of the
Scorpion and The Towers of Silence but introduces
only one new image, that of the coppersmith birds.
His characters function within his already established and explored metaphysical perimeters. What is
significant in A Division of the Spoils is that these
perimeters and symbols are applied to characters

195

outside the raj circle, emphasizing that Scott's analysis of this specific historical period contains an ultimate, universal truth about the human condition.

I

A Division of the Spoils gives the reader a final glimpse of the raj world at the close of their empire. The litany of raj shortcomings is much the same as in former volumes. The raj's austere manner--an icy stoicism in Millie Layton's case (pp.282-83)^2 and a kind of oriental detachment as in the Trehearnes' case (p.361)--was inevitably misunderstood by Indians who were themselves open and extreme in their emotional responses. Mohammed Ali Kasim believed that beneath the Spartan exterior English were really an emotional people (p.440), but most often their manner proved problematic. Governor Malcolm cautioned Nigel Rowan to be more open, more personable because an austere manner was not appropriate in India (p.194).

The raj were blinded by an exalted sense of corporate identity. But their superior manner hid feelings of inferiority and insecurity (pp.291-92). Perron observed that raj women knew their place and expected everyone else to acknowledge it (p.18). But Perron also recognized that under their surface air of self-confidence and self-absorption lay an innocence and attendant uncertainty about the true nature of the alien world in which they lived (pp.17-18). He formulated a theory that the history of Anglo-Indian relations was determined in part by the bacterial infiltration of amoebic life into the bowels of the raj, causing even the most mild-mannered and considerate of men to become impatient and irascible (p.27).

Even in these final Edwardian days, there was a regal, disdainful air to the English ruling class, symbolically captured for Perron by the dazzling reflection of the setting sun on the dome of the governor's summer residence in Pankot. It was as if the raj ordered the sun to hesitate until they allowed night to fall (p.348). The same proud arrogance was apparent in the "renovated" Rose Cottage. Mabel Layton had allowed her home to blend with the garden, to absorb and be absorbed by the soil and the lush Indian plant life. She understood that survival meant change (p.140). But Millie transformed the cottage into her own image, to reflect her own values. Perron thought it squat, functional, and aggressive, anchored to the ground like a Hindu temple (p.281). But it was an English temple, testimony to the raj's functional solidarity. The secluded, tentative air was gone. The bungalow advertised the Layton family's presence. Millie erased the natural (to her inessential) accumulation of years and thereby transformed Rose Cottage into a monument, like one of the drunken tombstones in the churchyard. It was almost skeletal in its air of uninhabited emptiness. By erasing Mabel's distinct influence, Millie erased the bungalow's history, making it look like it could belong to anyone, or no one. She had intended the new facade to symbolize service, sacrifice, and integrity. Instead, she had exposed the raj's self-interest and corruption (pp.139-140).

In 1945 John Layton returned to this self-proclaimed monument to the permanence of English rule. He had undergone hunger and disillusionment, hardship and long, idle hours during which he would conjure up mental images of his women safe and secure amid the garden and pine trees of Rose Cottage (p.122). But the hero-come-home had become aware of the insecurity of any tenure (p.87) and must have viewed the solid, unshakeable facade with a sense of irony. The past was frozen in the form of stories and scenes which his memory sketched for him. He would never curl up with Jane Austin while sipping whiskey and fondling his black labrador (p.93). Such a frozen image may have expressed his desires while a prisoner, but it did not capture the essence of what "home" and "family" really meant. It was not a formula to secure happiness. Space and time separated John from his wife and daughters. He might forgive Sarah for her affair and abortion, but could never truly understand (p.401). He could console Susan in her bereavement and burden of responsibility, but he could never really share them with her. His family would never know the complete story of his imprisonment, only the short excerpts which he might choose to reveal (p.124).

Public displays of affection had always been difficult among the Laytons, but their long separation emphasized their inability to give of themselves openly and without reserve. John was even more restrained than Sarah remembered him, less able to express his affections and feelings, interiorly even more reserved: "as solid an edifice as the rock-face that marks the end of the line from Ranpur to Pankot..." (p.132), another tower of silence.

Pankot seemed to have shrunk since John Layton last saw it, in much the same way it appeared less inspiring, less welcoming when he returned as a young subaltern after World War I. He was present then when a widow and her six-year-old son accepted a medal for her dead husband. The ceremony was "splendid enough" but even then the young John Layton sensed a lack, a void in the raj code (The Day of the Scorpion, p.63). Now he was returning with a train-load of his wounded men, but without that six-year-old boy now grown and under arrest for having waged war against the Crown.[3] John Layton was haunted by a sense of disaster, having failed his men in Africa and seeing many of them killed and the rest imprisoned and separated from their officers. He felt dishonored by his own limited talent, a feeling which narrowed his self-regard (p.359). The myth of Man-Bap did not survive his years of prison, or if it had, John now felt that living up to it demanded more energy than he had (pp.358-59).

John Layton was prepared to play the part expected of him, to enter the raj stage "dressed for the part" and function true to form (pp.127,135). But his act had acquired a sense of charade because the code did not mean what it used to. Or more accurately, he still loved the myth but no longer believed in it. For Millie to offer "the shell of her flesh" (p.359) to the native women in the surrounding villages was an appropriate form of role-playing. But she never identified too closely with it (p.359). Man-Bap had been the source of John's inspiration, an inspiration which failed to give him the courage to ride into Muddarabad, the village of his lost sheep Karim Kahn. He could not guarantee to those people with his presence, with his own integrity, the truth of Man-Bap (p.360). He could not be a sign for them.[4]

From this disillusionment sprang a feeling of fatalism, of resignation. Sometimes John looked like a man with a secret he was waitng patiently to share (p.355), a truth about people and life which his hard

experience in war had taught him and which the world
needed to know. At other times he seemed like a man
empty of knowledge and recollection (p.355), despair-
ing of his contribution or of the world's willingness
to receive it. John realized that Merrick's interviews with the POW's would produce nothing. That was
part of the empty form, and he expected nothing more
(p.288).

Once he returned home, the emotional instability
John manifested in Bombay lay hidden "under the
carapace, the hardening shell of reaffirmation"
(p.287). His return from Germany did not appear to be
the God-send that his family needed. His absence had
kept them together, but his presence illuminated
their deep divisions (p.355), divisions which taught
Sarah that the greatest distances in India were not
physical but emotional, distances which divided
people and not places (p.131). The greatest distance
between herself and her father was caused by her
affair with Jimmy Clark (p.131), not because it was a
sin against God but rather an offense against the
code; a vulgar act of choice affirming common
pleasure, an insult to the responsibilities of her
class and position. Such "uneasy distances" between
Sarah and her father, who would not let her confess
to him; and between Sarah and her mother, who
continued to pretend it never happened resembled the
feelings of isolation and rejection Barbie experienced in trying to scale the towering fortress walls
of her silent God and of Mabel the rock.

> Everything has meaning for you, Gaffur: the petal's fall,
> the change of season. New clothes to celebrate the Id.
> The regard of princes.
> Rocks. These are not impediments. All water flows
> towards uneasy distances. Life also--(p.413).

It was difficult for Sarah to see beyond this impasse
into her own future. Pankot threatened her serenity,
but there was no clear alternative. As long as she
remained in India she could never dispel "the
powerful and terrible enchantment of inherited
identity" (p.137). She could never escape her
occupation which was becoming harder and harder to
explain and to follow (p.135). As long as she was in
India, Sarah would implicate herself in the raj's
dogged attempts to demonstrate that dim as the light
had grown it was still enough by which to see an
obligation. The raj were like artists "who carved

199

angels' faces in the darkest recesses of a church roof and countered the charge that people couldn't see them by saying that God could" (p.135). At moments of acute distress Sarah experienced destructive impulses, and desired "to tear the fabric of the roof and expose the edifice to an empty sky" (p.137).[5]

Yet Sarah, bitterly honest by nature, could see the value of those angel (or demon) faces carved in the dark, even if the light of the divine gaze or of human recognition would never discover them. Millie's stubborn silence regarding Sarah's abortion was more than a means of punishment. It was an exercise in survival, a case of adhering to the code in order to establish and maintain a posture of fortitude and composure. Her silence, her stubborn allegiance to the code, was Millie's version of affirmation, of carving angel faces in the dark.

As important as maintaining the silence was to Millie, it was equally important to Sarah that the silence be broken. To survive, Sarah needed to communicate with her mother, she needed consolation and forgiveness. Sarah considered such needs as a form of weakness and self-indulgence (p.137) and so could accept her mother's own weakness more readily. Instead of condemning Millie, Sarah admired her for her tenacious ability to survive, an art like carving angels in the dark, an art which they both exercised and needed to sustain. By this implicit form of acquiescence Sarah, too, affirmed those faces in the dark and carved faces of her own (p.137).

The tragedy, Sarah realized, was that their survival patterns seemed to be mutually exclusive. The other members of her family were as foreign to her as the coppersmith birds, whose calls resounded in the Pankot hills.[6] As Sarah sat in the car which had met and transported her and John Layton from the train depot to Rose Cottage, she considered the possibility that the coppersmiths, as they lulled her with the sound of their rhythmic tapping, might take some predatory advantage and turn into Barbie Batchelor's birds of "ominous intentions" (p.136). Sarah knew very little about these creatures and their capabilities, of their world and of the uncounted number of finite worlds like theirs which co-existed with her own. All creatures seemed intent upon survival, the coppersmiths and the members of her family. They were all tragically sealed in their own self-sufficient, separate worlds (pp.135-37).[7]

The only bond between them, the only reason for staying, was the burden of familial responsibility which Barbie warned her about: "some people are made to live and others are made to help them. If you stay you'll end up like that, like me" (p.402). Barbie knew that if Susan did not marry again, Sarah would never get away. They would all keep depending upon her for emotional support, for selfless devotion to their own selfish needs. Sarah would continue to pour herself out for them, riddled with the guilt of being born female, for being unmarried, and for ruining her chances to marry a decent man (pp.128-29,389,403). The Sarah whom Perron encountered at home with her family--subdued, oppressed, and shackled--was not the same young woman he remembered from Bombay (pp.285,341).

The news of an atomic detonation over Hiroshima filled Sarah with relief and hope that the end of the war was at hand. She might again have an opportunity for a life of uncluttered freedom, "open at last to endless possibilities" (p.119). She believed she needed to return to England because she could never be happy in India (p.102). With her father back she would be free at last to return home and find a man who was not

> tortured by an affection for a country I'd not been happy in and to which he would always be longing to return, as if to prove something to himself. I could finish with India before it had quite finished with me, rusted me up, corroded me, corrupted me utterly with a false sense of duty and a false sense of superiority (p.369).[8]

Both Perron and Rowan werre attracted to Sarah, to her enduring Layton face which possessed a natural and incontrovertible logic, and which in old age "would be marked by the serenity of understood experience and the vitality of undiminished appetite" (p.153). But Sarah was not aware of her attractive qualities, only of the hollowness of her gutted womb, of the haunting memory of the life never to flower, and of the lonely and loveless experience which marked its end (p.136); of the bitterness hardening

201

the edges of her personality (p.367) and of the growing and insatiable appetite for physical intimacy and pleasure which she had indulged with a Bostonian in Calcutta after her abortion (p.370). The newly-discovered world of pleasure taught her to smile. It was like a new faculty animating her entire being (p.372).

After The Day of the Scorpion and The Towers of Silence, which deal exclusively with the world and viewpoint of raj society (with the exception of the Kasim family), Scott choses to impose a new character upon the scene, a person who would not automatically revere their sacred history and code written in stone, and who would see beyond their insular viewpoint and prejudice with a perspective enhanced by historical knowledge, humor, and compassion. Guy Perron was born into a family as eccentric as it was aristocratic. His aunts and uncles were so influential that they could afford to pursue non-productive but certainly memorable enterprises. George was the oldest and inherited the family fortune which he methodically squandered in ill-fated investments (p.228). Charles was the balloonist, William the frustrated actor, Hester the crazed stamp collector, and Charlotte the one who loved people and their interests. They all had brilliant minds but unadaptable personalities (p.229).

After graduating in history from Chillingborough, Perron enlised in the army but refused a commission, a decision lauded by his relatives as appropriately eccentric (p.10). Leonard Purvis bitterly remarked that only a man born into the officer class could afford to decline the position without having his integrity and future usefulness doubted (p.25). Even though Perron was free from this danger, he was still careful to display proper military spit and polish to preserve the image of discipline and efficiency, and to ensure that no one thought him effeminate or cowardly because of his accent and his interest in history (p.11).

There were advantages to being an enlisted man. Perron never had to initiate anything or plan ahead (p.283). He did not have to make any decision when other men's lives would hang in the balance. And he enjoyed a greater measure of freedom and better opportunities to study human behavior in depth during an interesting period of history (p.10).

That had been Perron's intent when he came to India. He quickly realized that war did not function well as a foil conducive to understanding either human nature or India. The war was an under-rehearsed and over-directed amateur production badly in need of cutting (p.11). It ruined India for Perron, who during peaceful lulls found the East otherwise capable of putting his mind and body at ease with the sensuousness of its warm smell (p.37). The potential for a love affair with India was there, but Perron was afraid that the war would cause him to lose the confidence which the actual experience of India should instill. He wondered if he should return home to England, to a world of peace of mind and common sense, to regain the calm rhythms of logical thought (pp.11-12).

There were several events in Perron's life which helped drive him away from India in 1945. His encounter with Leonard Purvis revealed what life in India meant for Englishmen who were not there by choice. Purvis had been an economist who wrote a paper misconstrued to be about India by people in influencial circles. After a series of "interviews" Purvis found himself a commissioned officer in India without understanding how or why. He mocked his own passivity, describing the posture as restful and erotic like a wet dream with an asexual quality of involuntary obedience to a dominant force (p.26). Purvis' conviction that he was being victimized by a pointless fate was aggravated by an amoebic infection of the bowels. On the evening he was assigned to Operation Zipper and would try to kill himself, he expounded to Perron his views about Britain's Indian Empire, views shaped solely by economic consider-ations.

The war, Purvis believed, was a criminal waste of energy (p.213), and he resented having to pay for other people's mistakes. To be sent to India was a further manifestation of human folly. India was governed by people who could not pull their own weight at home (p.33) and who were still immersed in the nineteenth century "Singapore-mentality" (pp.28-29).[9] Purvis found the raj's administration to be "indolent, bone-headed and utterly uneducated" and the Indian populace "conservative and tra-dition-bound" (p.32). The combination was hopeless, ensuring an elitist bureaucracy out of touch with the social and economic thinking of the twentieth century and a native population which would still be feudal when the English finally had the good sense to depart (pp.32,34). The prospect of living (or dying) for such a futile cause drove Purvis to a successful second attempt at suicide. He was determined to do what he had to do (p.213).

Perron's Aunt Charlotte (who judged India's Viceroys to be full-fledged bunburyists) was a convinced Purvisite. She felt, as did most English, that maintaining control of India was no longer administratively possible or economically desirable. Such a position was pragmatic rather than moral and assumed that India had only drained the mother country of money and men. Perron knew that India had not been totally a burden, since England had reaped and enjoyed economic recompense from its investment for hundreds of years (p.33).

Unlike Leonard Purvis and Aunt Charlotte, Perron saw the issue of Indian independence as a moral question, but not in the same way Edwina Crane did. Edwina believed that the British were morally bound by their endless promises and by an unspoken spirit of allegiance to the liberal creed, both of which dictated the necessary and inevitable day of Indian self-government. Perron never addressed the question of whether Indians were capable or deserving. What did weigh on his conscience were the years of English exploitation, short-sighted bungling, and deliberate injustices for which he believed all Englishmen responsible. He also felt that those at home who voted for Indian independence in 1945 were responsible for the quarter of a million dead in the ensuing blood bath (p.230).

Although Perron agreed with Purvis' view of the raj's shortcomings, he also took into account their accomplishments and hardships. The raj had made India safe for people like himself and Purvis (p.35). They had developed a talent for survival, an ability to endure with style, which encountered in the person of Millie Layton inspired admiration and not pity (p.282). The strain under which the raj toiled was largely their own fault, and Perron tried not to sympathize too closely with their problems (p.104). To align himself emotionally with the raj would prove the end of his objectivity and destroy his chance to experience the real India.

Whenever he encountered the inconsistencies and inadequacies of the military tradition, Perron became depressed, overwhelmed by a feeling "that boded no good" (p.11), as when he observed the fleet preparing for Operation Zipper anchored off the port of Bombay. Mist and rain made the armada disappear and reappear as if by decree from the director of operations, a typically omniscient raj officer who fancied himself endowed with divine and infallible powers (p.11). One of the reasons Perron believed himself not of officer material was that he could not achieve the required heights of self-deception (p.10). The raj career officers deluded themselves that they knew all about their men, about their thoughts and attitudes, their families and background. The war made all of that impossible, but the officers did not face the truth. The majority of enlisted men, as Clark foretold, would vote for a Socialist government in 1945. Having experienced not the privileges but only the hardships of Indian occupation, they were not about to support an extension of their Churchillian officers' plush life-style (p.9).

The sight of John Layton's bush shirt draped over the back of a chair depressed Perron as did the sight of the Zipper fleet (p.88). It brought home to him the depravity faced and sacrifices made by people like the Laytons. But for what purpose? Their labors accomplished nothing for Leonard Purvis or for the INA prisoners Perron had seen on the Bombay docks, whose faces of vacuous expression bespoke a "peak of incomprehension" (p.43). The complex problems produced by years of mistakes impacting on an infinite series of misunderstandings could never be unraveled. Perron agreed with Count Bronowsky that historically the raj deserved no consideration of kindness (p.486,585).

Being assigned to Ronald Merrick's department was the primary reason why Perron chose to leave India in 1945. Perron had been asked to assist in Merrick's initial interrogation of the INA prisoner Karim Khan in Bombay and later ran into Merrick at the Maharanee's party. "...Already I was chosed," he told Nigel Rowan. "Fate. It has driven me to drink, to Bunbury and Aunt Charlotte, and to a refutation of Emerson" (p.215). The specific passage Perron had in mind was the "Society is a wave" paragraph which Barbie Batchelor had noted (The Towers of Silence, p.202):

> Society is a wave. The wave moves
> onward, but the water of which it is
> composed does not. The same particle
> does not rise from the valley to the
> ridge. Its unity is only phenomenal.
> The persons who make up a nation
> today, next year die, and their
> experience with them (p.215).[10]

"Emerson was writing for the Merricks and Purvises of
the world. The ones who get drowned. Merrick hopes
not to be. But he will be," Perron observed. The
reason was that Merrick was as "principled as a rock"
(p.217). He had been sucked in by all that
"Kiplingesqsue double-talk" that depicted plain,
ordinary greedy Englishmen as going into exile for
the "good of their souls and the uplift of the
natives" (p.217). Merrick really believed in what he
construed to be upper-class mores, of knowing oneself
superior to all other races and having the duty to
guide and correct them.

Perhaps Emerson had been too much of a peasant
to appreciate the significance of the raj-type
(p.217), Perron speculated.[11] The raj were built to
survive, as Sarah had realized years before. Even the
very train car they were riding in verified that
fact. To Perron it was symbolic of "our isolation and
insulation, our inner conviction of class rights and
class privileges, of our permanence and of our
capacity to trim" (p.216). The raj felt no moral
responsibility toward India, only the responsibility
of ownership. The raj were guilty of a fundamental
indifference to problems toward which they adopted,
or pretended to adopt, attitudes of responsibility.
They were, in fact, unprincipled. "Property...can
always be got rid of and new property acquired"
(p.216).[12]

Those people with principles, "rocks" like
Merrick, would sink to the bottom while the unprincipled raj ("the scum") would float to the top and move
on with the wave of change without regret or pangs of
conscience. No one of the upper class cared about the
empire and all that "God-the-father-God-the-raj"
"insular middle-and lower-class shit" (p.217). However, as a true Emersonian, Perron distinguished
Merrick's "principled" position from true,
peace-giving principles. Merrick's position was one
of prejudice rather than principle. Rather than

seeking personal, interior tranquility and control, Merrick sought to control others, deploying things and people "to his uttermost personal advantage and private satisfaction" (p.217). In the end, the result would be the same. Merrick would be overcome by the wave of change because he'd "spent too long inventing himself in the image to have energy left to realize that as an image it is and always was hollow" (p.217).

Perron was mistaken in grouping himself with the upper-class scum. He was too much of an individual, raised by an eccentric family which would never have conformed to collective class behavior. Perron would never move on with the wave like the scum floating on the top. He would never forget India. He had, even at this point, a highly developed and sensitive convic- tion of moral responsibility. He was one of those men Sarah feared, who was tortured by an affection for India and once away, would long to return (p.369).

Nigel Rowan, for all of his good qualities, tends to be more raj-like than Perron. After his conversation with Perron he returned to the coach where Merrick and the Red Shadow waited. Away from Perron, Rowan felt once more in control (a fatal illusion, according to Emerson) and felt under an "odd kind of compulsion to forget what he knew" (p.222). He sat in apparent repose with Merrick, momentarily relieved of the pressures that were piling up and undermining his confidence:

> a feeling accentuated, perhaps, by the way the coach absorbed and muffled the vibration and clatter of the wheels without diminishing the flattering sensation of a speed and movement forward that were absolutely effortless (p.222).[13]

Rowan was eager to move on, away from the distrubing sense and burden of moral responsibility to the Layton family and to Hari Kumar to act upon what he knew to be the truth about Ronald Merrick. At this moment it was far easier to feel safe, insulated, and in control, literally to move on with the wave instead of taking a stand and rising or falling by what he believed was right.

Sarah felt that not only did Merrick believe in the "Kiplingesque double-talk," but he loved it as well. He wanted to warm his hands at the dying fire of Man-Bap and envied those who were able to, like the Laytons and Teddie Bingham. As his Christian name signified, Ronald Merrick was "someone with power who Rules" (p.523), born with that right and power by virtue of his skin color. He had an inflexible and unshakeable sense of his own authority. But his physical courage and his tenacious will to better himself could not be confused with moral courage, as Sarah tried to convince her father (p.381). Merrick was not driven to do the right thing at any cost. He was compelled by a rigid, single-minded determination to abuse and twist all things and all people to his personal advantage. He was incapable of willing anyone else's happiness. As Sr. Ludmila had understood years before, Merrick could never love, only punish (The Jewel in the Crown, p.167).

Because he observed the raj code from afar, from a lower station in life, Merrick had only a superficial grasp of the form but not the content of the raj's real and imagined virtues (p.584). Through years of grasping, working, and scheming, he manufactured an exterior form which conformed perfectly with the shells of those he envied. But the raj's time had passed, their Edwardian sun was setting, and Merrick was "the man who comes too late and invents himself to make up for it" (p.214). It was Merrick drawing Merrick: adjusting, molding, creating a self he thought would count, just as Susan did.

Even Perron and Count Bronowsky admitted that the outer casing was almost perfect. His handicapped arm and scarred face fitted so well with his cultivated image that they seemed like deliberate inventions rather than unfortunate accidents (p.178,214). The Count remarked that the injuries were so appropriate, the deformities so eloquent, Merrick might have had to add them deliberately if they had not appeared through the course of events. He wore his wounds like a stigmata so that the world would notice and pause, witnesses to the graphic proof of the truth he wanted to personify (p.214).[14]

Merrick was so obsessed with inventing himself according to the "God-the-father-God-the-raj" image that he did not realize the image was hollow (p.217) and that he had become "one of your hollow men"

208

(p.178), as Count Bronowsky expressed it. Recognizing such hollowness involved the faculty of moral judgment, which men like John Layton still possessed. He had the moral courage to face the hypocrisy, the waste, and the pretense. But Merrick had neither the moral faculty nor the moral courage to perceive or to care that there was nothing to him at all.

Merrick lamented that there were so few "real" white men like himself, like Generals Dyer and Reid who took seriously their responsibility to guide and correct (p.218). The raj had been contaminated by liberal bilge from England which corrupted their ruling principles based on racial superiority (p.217). The upper class had abandoned the code and did not deserve its power and privileges. Merrick revealed his festering envy and inferiority complex when he remarked to Perron at the Maharanee's party: "...It's at the top you find the scum..." (p.63).

What Merrick would never have admitted, as Leonard Purvis could not admit, was that the raj made the world safe for him. Their India made him what he was and gave him his distinction (p.385). He was protected by "shadows of doubt" (p.161) cast by the raj's unspoken prejudice in judging between his word and the word of the black man. Merrick was protected by the "iron system of the raj itself" (p.161). If this system was ever weakened by the growing conviction of his guilt, his heroic action of saving Teddie would ensure that action would never be taken against him.

Perron witnessed Merrick victimize Karim Khan. He believed Merrick hated and intended to punish the Layton family. He heard the story of how Merrick destroyed Pinky and read how he tried to destroy Hari Kumar. Perron was himself one of Merrick's chosen victims and during his brief posting with the man became convinced that Merrick was consumed by self-hatred. "Self punishment being out of the question, Merrick punished the men he chose" (p.315).

It was apparent also to Perron that Merrick's primary victim was Teddie's child Edward (p.327). Perhaps Merrick had been humiliated more that he indicated to Sarah by Teddie's cold, polite rejection after the wedding. Or perhaps his level of contempt for Teddie's "amateur" values was fueled beyond measure by the Muzzie's obvious distrust. Influencing and molding the young child according to his own sinister image would surely be the ultimate means of punishing Teddie. Given Merrick's sexual persuasion, he would never have a child of is own. Being with Edward gave him the only opportunity he would ever have to create and guide and thereby ensure that the line of "real" white men would be perpetuated.

Merrick was not deterred by the number of people who stood in the way of this goal. He eagerly devoured them with ruthless calculation. John Layton inspired Merrick's contempt because he exemplified the type of upper-class white man who betrayed the code. He was too soft, too emotionally involved with his men, like Teddie, and too naively sure of the unbreakable bond between an officer and his men. John Layton also possessed everything Merrick coveted: rank, revered reputation, money, and privilege, but he did not have the "guts to live up to it" (p.218). Merrick must have sensed, too, that beneath the Laytons' regimental skin was the unspoken conviction that background and blood really did matter (p.381).

In order to punish John Layton, Merrick "chose" Havildar Karim Khan, the only INA prisoner from Layton's 1st Pankot Rifles to fall into his hands. Merrick fabricated slanderous lies to explain why Kahn defected to the INA forces. He told Perron that there had been reports linking Khan's name to an incident of recruitment by torture at Königsberg (p.96). Merrick even suggested that Khan may have proved a coward on the field of battle and joined the INA's so he would not face the people who witnessed his cowardice. Perhaps Khan had lived under his father's shadow, Merrick continued, and had his father's example "rammed down his throat day after day" (p.52). During the interview which Perron witnessed on the docks of Bombay, Merrick initiated his relentless program to shame and insult Khan, hoping to break his pride and emotions, to gain informatin about the INA, and to frustrate John Layton's hopes of reconciliation. Merrick impressed upon Khan the vision of his Colonel Sahib, of his family and friends filled with sorrow and shame: "The wild dogs in the hills will be silent and your wife will not raise her head" (p.49). Everyone in the room knew that if Havildar Khan broke down before Colonel Layton it would be an honest expression of remorse and shame. But if he wept before Merrick, it would be from humiliation and insult. Merrick's rhetoric might have been moving but it was an act of deceit, a lie. The wild dogs in the hills would keep silent not out of sorrow but only when their bellies were full. Khan regarded Merrick with contempt (p.49).

But Khan's level of contempt could not match Merrick's. Khan eventually broke under the examiner's constant barrage and hanged himself from shame and despair. He simply fell into the hands of the wrong man, just as Pinky did. Merrick trapped Pinky with his own desire for "a bit of love" by bating and then exposing him only because he wanted to read Susan Bingham's confidencial file (p.272). Pinky's anguished cry, "Why me?" (p.267) only illuminated Merrick's sinister, deprived interior and his inevitable choice to take "the tragic and twisted way," by continually creating "situations" which gave rein to his contempt for anyone he could intimidate or bully (p.239).[15]

As one of Merrick's victims, Susan was ready made (p.285). Despite the recuperation from her breakdown and her re-entry into sanity, Susan was still drawn to the center of "the powerful and terrible enchantment of inherited identity" (p.137). She needed to feel she belonged so as not to be like a drawing that could be rubbed out (p.138). But since her return home Susan repeatedly protected herself from human interaction, constructing barriers of hostility between herself and Sarah (pp.125,365). Susan still had the power to attract people to herself but the knowledge that she did terrified her (p.126). She never really believed in her own value, and her insecurity must have rivaled even Merrick's inferiority complex. When her father returned from Germany, Susan offered him a new puppy, the ghost of her dead husband, and a grandson--immediate explanations and proofs of her existence and a promise of continuity for them both (p.142). Yet such an offering was not a gift from her very self to another person. It was another "grim and conscious exercise in personal survival" (p.138) just like spilling her coffee at the Trehearnes': Susan drawing and re-drawing Susan.

What she needed, and what the new Rose Cottage could not offer, was an environment which not only highlighted her virtues of beauty, youth, and charm, but which also provided a camouflage to hide her from the hands of the erasers (p.138). Millie's self-fashioned home was a bold statement of the raj truth, of harsh reality, hardly a fitting site for Susan to play her game of pretend securely.

When Perron was invited to dinner with Rowan at Rose Cottage and met Susan for the first time, he was appalled at the thought of her falling into Merrick's grasp. She was so vulnerable, so frightened and insecure, that she would have died from exposure to the circle of flames without the extreme degree of self-centeredness she wore like an extra thickness of skin (p.285). Rowan and Sarah both wanted Perron to speak up against the marriage and warn the Laytons of Merrick's insidious character. But at this point Perron was neither willing nor prepared to play the role of prophet as one who would proclaim the truth. He refused to enter into the raj's troubles, to endanger himself by coming too close to this family enclosed in its own private little drama, each member living in a self-contained world like a Chekhovian character (p.285). When he congratulated Susan on her engagement "...my quiet little speech splashed as loudly as a stone thrown into a placid pond on a summer night" (p.286).[16]

Perron's act of omission contributed to the strength of Merrick's hold on the Layton family. He was one of the few capable of defying Merrick, and he chose not to do so. In this way both Perron and Rowan were deserving targets of Merrick's contempt. Susan and Ronald would marry in February, 1946, and seal Edward's fate. By the time Perron saw him again in August, 1947, the child had undergone an amazing metamorphosis. Merrick had always inspired Edward's confidence (p.278), but by then he had molded the child into a little Pathan who was not only confident but bold, seemingly arrogant and fearless. His stepfather had even given him Barbie's Queen Victoria picture depicting Man-Bap to inspire his stepson and perpetuate the myth.

By entering into the Layton family, Merrick succeeded in victimizing Sarah even though she refused to be drawn into his interior hell like Susan was. Sarah had naively assumed that she was safe from him because he knew of her dislike (pp.380,391). Far from protecting herself and her family, Sarah's dislike inflamed Merrick's attention like a challenge. It helped affirm his existence just as

Perron's antagonism would later on. Whether or not
Rowan was too "decent" a man to marry Sarah because
of her sordid past, he would never have entered into
the Layton family once Merrick was a part of it
(p.334). Merrick was able to ruin Sarah's prospects
of happiness after all.

When Rowan and Perron met again in Mirat after
Merrick's death, Rowan wondered whether he had in
fact been "chosen" in a more direct way. Merrick
could have discovered that he had interviewed Hari
Kumar in Kandipat prison and that he knew but hid the
truth about the arrest and interrogation (p.566).
That Rowan knew the truth would have pleased rather
than alarmed Merrick. That Rowan hid the truth would
inspire Merrick's contempt and goad him into further
acts of punishment and cruelty.

After ensuring Rowan would never marry Sarah,
Merrick chose to punish him further through Laura,
the woman who eventually became Nigel's wife. In
Mirat Merrick often dropped in on Laura while Nigel
was away, and soon their names became linked
together. It pleased Merrick to be known as The
Other Man (p.566). During one such visit Merrick
killed a snake that Laura found in her tub, and later
that evening she confided to him some of her POW
experiences which she had kept hidden even from her
husband. Merrick seemed so approachable, so under-
standing--the one person scarred and deformed worse
than she was (p.564). Perron suspected that Merrick
may have come across the records of Ratcliff's death
while searching out INA evidence in Malaya (p.565),
which would enhance his apparent ability to "understand" Laura just as he "understood" Susan.

It was not difficult for Perron to attribute the
most sinister motives to Merrick's simplest actions
because he had worked intimately with the man.
Perron suspected that he had originally been chosen
because Merrick discovered he had attended Chillingborough two years ahead of Hari Kumar (p.51). But
Merrick retained him because of Perron's dislike for
him.[17] Antagonism affirmed his existence, helped
Merrick to draw Merrick.[18] He did everything in his
power to fuel Perron's hatred. He tried to control
Perron's life and posted him in the NCO's Mess in
Pankot amid a nest of his enemies (p.248). When
Merrick was suddenly called away, Perron had the
pleasure of doing some punishing of his own when he

caught the Red Shadow stealing: "Fart in the holy silence of the universe and limp pudenda on the body of the false prophet" (p.254). All of Perron's dislike and distrust for Merrick was transferred to and unleashed upon the Pathan.

Being one of Merrick's victims made Perron hate being in India. Because of him Perron surrendered his chances with Sarah and for the moment gave up on a land that could have made him happy. Even his "homecoming" in Mirat in 1947 was ruined by Merrick's death (p.512).

In his confrontations with Merrick Perron suffered little in comparison with other victims and in light of Merrick's insatiable capacity to destroy and to deceive. Ronald Merrick was not truly a dedicated "God-the-father-God-the-raj" figure like John Layton, but he certainly was the Father of Lies. One of his major talents and most unsuccessful plates of armor was his ability to cast light on his own actions so that they appeared logical and sensible rather than diabolical (p.382). During his interview with John Layton, then Merrick asked for permission to marry Susan, the Bibighar incident was discussed but revealed in such a way that John was impressed with how caring, civilized, misunderstood, and principled this man of integrity was. Merrick could lie, shade and twist truths and half-truths to help create the image he desired, which would change in chameleon fashion with whoever he happened to be dealing. Merrick was convinced, as he told Teddie after his lecture about the INA's, that the truth of a statement depended upon the light in which it was presented rather than how accurately it corresponded to reality (The Towers of Silence, p. 155).

After Havildar Karim Khan committed suicide, Merrick journeyed to Pankot to inform Colonel Layton personally. In so doing he increased his hold upon the family and displayed his "depth of feeling and concern" (p.219). While in Pankot he conducted, or more accurately, orchestrated interviews with the newly returned POW's. Perron, in watching the process, quickly realized that no valuable information would be forthcoming. It simply provided an opportunity for Merrick to be in the limelight, to manipulate people and things. There was no other

214

purpose to the interview than to move people into an order which made Merrick the dominating and controlling center (p.239).

Underneath Merrick's rock-iron, principled attitude was envy for the privileges others enjoyed, and a tribal-like memory (as Emerson might say) of a patriotic love of the superior-white-man myth. But in the depths of Merrick's depraved, twisted personality, what he took most seriously was his "unassailable right to deploy things and people to his uttermost personal advantage and private satisfaction" as Perron guessed Rowan's uncle did (p.217). In the contempt/envy game with the Layton family and with Rowan and Perron, Merrick was the victor and Edward the spoils.

It is impossible for the reader to imagine the kind of perverted pleasure it gave Merrick to make Susan touch his injuries. The woman who sheltered herself from anything difficult or unpleasant, who would be reminded of Teddie's death every time she even looked at Merrick and who was afraid of human intercourse, now lived with a monster. "The first time I saw his poor shoulder and poor stump, I cried," she admitted to Perron (p.529). But Merrick was patient and understanding. He could afford to step back and enjoy her horror and loathing, like basking in a mirror at his deformity. It was a long time before Susan could help with his arm, but when she did they were "closer than at any other time" (p.533).

Susan depended on her second husband for everything. He became the foundation of her emotional stability, seeming to guess things about her no one else had ever understood. "It was like living with someone who'd lived with you always, even in your secret life" (p.532). Susan never knew Merrick had read her private file at a terrible cost to Pinky. She only knew that Merrick was afraid of nothing and was fearlessly honest. People knew where they stood with him because, she believed, he never pretended to be or to feel anything which was not true about himself. It was a tribute to his distinction as a liar and to his hollow, cultivated image that she considered him the most honest of men. The reader must wonder about other intimate details of their marriage in light of Merrick's finally unleashed homosexual appetites which were hinted at in previous volumes.

There were four aspects of Merrick's behavior which revealed his dark nature. The first was his insistence on surrounding himself with men who hated him, like Guy Perron. It was the one sure way of measuring the effect of his actions. Perron's antagonism acted like acid on film, making his image emerge (p.239). He found Perron's hatred exciting, and rewarded it with gratitude and contempt (p.239).

The second characteristic was Merrick's sadistic need to manipulate people, his cultivated ability for seeing which key or combination of keys would open up a situation so he could twist it to his own purpose (p.271). It was not enough that he had achieved a position in India which in England would have been considered above his station. It was not enough for him to have a hand in the INA scandal and help topple the "amateur" approach of Man-Bap and the white man's rule. Inside Merrick, as in many successful men, there was a disappointed and envious one, moaning and groaning and plotting and planning (p.30). Merrick continually manipulated and bullied people, used and cornered them, thereby pushing his credibility to the limit while he courted disaster (p.271). This led Perron to recognize a third characteristic: deep down Merrick had a death wish.

Merrick knew that he was on "the list" for exceeding his authority in the 1942 riots. He smiled when MAK questioned him about recent acts of persecution such as the incidents which dogged him in Mirat (p.423). In fact, he seemed so proud to be on the list that MAK suspected the rumors about his conduct were true (p.425). In 1945, when members of the Indian Congress pressed for a witch-hunt to punish culprits like Merrick and in so doing heighten racial tension to a dangerous degree, the British destroyed all records of such offenses. This annoyed Merrick (p.519), because being on the list was another resource by which he could measure his effect. Despite his public posture of arrogance and defiance, Scott hints that inside, the man may have been tortured by his actions, no matter how adamantly he insisted that Hari Kumar was guilty. In The Day of the Scorpion he told Sarah that he believed people ought to be held responsible for their actions even if they were part of the establishment (The Day of

the Scorpion, p.223). When Count Bronowsky spied
Merrick picking up confetti outside the Bingham's
wedding reception, he cheekily observed that compulsively tidy people were subconsciously trying to wipe
the slate clean and give themselves another chance
(The Day of the Scorpion, p.188). While Teddie and
he were roommates in Mirat, Merrick admitted that he
started drinking in Sundernagar, the town where he
was stationed after the Bibighar incident in Mayapore
(The Towers of Silence, p.159).

    Another key element in Merrick's character was
his fascination with the Pathan image.[19] From as early
on as his posting in Mirat in 1942[20] Merrick would
dress as a Pathan warrior, complete with blackened
face.   Later, he was accompanied by a real
Pathan--Suleiman, the Red Shadow--handsome, predatory, a man to be distrusted (p.208).   Merrick
encouraged Edward to dress like and acquire the
fearless, arrogant manner of a Pathan. And it was a
Pathan who procured young, westernized boys for
Merrick during his last days in Mirat, including his
murderer. When the Chaukidar realized Aziz had been
with Merrick during the night he remarked: "he is at
heart a Pathan, and Aziz is a fine sturdy boy"
(p.590).

    It is significant that the appropriate symbol
Merrick used to convey his manliness and courage did
not come from his own white culture.   Merrick
identified closely with this image, and in his
twisted mind found adequate expression in this guise.
He would dress as a Pathan in the dead of night when
he believed he was alone, as if he were enacting a
private fantasy. He dressed as a Pathan to meet the
young men procured for him. And he molded Edward
into his own image as a Pathan. Susan shrieked when
she saw Edward in Pathan costume after Merrick's
death: "I only mean it was like seeing Ronnie again"
(p.532).

    There is no doubt that Merrick held blacks in
contempt. But his sexual use of young Indian men was
not merely a means of violating and humiliating an
inferior race whose males did not qualify as real
"men." As Count Bronowsky recognized, Bibighar was
very interesting in light of Merrick's sexual taste
(p.176). Merrick was repelled by and yet attracted
to Hari Kumar. He hated yet desired Kumar's body to
such an intense degree that Hari became an obsession,

a fixation, with Merrick (p.177). During the physical, "persuasive" phase of Hari's interrogation, Merrick ran his hands across the black man's bloodied buttocks and fondled his genitals (p.324). But the reader is not sure of Merrick's attraction until Aziz was invited into the master's bungalow. Aziz, like Hari, was young, handsome, and educated and the parallel is heightened when Aziz was discovered bathing his bruised and bloodied face after his second rendevous with Merrick (p.589).

While talking with John Layton, Merrick revealed new information about his life. His parents were both killed when he was fifteen and Merrick found himself alone, just as Hari was alone after Duleep's suicide. But unlike Hari, Merrick was sponsored by his headmaster, who believed this young history student showed promise. Merrick was able to matriculate and find a good job in India (p.382). Even though he found himself outside his class Merrick did not succumb to disadvantages and difficulties, but faced them head on. Not only racial hatred was the root of his contempt for Hari, but also the conviction that Hari gave up in the face of similar adversity. This resentment was intensified by the realization that in England Hari would have been the favorite in the historian's eye. To the liberal mind Hari would have been the symbol of England's virtue and Merrick would have been the invisible one. In India both were invisible; Merrick because he was not of the ruling class, and Hari because liberal values did not follow him to India. "They have wandered off the guideline, into the jungle" (p.314). The historian's gaze would fall on neither of them. "But throw a spotlight on them and it is Merrick on whom it falls. There he is, the unrecorded man, one of the kind of men we really are" (p.314).

But Merrick, too, was a casuality of his own interior evil just as Hari was. During his final days Count Bronowsky noticed that he was inwardly melancholy, and himself only when he was with Edward (p.584). He was convinced that Merrick sought the occasion of his own death (p.594) because his night with Aziz revealed something about himself he could not face. It was a revelation about the relationship between his homosexuality and sado-masochism, his sense of social inferiority and his grinding defensive belief in his racial superiority (p.594).[21] He finally realized, in a moment of profound peace, that

218

his obsessions involved an emotion besides contempt,
and involved an authentic human need (however per-
versely manifested and pursued) to love and be loved,
a need directed to and fulfilled by people whom he
despised, or believed he had to despise to be his
hollow self. To admit this peace meant discarding
every belief he had (p.594). So Merrick grew
impatient to die.[22]

After his riding accident immediately prior to
his death, Merrick kept insisting that someone had
intentionally startled his horse. Rowan suspected
that he wanted to be in the middle of a show down
(p.567).[23] No one would ever be sure if Merrick
recognized his final form of persecution, but it was
quite possible that Merrick knew he was being stalked
and that his murder was really a form of suicide
(p.586). It would have pleased him to be the cause
of a racial incident leading to explosive violence
and bloodshed.[24] Perhaps he wanted his death avenged
by the raj "emerging from the twilight and sweeping
down from the hills with flaming swords---" (p.595).
But the raj were not Pathans at heart like Merrick.
They were only survivers, and abandoned Merrick and
his kind to the waves of change, which consumed and
devoured those who did not rise to the top and move
on with the times (p.217).

II

The series of cartoons by "Shankar Lal" described in A Division of the Spoils reveals what
Scott considers the key historical issues in the
transference of power from British into Indian hands.
The first cartoon (p.4) depicted the struggle for
political dominance between Nehru's Hindu Congress
party and Jinnah's Muslim League, a struggle which
might determine Mohammed Ali Kasim's hopes for
office. Such internal division pleased Winston
Churchill, as the second cartoon illustrated (p.6).
From behind a pillar Churchill spied on MAK, the
Nawab of Mirat, and Mr. Jinnah feasting on "Islam"
while the body of "Free India" struggled underneath
the table, inferring that Congress' moves to force
the issue of independence might be halted by such an
alliance. A third cartoon (p.7) depicted the Muslim
League and princely states as the culprits in
blocking Indian unity and nationalism. Churchill's
hopes for continued British rule were toppled, not by

India but by England, with the election of the
Socialist party to power in 1945, an act which
guaranteed Indian independence. Self-rule would
finally be achieved, but accomplished only on
Britain's terms and in light of Britain's needs, as
Lady Manners lamented (The Jewel in the Crown,
p.475), as Jimmy Clark foretold (The Day of the
Scorpion, p.446), and as Leonard Purvis hoped (A
Division of the Spoils, p.32).

When the actual moment of independence came,
Shankar Lal satirized Viceroy Wavell, waiting for
cold weather to schedule elections, as a Rodin
"Thinker" with snow on his shoulders and a starving
child asleep at his feet with a begging bowl labelled
"vote" (p.475).   Wavell was also drawn as a
box-wallah selling wares to India's leading political
figures (p.475). The cartoonist treated the subject
of princely states (pp.478,479,483), the final example (Perron's favorite) showing the new Viceroy
Mountbatten as proprietor of Imperial stores holding
a "going out of business" sale. Several queues of
people waited outside.   Subsumed into the larger
store but perceptibly separate was "the Princes'
Emporium" holding "business as usual" (p.484).

There is no doubt that Scott believes Indians
equal in dignity to the British and capable of
self-rule. But he exhibits grave moral objections to
the reasons for and means of transferring power from
the raj to a disunited and volatile black populace.
The British, once the question was settled, instantly
withdrew their interest and influence. "We are all
emigrés," Count Bronowsky mused (p.576), and the time
had come to debark. Once the raj's state of exile
ended, none of India's problems seemed relevant or
serious any longer. Feelings of a mutually shared
past held the emigrants together but the prospect of
an uncertain future drove them apart. They distrusted
each other's motives and buried feelings of guilt
(p.580). The need for solidarity was gone (p.576)
and with it the pretense for cooperation with or
admiration for each other. The raj would endure, as
Sarah and Perron understood. They were built for it
(p.402). But they left behind them a multitude of
problems, largely of their own making, which would
plunge India into chaos.

One of those loose ends was the INA question.
Strictly speaking, the INA prisoners who returned to

India after the war were disloyal to the British Crown and therefore a British problem. But the whites were not prepared to put thousands on trial for the sake of their own principles, and chose instead to single-out only a few to face the full force of white man's justice; those suspected of using torture for recruitment purposes.

For the English back home, like Perron's Aunt Charlotte, the INA phenomenon was another indication that their administrative and political hold on the hearts and minds of their subjects was slipping fast and could no longer be maintained (p.228). To the leading Indian political parties vying for power, the INA's were folk heroes (p.520), and the issue became a sweet political pie to be divided and fought over. It would have meant political suicide for any party or any leader not to show support for the INA's (pp.429,460).

But that was exactly what MAK had to do, and he risked losing all political influence because he did not want to live with a single moment of short-sightedness (p.461). He was willing to privately help his son Sayed with his own defense but would not publicly support his actions (p.447). During their meeting together, MAK advised his son to weed out emotional issues and personal grudges in his testimony. It did not matter that the British never wanted nor trusted Indian officers and often abandoned them in battle--though it was true (p.432). Whatever personal injuries Sayed suffered were irrelevant to the legal issues. At best, Sayed's defense lay in his concern for the welfare of India if it would fall into the hands of the Japanese, which in 1942 appeared to be an imminent danger. In order to prevent terrible atrocities Sayed chose to march with the Japanese and so sacrifice his personal integrity as an officer for the sake of his country (p.434).

Sayed was guilty of treason, MAK told him, no matter what his reasons. He had treated his oath of loyalty as if it were nothing, and he could no longer be a soldier either for the Crown or for a free India. The INA, no matter how popular or heroic their actions appeared, had fought on the losing side. Even after the British had gone, the members of the Indian army who had remained loyal would never accept him back into their ranks. Sayed's life was wasted. He had trained to be a soldier and now could not serve

221

his country in that capacity (pp.430,448,450).

Even though most of MAK's own political actions
were aimed at ridding India of the weight of the
raj's presence, he had never waged his war at the
expense of his principles (p.448).[25] He would never
trim those principles to his private political
advantage, not for the INA's and not for the
unity/partition question. He wore his "crown of
thorns" Congress cap to the end (p.415) even if his
sons and the entire country thought him a fool.[26] He
chose temporary rustification (p.461) rather than
compromise.

Another loose end to the British reign in India
was the over six hundred princely states. This issue
illustrated the interplay between the light of good
intentions and the dark of doubt and error in the
political arena (p.302). Liberal historians would
laud British withdrawl, but what about their sacred
oath to the princely states which, since 1857, had
been assured of their independence and autonomy? The
Nawab of Mirat believed that the British were cunning
enough to ensure Mirat's continued existence even
after they withdrew. But the Count knew, as Sayed
knew, that the British trimmed their principles to
suit their own needs (p.173,449).

The general feeling at home was that the
existence of princely states which was based on
autocratic authority contradicted the goals of free,
enlightened self-rule which British influence and
withdrawal were all about. They could therefore
uphold their principles even when they abandoned
these states (p.517). It was true that many were
"constitutionally backward" (p.159) but it was also
true that the British (like Rowan's uncle Thomas
Crowley) tended to regard Indian princes as willful,
spoiled, backward children (pp. 165-66). The state
of Mirat, through Count Bronowsky's labors, had
become modern and enlightened. The Count knew that
Mirat could not remain separate forever. But he hoped
that Hindus and Muslims could continue to live
harmoniously under the Nawab and not choose Gandhi's
promised democratic millenium or Jinnah's theistic
paradise state (p.172). But under advisement from
Rowan and eventually Count Bronowsky, the Nawab
acceded to the new Dominion of India. Mirat would
become part of the provincial administration of
Ranpur and elect representatives to the legislature

(p.577).

An editorial entitled "Pandora's Box," which Perron read in 1947 on his return to Mirat, expressed the belief that all those evils "that have afflicted this country probably since time began" (p.546) but which had been imprisoned under British power and law, would now be released by mandate of ignorant British voters. While captured in Pandora's box these evils had multiplied, and now everything would be released and let loose on India--everything except hope (p.546).[27]

India stood poised on the edge of the modern world. In one sense it was never a nation, simply a geographical collection of feudal states. Purvis criticized Gandhi and his spinning wheel for keeping India "stuck in the mud" (p.34). In journeying from Mirat to Ranpur a traveler would view mud huts, "buffalo wallowing in celebration of their survival from the primeval slime; men, women, and children engaged in the fatal ritual of pre-ordained work" (p.115). For these people Indian independence meant nothing. It would not change the pattern of their lives: back-breaking toil, hunger, disease, and futility. The "heavy darkness" of an ancient and endless past pressed in everywhere in India's archi- tecture and customs, reminiscent of tombs and dun- geons (p.541).

To be a modern nation India would have to deny its past, a past rich in religious and cultural diversity, a past wherein Hindu and Muslim could live together until the British convinced them they could not. India would always be torn between a past as endless as the vast stretches of plains, and an uncertain future. In one pocket it kept an onion and in the other the formula for splitting the atom (p.199).

In one sense cutting the umbilical cord to its past was an easy task for India. The historian Perron was oppressed by the way knowledge of the past impinged so little on the present. In India the sense of the present was so strong that the future seemed unimaginable, and the country remained curiously immune to the pressures of one's knowledge of its history (p.12). There was no connection between the India he was in and the India that was in his head (p.13). He was afraid that exposure to the real

223

India would deprive him of his historical perspective, of those nice, neat answers he had learned in the hermetically sealed world of school (pp.12,287).

But the raj, too, were guilty of ignoring their past by denying their ties to India. For the last one hundred years India had been a part of England's idea of itself and India was forced to be a reflection of that idea. Until 1900 England felt it was right to possess India, "like a special relationship with God" (p.109) but after World War I the feeling was that India was no longer a credit to the Empire. From then on the idea the English had of themselves involved letting India go.[28] For the people at home India was no longer a part of their lives, although they would continue to decide its fate in their ignorance and indifference (p.231). Those who came out to India became detached from English life and from the English idea of life. In their insularity the raj were cut off from their source (England) and from India. The fate of India was not a matter of conscience because in the mirror image of themselves the English no longer beheld India.[29] But England was still in India's mirror because the occupation was not an idea but a harsh reality (p.109).

In dealing with the common Englishman in India, Perron discovered that most of them were indifferent to their history. It was irrelevant to the things they wanted for themselves and as such could be casually discarded (p.88). But whether or not they realized or accepted the fact, India was a part of England. It was there "in the skull, and the bones of the body. Its possession had helped nourish the flesh, warm the blood of every man in the room, sleeping and waking" (p.107).

Perron embraced India as part of his inheritance (p.111), but he might never find India through the world of the raj. During his tour with Sarah of the Governor's summer residence in Pankot, Perron felt that he passed through a maze, a "nest of boxes" which room by room severed him from "the source" (p.349). In the Moghul room, decorated to house visiting princes, Perron at first seemed to be released "from the stupefying weight of nearly a century of disconnexion from the source" (p.349). But the room was musty, the fixtures full of dust and stale, perfumed scents. "But the Moghul suite was no less burdened by that weight: it was the inner box"

224

(p.349). Emerging from the palace Perron could hear
the coppersmith birds, a symbolic reminder of a
reality he had already understood as true: that
people, like himself and Sarah; and countries, like
England and India; led parallel but rarely intersecting modes of existence.

Later, in contemplating his return to England,
where the affairs of India would count for little and
seem to belong to another world, Perron thought of it
also as his "source" just as India was (p.352).
Therein lay an important truth: never to know India
meant never to fully understand England or himself.
The loss would be irreparable if England chose to
deny the importance of its years of cohabitation with
India or relegated their relationship to the soon to
be discarded past.

But the past could easily be ignored because it
could so easily be left behind, just as the train
could leave the body of the victim behind with a
smooth gliding motion as if the train, the wheels,
the lines were not made of metal but of something
greasy and evasive (p.116). The train moved away from
the spot, like the present from the past, with a
mechanical anxiety to get away:

> before blame is apportioned and re-
> sponsibility felt. Increasing speed,
> the train puts distance between it-
> self and the falling body and between
> one time and another so that in the
> mind of the traveller the body never
> quite achieves its final crumpled
> position on the ground at the feet of
> the attackers (p.117).

The British will leave India to its bloody fate
as part of its past, just as the train could leave
the falling body frozen in space and time. There were
"uneasy distances" as Sarah knew between people.
There were uneasy distances across the vast physical
spaces of India which the trains did little to
bridge. And there were uneasy distances between the
past and present. Only by knowing and appreciating
history and striving to intersect with lives coexisting with one's own could men overcome those uneasy
distances which plagued them.

As in his analysis of the nature of history in

the previous volumes, Scott closely examines the roles of fate and free will in A Division of the Spoils. There is a pronounced sense of destiny and of fate, as if time moves forward with deliberation and intent. Destiny is Emerson's wave of change disrupting individuals mercilessly and indiscriminately. This wave operates independently of man's knowledge of its origins, e.g., of his own past. Man is like the goat herders who passed across the railroad tracks "drugged by the heat and the singleness of their purpose" without so much as glancing at the waiting train, and totally unaware of and indifferent to the fact that the body could have fallen there (p.116).[30] Sometimes this wave of destiny lulled its victims with a sense of repose,[31] as when Rowan and Merrick traveled together to Pankot with "the flattering sensation of a speed and movement forward that were absolutely effortless" (p.222).

But at other times destiny was not such an attractive mistress. Rowan also felt that things were out of control or that he was out of control, as when he listened to Guy Perron's rantings against Merrick. There were forces and pressures working upon him that undermined his sense of confidence (p.222), factors which he could either ignore or confront with little hope of success.

Count Bronowsky regarded destiny so apparently random as shaped by someone or something from the beginning. The "dark young man of random destiny and private passions," the would-be assassin who waited for the Count in the snow on a Russian night, had been moving toward him from birth. The Count, too, had been waiting for him: two coppersmiths of parallel existences who would violently interact in a brief, explosive confrontation. Count Bronowsky regarded himself as the agent of his assailant's death, and expected that somewhere in Russia, Europe, or even India another young man would be called from birth to avenge the death of the first (pp.169-70).

Perron, too, felt that a power beyond his own designs was shaping his life. He was fated to be on the docks of Bombay that night he first met Merrick (p.215). The deciding factors of whether or not he would see Sarah again after their tour of the Governor's summer residence went beyond the intentions and desires of either of them. He felt, as they walked across the lawn back to the guest house, that

226

they were going "further, much further, on separate
roads that may never cross again" (p.349).

Just as he finds incontestable evidence of fate
in history, Scott also finds evidence of the power of
free will, which shaped the course of events and
determined an individual's unique contribution to
history. If Colin Lindsey had chosen to recognize
Hari Kumar on the Mayapore maidan in 1942 there would
have been no Ronald Merrick in Hari's life, and no
Bibighar (p.314). Without Bibighar Ahmed Kasim would
not have been riding with Sarah and Susan by train to
Pankot with an urn containing Merrick's ashes.
Ahmed's final train journey, a single-minded, rail
pathway to his death, was a product of a complicated
network of free choices and the impersonal forces
launched by those choices.

Confronted by a fate not of his own choosing,
Ahmed could still exercise his free choice even
though the defining perimeters of that choice were
very narrow. He could barricade himself in the first
class carriage and perhaps save his life by endangering his friends, or he could surrender himself into
the hands of his murderers for the sake of the
others.

> The victim chose neither the time nor
> the place of his death but in going
> to it as he did he must have seen
> that he contributed something of his
> own to its manner; and this was
> probably his compensation; so that
> when the body falls it will seem to
> do so without protest and without
> asking for any explanation of the
> thing that has happened to it, as if
> all that has gone before is explan-
> ation enough, so that it will not
> fall to the ground so much as out of
> a history which began with a girl
> stumbling on steps at the end of a
> long journey through the dark
> (p.117).[32]

"It seems to be me they want," Sarah heard him say.
Then he smiled, conveying a look of recognizing some
kind of personal advantage (p.118). With a shrug he
freely left the carriage to meet a pre-ordained fate,
and by so doing helped determine the fate of others.

The smile might indicate that free choice shaped by moral imperatives would reap its own reward, just as choices reflecting selfish and bigoted motives would poison the destiny of many lives far into the future.

The confrontation between Merrick and Perron was, on one level, a duel between two students of history. One would seek, by creating "situations" between himself and his chosen victims, to defy impersonal forces produced by other people's cowardice and in doing so become a master of history. While Merrick sought to make history Perron sought to understand it. Knowledge of the past enriched his experiences of present reality. Familiarity with history as an academic discipline enabled Perron to understand that English history had been interpreted by liberal historians in a way which reflected their own beliefs rather than the real past. As Robin White said, they tended to sieve the facts through their own set of prejudices (The Jewel in the Crown, p.357).

It took self-confidence and a sense of moral superiority for Perron's insular forebears to create its vast empire (p.110). That same moral confidence selected and spotlighted privileged subjects according to its own liberal prejudice. Given two different Englishmen, Merrick and Kumar, it was on Coomer that the historian's eye lovingly fell. He was a symbol of their virtue. In England Merrick was invisible, a victim of his mother country which denied him the advantages and privileges which Coomer initially enjoyed. But in India Merrick would be spotlighted, the man who lacked the liberal instinct "which is so dear to historians that they lay it out like a guideline through the unmapped forests of prejudice and self-interest as though this line, and not the forest, is our history" (p.314). But Merrick knew that the jungle was the true arena and that prejudice and self-interest were the norms of human behavior and not the embarrassing exceptions. Sarah, who saw through the raj myth, knew that Merrick's interpretation was more correct than the liberal one. Merrick's actions and prejudices reflected who the English really were. He was their dark, arcane side (p.314), a side which liberal historians preferred to overlook.

Bibighar was metaphorically the source of eternal life for Ronald Merrick, who would otherwise be unrecorded, lost in the bureaucratic crowd of white faces. Through the events of Bibighar he loomed large in the consciousness of black and white alike, rising from the invisible ranks to be regarded either as a salvific or demonic frigure. Whether early on in Mirat, or during the Bingham's wedding, in Delhi or while talking with MAK, Merrick's identity was obscure until the utterance of a single word which inevitably brought a smile to his lips: Bibighar.

Scott gives a blasphemous twist to the opening lines of St. John's Gospel: "In the beginning was the Word. "Symbolically, the utterance of the Word "Bibighar" created Merrick. His actions during the events of Bibighar attained for him the reputation he needed to solidify the image of his hollow self. He was the image of the Word, the image of an idea. He was the anti-Christ. This treatment is developed through continued reference to Merrick's depraved nature. His photographic likeness was described as "sinister" (p.506), and the disfigurement on the left side of his face reflected something inexpressible about the right (p.69). He would never be capable of promoting anyone's happiness, not even his own (p.178) because he could not love, only punish. The Christian Word as manifested by the Christian Savior was the antithesis of what Merrick wanted to make of his life and how he would influence the lives of others. His scars were manifestations of his interior deformity, not glorious wounds of a resurrected body. For some fateful purpose Merrick's and not Teddie's life was spared. Learning to cope with his "stigmata" (p.214) was like starting a New Life, and Susan would touch and explore those wounds and thereby find New Life by re-establishing human contact.

Yet ironically the logical conclusion of Bibighar was Merrick's death and not his eternal life (p.585). Pandit Baba and the men after him who hounded and persecuted Merrick were not interested in the triumph of justice and virtue (p.171). They wanted to exploit Bibighar and later Merrick's death only for political purposes.

As long as Hari Kumar was alive, the tragic

legacy of Bibighar would continue to influence the fate and consciousness of a wide circle of people. At first Guy Perron refused to be touched by his fellow Chillingborughan's misfortune, just as he was reluctant to take raj problems too much to heart. "It meant nothing to me" (p.291). Even after reading Rowan's confidential transcript of the interview, Perron had too many unanswered questions. He found Hari's stubborn silence incomprehensible (p.337).

Yet Bibighar pressed around Perron from all different quarters of his life. Merrick "chose" him just as he had chosen Hari, and at the peak of this "punishment" Perron would come to identify strongly with Hari Kumar. After saying good-bye to Sarah when they visited the summer residence, a trick of light made his hands look brown while buttoning the cuffs of his sargeant's sleeves (p.351). Later that night he would have a dream:

> They had emerged, erupted violently, from the shadows of the Moghul room, attacked me, pulled me away, hit me in the face. Later when they had gone and we held each other again I said: Let me take you home. She said, No. No. We haven't seen each other. We haven't seen each other since the night we visited the temple (p.351).[33]

It was Merrick who first brought Hari Kumar to Perron's attention and out of his dimly remembered past. After witnessing the INA interview on the Bombay docks, Perron dreamed about Hari playing cricket, seeing his dark-skinned, handsome face full of determination as he hit ball after ball. To misjudge, mistime would mean misfortune. "Suddenly the face vanished. A flurry of birds, crows, rooks, rose from the surrounding elms, startled by a sudden noise, although there had been no noise. And they were not elms but palms; and the birds were kite-hawks. They circled patiently" (p.111). Already Perron's subconscious was warning him that Hari's disastrous fate was not of his own making.[34]Soon after his dream he met Ahmed Kasim at the Maharanee's party, and "for an instant he had an absurd notion that the young Indian was Coomer" (p.54).[35]

Nigel Rowan had been deeply affected by his interview with Kumar. He hoped to inspire trust, like a typical member of the raj, but at the outset of that meeting he believed that Hari was probably guilty of rape. By the end of the interview Rowan was convinced of Kumar's honesty and innocence. Still, his ideas about Bibighar were "woolly" (p.315). Because Rowan was not a man of action, he hoped that Perron would somehow help Hari put a stop to the train of tragic events in his life just as he hoped Perron would stop Susan from marrying Merrick (p.315). In a sense both were trying to use Hari so that their guilty consciences would be placated. But Hari kept to himself, refusing to be used for anyone's moral or political cause. He was adamantly his own kind of Indian (p.519) and, like the Moghul Room, would not bring Perron or Rowan to the "source." They would never find India or do penance for the sake of India through Hari. He would lead his own "coppersmith" existence, a parallel and coexisting but never intersecting life.

Perron underwent a metamorphosis while in England between 1945 and 1947. He found that he could not leave India behind. He was one of those men Sarah wanted to avoid, a man "tortured by an affection" for India to which "he would always be longing to return, as if to prove something to himself" (p.369). Not only India but Bibighar mattered to him. He had taken them to heart and before his departure would hunt out Hari Kumar as one Chillingboroughan for another.[36] Perron is Scott's prophet figure--one who proclaimed the truth. But his vision was not fired, not purified, until Bibighar changed and enlarged him. He was wiser because of it, and could finally find happiness and enchantment in India (p.539).

The garden imagery surrounding the description of Mirat is unmistakable.[37] The palace courtyard was bathed in brilliant sunshine and color. Water splashed in the fountain, and a white peacock strutted undisturbed (p.580). According to ancient lore, the Nawab's reign would last as long as there was water in the lake (The Day of the Scorpion, p.136). Symbolically, the Nawab's lake was the place of living waters. Mirat, as a princely state, still mirrored something of the old India (p.536). The picturesque splendor and luxury had not been completely contaminated by Western influence, and in Mirat both Ahmed and Sarah discovered that illusive happiness which the rest of India could not offer them. For a few brief months Sarah was not on show, having no official authority as a member of the raj. She was free to serve , not out of duty but choice; free to help poor Shiraz struggle out of her cocoon of unhappiness, free to do hospital work, free to perform tasks for the Count and the Nawab which quickly made her indispensable (pp.560,574). Ahmed, too, found fulfillment and happiness in the early hours of the morning, cantering in "a game of love" with his hawk (p.538).[38] For Ahmed, Mirat provided a thin wall between himself and the political turmoil which engulfed his family and the rest of India.

When Perron arrived in Mirat, he was glad and enchanted to be there, but felt excluded from "the mystery, the vital secret" of their happiness (p.516). Scott chooses not to reveal the reasons for or means to their happiness. At this point he refrains from entering intimately into Sarah's feelings and thoughts, as if her path to happiness were so private, so unique, that it would not help anyone else to reach the Garden. Without a religious or philosophical formula which could apply universally to all people, there is no sure way to the paradise of love, happiness, and peaceful enchantment. Every man must find his own way to the "secret garden of happy center." There was such a place, Scott says, such a state, but there is no universal formula as in the days of the Christian faith which offered each man safe passage there. For a brief time in Mirat there was a state where black and white, English and Indian, lived and loved in happiness.

The short days of Paradise rapidly came to a close even as Perron arrived.[39] The serpent had also freely moved in the Garden, and from the moment of his death violence threatened to engulf Mirat. There the bloody results of the British's irresponsible withdrawal and the last violent effects of Bibighar would achieve its culmination. Merrick the punisher would become the punished, with the word "Bibighar" scrawled on the mirror above his bloodied corpse (p.570). Ahmed would be victimized by historical circumstances, circumstances which would engulf thousands of others before partition was completed in a scene which would become commonplace.[40]

Sarah would never forgive herself for letting Ahmed leave the carriage to be hacked to pieces. He had been killed by a religious conflict in which he had never seen any value, which he never took

232

seriously, and which the raj never did anything to solve but only intensified (p.616). "We just let him go. We all of us sat here and let him go" (p.607). No matter how well-intentioned the whites were, they all let the black man go to his bloody fate. The unspoken assumption was that Ahmed, who had shared the white man's salt, should offer himself as sacrificial victim. He was morally obliged, duty-bound by the code not to let any harm come to the white sahibs (p.617). Sarah hated herself for letting skin color decide who would survive and who would not, for playing the brave little memsahib at Premanagar, enacting the "bloody code" (p.617). When Perron left her to return to Mirat and asked to see her again, Sarah responded, "What is there to see?" (p.615)[41]

But Sarah's bitter self-flagellation did not do justice to Ahmed's decision. It was a gesture finally made full, the fulfillment of a gesture which began with reining in their horses and finding no words to break the silence. At the end of his life Ahmed had changed. He loved Sarah though (she said) they were not "in love" (p.616). There was a special empathy between them (p.540). They both were rebels who broke away from a "received" life (p.616) and found happiness together. Ahmed and Sarah achieved the level of friendship which eluded Hari and Daphne.[42]

Ahmed was the very man whom his father considered "indifferent to everyone," dutiful but not affectionate (p.410). This was the young man who, in The Day of the Scorpion (p.101) described being caught in a riot and revelling in the opportunity to lash out in self defense and leave at will. "One did not feel...that one had to take sides, one merely hit out in one's own defense, and there wasn't any moral problem to puzzle out." Now this same man freely gave himself over for the sake of others, not out of duty but out of love. "It seems to be me they want," he said, and smiled as if he recognized some kind of personal advantage (pp.117,617). He could make a choice as an equal, a choice not shaped by racial or political motivations, resulting in an act of courage by one person for another, an unselfish and (finally) full gesture of one friend to another. In the moment of his death Ahmed attained the freedom denied him in raj India.

Scott's criticism of the raj is ultimately

vindicated in A Division of the Spoils. Most of them
had no lingering sense of moral responsibility. They
would leave unmoved and unchanged by their Indian
connection, e.g., the coppersmith syndrome. From the
violence and chaos left in their wake, it is doubtful
whether India was better off, elevated from the
primal slime, for having cohabited with the white
man.

This is not to ignore the damage done by Indian
political officials and the black mobs who could be
swayed and used by self-serving gurus. Nor does it
ignore the hardships that India life imposed upon
black and white alike. MAK and Sarah both refer to
the "Indian" effect as a state of rustification. In
1945 Sarah wanted to leave before India "had quite
finished with me, rusted me up, corroded me, corrupted me utterly with a false sense of duty and a
false sense of superiority" (p.369). MAK's inability
to support the returning INA's in 1946-47 and the
moral necessity to labor against the emotional
current of the times, led him to abandon his
immediate political hopes for himself and his country
and enter into a state of "temporary rustificaton"
(p.461).

MAK never quite appreciated Ahmed's observation
that politics is ultimately useless, irrelevant to
the terrible problems of the human condition, because
it would not keep people from starving or killing
each other (p.457). The British may have prided
themselves on their liberal, enlightened legacy, but
if politics and government were their only lasting
and substantial gifts to India, their entire reign
was an unjustifiable sham.

The tragedy of the British/Indian experience is
not to be measured by the number of dead resulting
from the disastrous partition of 1947. The real
tragedies were the personal ones: Ahmed's death,
Sarah's heart-break, Hari's empty and hopeless fate,
Merrick's opportunity to use the white man's position
for his own evil obsession. As Perron realized, it
was logical that Merrick and Kumar would meet. They
had met before, countless times. "You can say they
are still meeting, that their meeting reveals the
real animus, the one that historians won't recognize,
or which we relegate to our margins" (p.314-15). The
liberal historian had pretended "everything was
lovely in the garden" (The Towers of Silence, p.326)

234

but the real truth was expressed by Bibighar. Bibighar reveals the truth about this specific historical subject and period, but also casts light on a lamentable characteristic of human behavior severed from divine influence, and it is this truth which travels by waves through ever-widening circles to influence every reader.

By tracing the effects of Bibighar, Scott has illustrated the vast reaches of moral choice. He has explored the overwhelming repercussions of good and evil which extend to sinner and victim, black and white alike. The list of victims who suffered an unjust fate is as long as the catalogue of moral choices and historical conditions which brought about that fate.

Count Bronowsky wisely observed that it was not a country that the exile lost, it was not even a home, but only a part of a home, a room, or perhaps a window in a room that he had to leave behind, and which haunted him (p.580).[43] Aside from people like Guy Perron, who recognized India "in the skull, and the bones of the body," who realized that India nourished the flesh and warmed the blood of every Englishman there (p.107), it is difficult to imagine any of the raj sustaining a substantial loss in leaving India.[44] Who of them will write about India the way Hari wrote about England, for which he yearned as for a lover:

> I walk home, thinking of another place, of seemingly long endless summers and the shade of different kinds of trees; and then of winters when the branches of the trees were bare, so bare that, recalling them now, it seems inconceivable to me that I looked at them and did not think of the summer just gone, and the spring soon to come, as illusions; as dreams, never ful-filled, never to be fulfilled (p.557).

Hari lamented the passing of an experience and of the hope of that experience ever being completed in his life. He would never see the cycle of seasons come full circle and achieve a wholeness. Hari's window on the world was closed and darkened because of his bitter experiences and his loss of lover, child, and country. Just as there would be no chance for a peaceful solution to India's problems, there is not a hopeful one for Hari's. In his essay on "love," Emerson says:

> The world rolls; the circumstances
> vary every hour. All the angels that
> inhabit this temple of the body
> appear at the windows, and all the
> gnomes and vices also. By all the
> virtues they are united. If there be
> virtue, all the vices are known as
> such; they confess and flee (A
> Division of the Spoils, p.347).

The raj virtues, lauded by Kiplingesque and liberal historians, are revealed by Scott as imaginary. Rather than exposing the vices they are shown for what they truly were: demons masquerading as angel faces carved in the dark (p.137).

Leonard Purvis believed that the study of history is the study of human folly (p.27). Gandhi was not so quick to judge: "God alone throws light on any matter and in this light we may from time to time perceive the truth" (p.8). Of all the conclusions the reader may draw from Scott's Raj Quartet, one is unavoidable. According to Greek Mythology, Philactetes (Hari's pen name) was a great archer, a friend of Hercules. He was abandoned by his friends on an island when his Greek comrades decided they could not tolerate his stench emitting from a disease he contracted. Eventually his Greek comrades realized they needed him after all and came to his rescue (p.572). The pathetic end to Bibighar will not be as happy. Hari, abandoned by his own in India because of his black skin, would not be rescued by the English. They would never return for him, never realize their loss at having severed his kind from their lives. As Purvis said, "I simply shall never be able to forgive it" (p.27).

The long history of the British/Indian relationship is an important and valuable part of both their pasts. Scott, for one, does not regret knowing India which shaped his skull and the bones of his body, which nourished his flesh and warmed his blood (p.107). Emerson says that the poet may put the key into men's hands (The Complete Essays, p.324), and

236

that the poet "is the true and only doctor; he knows and tells; he is the only teller of news" (The Complete Essays, p.322). If there is any sense to history, any message, it is not a case of the facts speaking for themselves. Its meaning is made by and within people. There is a continuum of time only in the aware eyes of an historian like Perron or wise women like Sr. Ludmila and Barbie Batchelor, or a poet like Gaffur:

> Fleeting moments: these are held along time in the eye,
> The blind eye of the ageing poet,
> So that even you, Gaffur, can imagine
> In this darkening landscape
> The bowman lovingly choosing his arrow,
> The hawk outpacing the cheetah,
> (The fountain splashing lazily in the courtyard),
> The girl running with the deer (p.623).

FOOTNOTES FOR CHAPTER IV

[1] This volume resembles The Jewel in the Crown in the way it retells stories which the reader has already witnessed: the meeting between Sarah and the Count and the interview between Rowan and Kumar are seen through the eyes of Nigel Rowan.

[2] All page references in this chapter, unless otherwise noted, are from Paul Scott's A Division of the Spoils (New York: Avon Books, 1975).

[3] During the ride from the train depot to Rose Cottage, both Sarah and her father were pressed back against the seat, being drawn into a situation in the same way Sarah pressed back against her chair while talking with Ronald Merrick, and Barbie pressed back in the tonga while riding down the hill with her trunk.

[4] The description of John Layton, sitting on his horse on the hill-side trail, unable to ride into Kahn's village, is especially pathetic when contrasted with the description of a younger John Layton who was welcomed into the villages surrounding Pankot because he was the sahib "who knew best how to tell the story of Subahdar Muzzafir Khan Bahadur's gallantry" (The Day of the Scorpion, p.69).

[5] Such metaphysical statements are rarer in this volume than in the previous two. The absence of God from human activity is now treated as a foregone conclusion. One of the few references to the subject occurs when Perron prayed just before his take-off on a plane leaving Ranpur. "These were nowadays his only offerings to God. It was inconceivable to him that the prayers could be heard because he felt that if there were a God, God would be praying too, watching these extraordinary machines shudder and flutter their frail way along the tarmac toward the lit runway" (pp.618-19).

[6] Perron heard the coppersmiths when he first arrived in Pankot (p.233,236) and as he and Sarah toured the Moghul Room of the Governor's summer residence while he reflected on the cultural and

238

historical gaps between the raj's world and both England and India (p.349). Sarah became aware of the coppersmiths again while she breakfasted with her father at the Dak Bungalow and tried unsuccessfully to warn him of Ronald Merrick and to confess to him about her affair and abortion (p.375).

Perron also meditates on such mysterious worlds within a world which appear hermetically sealed and seem as if they are composed entirely of a nest of boxes (p.249-50). When he visits, the Moghul room with Sarah, he recognizes it as disconnected from the source: the inner box of the nest of boxes (p.349).

[7]Daphne Manners was also very aware of such small, ingrown little worlds (The Jewel in the Crown, pp.33,378,379,427,462). In the Raj Quartet there is no continuum of time (between India and England, between members of the raj and their Indian subjects) or of space (among the members of the Layton family, between Guy and Sarah).

[8]When Sarah says "India" she thinks raj-India, and with this in mind her analysis is true. Perron knew that Sarah deserved better than the raj world (p.103). But Sarah would not have been so unhappy if there had been sufficient "Indianization" of her class (p.158) or if she had discovered the real India (as Daphne did) and as she would later come to know and love in Mirat.

[9]Purvis' equivalent of Jimmy Clark's description of nineteenth Century Edwardian sunlight. Clark would have agreed with most of Purvis' judgments, and it is fitting that the Maharanee thought that Purvis must have been one of "Jimmy's many friends (p.39).

[10]After a short paragraph describing Barbie's imaginery silence, Scott quotes another passage from Emerson's essay on "Self-Reliance," which begins: "In the will work and acquire..." and ends: "Nothing can bring you peace but yourself. Nothing can bring you peace but the triumph of principles" (The Towers of Silence, p.202).

[11]It is clear that Scott does not intend this qualification to be a refutation of Emerson. The entire conversation between Rowan and Perron on pages 215-217 follow Emerson's last three paragraphs of his

essay about "Self-Reliance" (see The Complete Essays, pp.168-69). Perron quotes the "society is a wave" passage, describes the raj's attitude toward its imperial property, and outlines the nature of Merrick's "principles." After the paragraph on society in the original source, Emerson discusses the evil of possessing property (property does not add to a person's stature; reliance on property is the want of self-reliance; what a man is counts, not what he has) and then concludes the essay with the paragraph on peace through the triumph of principles.

[12]Because the raj type will always survive and be perpetuated, the cyclic nature of history is re-enforced, and the danger of Merrick and Kumar's meeting again and again is increased.

[13]This description resembles the movement of the train away from the fallen body in the prophecy (pp.115-117): "Suddenly you had the feeling that the train, the wheels, the lines, weren't made of metal but of something greasy and evasive" (p.116).

[14]With such descriptions Scott indicates that Merrick was more than a man without a conscience, more than evil, more than demonic. He was an anti-Christ figure, complete with wounded face and arm which Susan would fearfully touch just as St. Thomas touched Christ. "He seemed to guess things about me no one else in the family ever guessed...the nice things and the not so nice things. Even things you'd forgotten and even the things you dreamt" (pp.532-33). This passage from the conversation between Susan and Perron recalls the Samaritan woman at the well and her account of the meeting with Christ: "He told me everything I ever did" (John 4:39).

[15]Sr. Ludmila recognized Merrick's "determination to miss nothing, a madness" (The Jewel in the Crown, p.135).

[16]Sarah felt that it was no business of hers whom Susan married (p.385). A conspiracy of silence surrounded Susan and Merrick just as it had surrounded Daphne and Hari. Rowan, Perron, and Sarah were all guilty of helping to seal Susan's fate: an example of how the human will shaped destiny. The

image of the stone tossed in the pond suggests that this is one incident when Perron acted as "principled [prejudiced] as a rock" (p.217).

[17]It must have pleased Merrick to have the aristocratic Perron salute and call him "sir."

[18]As Daphne observed years before, to be rejected was "one of the easiest ways of making your mark" (The Jewel in the Crown, p.412).

[19]Pathans were Afghani in origin, of Indo-Iranian stock. They were fierce warriors, impossible to subdue. Continued British efforts to incorporate them peacefully into the empire were not successful.

[20]It is possible (but not documented) that during his spying forays in Mayapore he utilized this disguise.

[21]Although it is intended that the reader believe Count Bronowsky's rendition of Merrick's state of mind, the truth is not revealed with absolute certainty. Intimate knowledge of Ronald Merrick was elusive, even inaccessible: "as obscure as the dark side of the moon." (p.161).

[22]The mystery of Ronald Merrick's personal thoughts and feelings is never revealed. The reader is never given first-hand knowledge of this character. From the beginning Merrick was "thicketed around with his own secrecy" (The Jewel in the Crown, p.159), and it is therefore difficult to appreciate the full meaning of Count Bronowsky's insight especially with regard to the relationship between Merrick's homosexuality, sado-masochism, sense of social inferiority and racial superiority.
 It was the Count's guess that sleeping with Aziz was Merrick's first complete homosexual experience. Because Aziz was young, handsome, black, and (secretly) educated the parallel to Hari Kumar is obvious. Count Bronowsky believed that his homosexuality must have been apparent to Merrick for many many years (p.594). But Sr. Ludmila had not been so sure, wondering if he had ever leapt into the depths of his own private compulsion, (The Jewel in the Crown, p.159). As in the case of meeting Aziz for the

241

second time, Merrick's homosexual dealings could be used as a form of punishment and an expression of power and contempt. Yet Sr. Ludmila recognized "in an unnatural context, the attraction of white and black, the attraction of an opposite" (The Jewel in the Crown, p.159). Hari was at once the Other, black and socially superior in education and background; and yet the same, an expression of Merrick's self, because he was a man and and outcast, and because he, too, was consumed by interior darkness.

The sadistic aspect of Merrick's personality must have involved the "grinding defensive belief" in his racial superiority" (p.594) which he had learned in India as a white man in control of a black man's country (The Jewel in the Crown, p.159). He used blacks and whites who weren't "real" whites without any obvious indication of guilt. His inclination to punish rather than love, which Sr. Ludmila recognized, extended even to himself. Perron believed that his sadism grew out of frustrated masochistic tendencies, stemming in part from his years in England and his obsessive sense of social inferiority. Merrick was painfully aware of his inferior class and education with any white man he met. He was his own subject of hatred and contempt and transferred those feelings to blacks, because the raj myth had guaranteed him that all blacks were racially inferior.

It is not known whether Merrick recognized this evil deformity, this consuming interior darkness before his rendevous with Aziz. But it was Count Bronowsky's belief that he found a brief moment of peace with the black youth and was appalled by what that meant. For once Merrick did not control, was not the master of "the situation." Through no design of his own he achieved some level of an authentic human relationship, of interior peace, and did so because of a black person. The falsehood of his entire life, of the raj myth and of his own monstrous evil came crashing in on him. As a self-fashioned myth-breaker he had broken his own myth. As Emerson observes in his essay on "Compensation:" "Inasmuch as he carries the malignity and the lie with him he so far deceases from nature. In some manner there will be a demonstration of the wrong to the understanding also; but, should we not see it, this deadly deduction makes square the eternal account" (The Complete Essays, p.186). Merrick's unnatural obsession was a perversion of nature, like men running on all fours. The raj had never come out of the jungle. They were not civilized and therefore not superior in any way. The revelation was "appalling," and the following night Merrick beat Aziz with his fists to invite retaliation. He knew he was going to die, and would rather face such a fate than live with this self-knowledge. Yet he hoped that his death would spark a racial incident, and that the raj would emerge from the twilight and sweep down from the hills with flaming swords to avenge his death (p.595) just as Teddie hoped the two missing INA's would answer his call. Neither could live with the knowledge that the myth was dead.

[23] When the English voted to grant Indian independence in 1945, Merrick's faith in the white man's code and wisdom must have been shattered much like Teddie's faith was shaken by the INA problem, Susan's faith by Teddie's death, and Edwina's faith by Mr. Chaudhuri's death.

[24] Merrick was always aware of the political significance of Bibighar, an awareness which Hari Kumar never achieved. For Merrick it was part of "the situation," and a manifestation of his self-obsession. Even in death he wanted to stir things up, to be at the center of controversy, to be spot-lighted.

[25] For a brief moment, while MAK contemplated the prospect of being Governor of Ranpur, "the temptation of the peak--that splendid heady upper air, that immensity of landscape--made his head sing" (p.464). But MAK resisted the temptation to float to the surface and join the company of unprincipled people, choosing to remain anchored down by his principles. Such a possibility was simply "water under the bridge" like the turbulent water of the riots in 1942. It would be foolish to disturb it (p.463).

[26] MAK and John Layton were very much alike. Any reminder of prison guards, locked doors, or guns made MAK uneasy just as the barking dogs upset John (pp.368,426). They both lived to see their hopes dashed, their most cherished beliefs and dreams turned into mythical illusions. For John it was Man-Bap, for MAK it was a united India. Each felt the weight of "uneasy distances" between themselves and their offspring. Sarah understood that Man-Bap was a myth, but did not share her father's anguish. Neither of MAK's sons believed in his dream of a united India

243

although it was consolating to know that Ahmed "expected and wanted" MAK not to go over to Jinnah's Muslim League (pp.454,457,467,449).

There are other minor parallels between MAK and other characters. While in prison, both MAK and Hari Kumar had an identity, not in their own right but in opposition to the raj (p.331). MAK described himself not as a martyr but as a pragmatist, much the same way Lili Chatterjee described Gandhi (The Jewel in the Crown, p.77).

[27]Pandora's Box is mentioned in two earlier volumes. In the first book Lady Chatterjee compares Daphne to Pandora "We were all afraid for her, even of her, but more of what she seemed to have unlocked, like Pandora who bashed off to the attic and pried the lid of the box open" (The Jewel in the Crown, p.118). When Barbie unlocks her trunk of relics to find Edwina's Queen Victoria picture to give to Ronald Merrick she "raised the Pandora-lid" (The Towers of Silence, p.386).

[28]Perron's analysis coincides with MAK's: "they will only see that there is no future for them in India when India no longer fits into the picture they have of themselves and their current obligations" (The Day of the Scorpion, p.40).

[29]What was logically left to them was a position like Millie Layton's. She never confused a sense of history with nostalgia, the desire to live in the past. In the circumstances which closed in upon the raj, she foresaw a challenge of survival. She was determined to survive the changes and defeat the forces aligned against her, no matter what she had to compromise to do so (pp.282-83).

[30]In this section (pp.115-118) the feeling of fate is intensified by the fact that it is written as if Ahmed's death has already been accomplished. But at this point in the book the act of violence is still an unknown element of the future. These passages prophesy an event which has already been fated.

[31]In this sense, all men are symbolically being stalked in the "old Thuggee way" (p.596), when the Thugs would travel with their chosen victims to lull

244

suspicion (p.597).

[32]The bodies of both Merrick and Ahmed Kasim fell out of "a history which began with a girl stumbling on steps at the end of a long journey through the dark" (p.117). Above Merrick's corpse was scrawled the word "Bibighar." Though the motives of their killers may have had nothing to do with the event in Mayapore, 1942, the cause and effect is still at work. The difference between Merrick's and Kasim's death was that Ahmed, as Scott says, found compensation in his death, whereas Merrick's takes on the form of retribution. That small area of freedom which Ahmed enjoyed at the moment of his death; that small, brief act of dominion, was used for a virtuous end. All of Merrick's choices expressed by action indicate that his acts of dominion and freedom were used to control others.

[33]Scott expands his character parallels and his metaphysical symbols to apply to Guy Perron. During his visit to Mirat, Perron also had a nightmare in which he was a huge butterfly "that beat and beat and fragmented its wings against the imprisoning mesh of the net" (p.573). This new application indicates that Scott's message is of universal dimensions, beyond the boundaries of raj society. Scott reiterates man's metaphysical state of abandonment and isolation on the night when Perron discovered the truth about Merrick's death, when he witnessed people's lives changed forever by an apparently impersonal fate. It is also the night before Ahmed would be killed, when he would fall out of a story which began in Mayapore five years earlier. Perron feels trapped, helpless, much the same way Barbie did: "One may carry the Word, yes, but the Word without the act is an abstraction. The Word gets through the mesh but the act doesn't. So God does not follow." (The Towers of Silence, p.342).
Perron's dream wherein he was a principle participant in the Bibighar tragedy is especially significant because Perron never read Daphne's diary and therefore did not have access to the details revealed in the dream. It is a case of Perron sharing in the experiences of the past in true Emersonian fashion.
Sr. Ludmila had also entered into Hari Kumar's experience in a similar way. It is her recreation of Hari and Colin Lindsey meeting on the Mayapore maidan

245

which the reader shares rather than an omniscient historical account. This recollection of Sr. Ludmila's was really Kumar's. "From Kumar I have inherited it. And feel almost as if I had been there. Am there. Towards evening. In Kumar's body" (The Jewel in the Crown, p.282).

In many ways Guy Perron appears to be an Emersonian individualist, from being part of an aristocratic family too eccentric to behave like typical upper class, to his sense of moral responsibility which made it impossible for him to float to the top with the raj, or sink to the bottom with Purvis and Merrick.

[34]After hearing Rowan remark that Merrick had a knack for making a game seem important (p.278) Perron associates the invisible bowler of his dreams about Hari Kumar with Merrick. Merrick's choosing Hari as he washed under the tap in the Sanctuary was the "first ball of the over" (p.315). Perron would dream repeatedly of Kumar "sweeping and cutting and blocking that merciless succession of contempuous deliveries" that came from the same hand (p.337).

[35]Perron comments that Rowan "would remain appalled and puzzled, a man with a conscience that worked in favour of both men; more in favour of Kumar than of Merrick; but Merrick was given sufficient benefit of the liberal doubt to leave Rowan inert" (p.315).

[36]At the last minute he was sickened by his own raj-like, altruistic motives and decided not to intrude on Hari's privacy.

[37]Scott's garden imagery, which began with the ruined garden of Bibighar (the site of love made manifest) and which continued in Susan's illusory "secret garden of happy center" and Mabel's now violated rose garden, achieves its apotheosis in the description of Mirat. But the sins of the raj contaminate even this Garden. As Lady Manners reflected, the world would grow suddenly dull "because the beloved, thank God, has gone, offering his killing and unpredicable and selfish affection elsewhere" (The Jewel in the Crown, p.476). By fearing rather than loving what was different, the English never truly became "bone of India's bone," and the

co-mingling between the two countries was more an act of violence than love. The English nation, like their white judicial robot, could not distinguish between love and rape, and only understood a physical connection (The Jewel in the Crown, p.452-453). The two nations, these would-be lovers, never experienced that brief moment of paradise that Daphne and Hari shared, when Daphne traced the miracle of Hari's black ear. England and India could have known Paradise but did not, and now it was too late. This garden, too, is lost. The ancient Biblical allegories describing man's fall into sin are realized again and continually: Scott coming full circle.

[38] Bird imagery in this volume relates to Perron's experience in a plane, which gave him "this sense of exaltation" because there was not a visible horizon (p.619). Such a flying sensation belonged to Sarah when she galloped with Ahmed for the first time: breaking free of her environment. India, the land of birds, could grant them this freedom.

[39] Impending death was symbolically foretold even while Perron traveled by train from Ranpur to Mirat. He woke in total darkness and heard the packs of wild dogs hunting on the plains (p.496).

[40] The section (pp.115-118) which foretells of the victim's death can be understood literally to apply to Ahmed's death, or allegorically to signify the conflict between Muslims and Hindus which was caused by British policy during their rule and withdrawal.

[41] This passage captures the difference between Perron and Sarah. Throughout the Raj Quartet Sarah had difficulty acting according to her thoughts. Too often there was a difference between how she behaved on the inside and the outside. Ahmed's death brings home that disparity to her. The reader hopes that she will be restored rather than destroyed by this great suffering, and attain the level of peace which Perron seems to have achieved. See page 623.

[42] Sarah appears to have achieved a "wholeness"--Daphne's kind of wholeness. Like Daphne, Sarah did volunteer work in the hospital, and wanted to work in the leper colony, just as Daphne worked at the Sanctuary.

[43]This passage recalls Sarah's reflections on the neo-classical facades of a vanished age of reason which she viewed from Aunt Fenny's bedroom window: "My history, rendered down to a colonnaded front, an architectural perfection of form and balance in the set and size of a window" (The Day of the Scorpion, p.422).

[44]Perron's feelings seem to be mixed, much like Scott's own. "He walked the few yards to the wall of the esplanade, with its view on to the Arabian Sea; and its smell. Disgusting. Peaceful. I shall never go back home, one Perron cried. The other said: Take me back, for God's sake" (p.486). Yet Perron's attraction to India is reminiscent of the stranger's in The Jewel in the Crown. This stranger, like Paul Scott himself, returned to India after an eighteen year-long absence. And this stranger was inspired by "a pervading redolence, wafting in from the silent, heat-stricken trembling plains; from the vast panorama of fields, from the river...A smell...It translates itself from repellent through almost attractive because familiar stages into an essence distilled by an empirically committed mind" (The Jewel in the Crown, p.100). On renewed association, the returning traveler will cry "possessively, even gratefully: Ah, India!" (The Jewel in the Crown, p.101) This stranger, unlike Hari Kumar, did not find this smell "stagnant, heavy, a conductive medium for stench" (The Jewel in the Crown, p.238). Rather, he found that the heat of India brought out the essential fragrance of the land like "the warmth of a woman's skin releasing the hidden but astonishing formula of an unusual perfume" (The Jewel in the Crown, p.101). The stranger, whether speaking for only himself, or for Paul Scott or even Guy Perron, loved and needed the smell of India: "It is not only the smell of habitation. It is the smell, perhaps, of centuries of the land's experience of its people" (The Jewel in the Crown, pp.192-93).

CHAPTER V

CONCLUSION

There are several misconceptions of the past detailed in the Raj Quartet. One of those misconceptions was Merrick's belief in "kiplingesque double-talk": his firm conviction of a body of half-truths and myths fabricated by the middle class about the behavior and responsibilities of the upper class, the "scum" at the top. Merrick worked to perpetuate the Edwardian sunlight of the nineteenth century, but on his own terms. One of his greatest sins was to impose the prejudices and practices of the past upon the present. In enacting his own philosophy of history Merrick was paradoxically master and slave of the past. By creating "the situation," he wanted to direct and determine the flow of events. But by misinterpreting the role and nature of the raj and choosing to cultivate his image, his hollow self, according to that misinterpretation, he in fact became a victim and a perpetuator of all that was wrong about the English in India. He was the "dark, arcane side" of the raj. He took their attitudes and behavior seriously, and pushed them to their logical conclusions. In doing so he tried to make a religion out of human institutions. The will behind such an intent and practice is traced by following the trail of fallen victims in the wake of Merrick's passing.

Perron had his own set of illusions about people and places in history.[1] As a child he thought of the Arabian Sea as a most romantic-sounding place, but his experience of the real thing (an unfriendly vista) proved a bitter disappointment A Division of the Spoils, p.12). Leonard Purvis knew little about history but refused to learn from the lessons of his own experiences. Every time the phantom voice called him about a position which would "interest" him, Purvis took the bait, convinced that past experiences could not possibly be repeated. "One has the

249

hysterical belief in the non-recurrence of the abysmal" (Ibid., p.28).

Guy Perron referred to the perpetually moving stream of history. While he sat in Beamish's office with Purvis he tuned into his "other" ear: "the one that caught the nuances of time and history flowing softly through the room, a flow arrested neither by Beamish's concerns nor his own sense of obligation to further them by putting himself at Beamish's disposal" (Ibid., p.14). In the Graces' apartment, as he sat studying John Layton's bush shirt, Perron tried to tune into the "perpetually moving stream" but caught nothing. Instead, he was struck by the "grand irrelevance of history to the things that people wanted for themselves" (Ibid., p.88). Later that evening Perron again tried to "obliterate from his mind all the disturbing residue of the day's malfunctioning and so leave it free to crystallize, to reveal the point reached in a continuum he was sure existed but, in India, found so difficult to trace" (Ibid., p.108). The question is whether this continuum actually exists, and what its nature is.

There is no continual flow, no intersecting of existences between England and India (Ibid., p.109), just as there is no connection to "the source" (Ibid., p.349) socially or culturally. The coincidence of existing at the same moment in time and space is no guarantee of interrelating: the coppersmith syndrome (Ibid., p.137).[2]

The continuum of time is further cast in doubt by the prophetical train journey in A Division of the Spoils. The passage of time is not such a simple phenomenon that an "X" on Purvis' calendar could accurately measure its progress. As the train pulls away from the place where the body falls, it puts dis- tance between "one time and another so that in the mind of the traveller the body never quite achieves its final crumpled position" (Ibid., p.117). For men who travel in time, temporal moments are either frozen in the mind (as the body never reaching the ground) or continually and eternally present (as the body forever falling). If the past is frozen or eternalized there is no continuum, and even the events of the future in relation to the present can seem unimaginable (as Sarah's anticipation of the day after reunion with her father, Ibid., p.125). John Layton's actual home-coming was not characterized by a natural evolution from a sequence of haphazard events (Ibid., p.142). The reunion was a staged scene, with the star performance by John Layton and the stage directions bearing the familiar mark of Susan's prearrangements in an attempt to reduce reality to manageable proportions in a series of tableaux (Ibid., p.142).

The only continuum which is presented as reliable is the continuum of intent. Count Bronowsky and the young man of passion moved toward each other step by inevitable step meeting in a violent confrontation too coincidental not to be considered preordained. (Ibid., p.169)

Scott's philosphy of history assumes that the past is frozen. The interview with Hari in Kandipat prison "illumined nothing except the consequences of an action already performed and a decision taken long ago. These could never be undone or retracted. In the world outside new action could be taken and new decisions made. But the light of what had been performed would glow on unblinkingly, like radium in a closed and undiscovered mine" (Ibid., p.302). Scott is adamant about knowledge of the past being a rich and important resource. The sharing of a common past is what animates and unifies emigrants (Ibid., P.580). India's past was especially rich: layer upon layer from a myriad of cultures. The fort at Premanagar was built by the Rajputs, conquered by the Moslems, invested by the Mahrattas and acquired by the British--so much, MAK reflected, contained in one place (Ibid., p.413). Yet those who lived only in the past, like Major Tippit and Ronald Merrick, are prisoners just as Hari was a prisoner in Kandipat prison.

In implementing one of his structural patterns from The Jewel in the Crown, Scott emphasizes the cyclic nature of history in A Division of the Spoils. "Tonight I miss him," the Count confesses to Perron after Merrick's death (Ibid., p.573). During the next several pages their conversation is interspersed with Perron's recollections on the events of the day at the end of which the count's confession is repeated: "Tonight I miss him" (Ibid., p.580). The reader is no farther along in the plot (e.g., in the book's time continuum) but he is in understanding. This is what Scott demands of England. If, after hundreds of years of influence in India, the raj found itself still at point A rather than advanced to point B or C (as the editorial implied about the problems which Britain first encountered being locked away in Pandora's trunk to be preserved, multiplied, and finally liberated in 1947, Ibid., p.546) then at least they should have grown in understanding, wisdom, and self-knowledge, or what Scott refers to as "grace." The mistakes of the past must not be repeated, Scott admonishes, or the chain of tragic events will never be broken. Merrick and Kumar will continually confront each other, and victims like Ahmed will perpetually be caught up in and fall out of a history "which began with a girl stumbling on steps at the end of a long journey through the dark" (Ibid., p.117).

* * *

In A Division of the Spoils Nigel Rowan and Governor Malcolm enter into a discussion of Einstein's theory of relativity in connection with believing Hari Kumar's testimony given in Kandipat prison. Sometimes, Malcolm explained:

> when faced with this apparently insoluable and intricate problem of reaching a solution through the thickets of departmental vanities he applied his own theory of relativity, which was that although people seldom argue a point but argue round it, they sometimes found the solution to the problem they were evading by going round in ever increasing circles and disappearing into the centre of those, which, relatively speaking, coincided with the centre of the circle from whose periphery they had evasively spiralled outward (p.332).

This image of coinciding, ever expanding and interrelating circles describes the structure of the Raj Quartet. With the initial intent of exploring an incident of rape in the native town of Mayapore, Scott has succeeded in creating a complicated thematic and symbolic structure of concentric and converging circles. In tracing the circumference of

252

the Bibighar circle, Scott thematically intersects
with circumferences of related circles which cast
increasingly wider arcs.³ In exploring the centers of
these circles Scott not only touches upon questions
of universal magnitude, but unlocks all the rich,
elusive mystery of the original circle.⁴

Scott's structure can also be compared to a
"nest of boxes" (Ibid., p.349) in which the reader is
released, and through which the reader searches until
he finds the prize: the hard core of truth gleaned
from the intricate and masterful maze of subjects,
images, and symbols comprising the Raj Quartet.

In studying Scott's work the reader appreciates
that he will never exhaust its meaning and message.
But there are some fundamental truths, a few circular
centers which the reader repeatedly encounters. One
such truth is that man, despite his long past, has
not "grown up," has not advanced. He has devised more
sophisticated toys for amusement and warfare (Ibid.,
p.528) but he has not really emerged from the jungle.
The civilized veneer is paper thin. The educated and
powerful quibble among themselves like children (The
Day of the Scorpion, p.105) and those nations which
enjoy technological superiority subjugate other
nations. This form of authority through power, in the
case of the British in India, was expressed in the
child/parent relationship: Man-Bap. The English tried
to guide and correct by instilling trust, but they
could not even trust themselves (A Division of the
Spoils, p.519). Life in India was a game (The Day of
the Scorpion, p.71) and to play one had to be like
everybody else (Ibid., p.357).

Prejudice is a manifestation of man's moral
state of infancy. It involves the primitive instinct
to attack and destroy what is different or unknown
(The Jewel in the Crown, p.428). Prejudice springs
from fear and the need to feel safe (Ibid., p.15).
It is a fifth-rate passion, "appropriate only to a
nation of vulgar shopkeepers and a nation of
fat-bellied banias" (Ibid., p.476).

But that hump of prejudice will never disappear
in a godless metaphysical setting. Without divine
fatherhood men are not born brothers; they are not
innately equal and will not be bound together by love
but only by comtempt and envy. Without divine
fatherhood men are orphans, a condition compounded by

253

the homeless existence of raj exiles. They refused to become "bone of India's bone" (The Day of the Scorpion, p.358)[5] and remained on the fringes of a potentially rewarding and nurturing relationship. Both India and England could have been immensely richer, but neither realized the immeasurable waste.

> You settle for the second rate, you
> settle for the lesson you appear to
> have learned and forgot the lesson
> you hoped to learn and might have
> learned, and so learn nothing at all,
> because the second-rate is the
> world's common factor, and any damn
> fool people can teach it, any damn
> fool people can inherit it (The Jewel
> in the Crown, p.476).

Both Britain and India could have been immensely richer for the experience of co-mingling. All whites could have been drawn out, enlarged, and joyful like Daphne Manners for having loved blacks. Members of both races could have "entered into their body's grace" like Sarah, or discovered even a small, private area of freedom within the stockade like Teddie and experienced that "legitimate, endorsed, blessed" joy "with nothing murky or restricting perched on its shoulder" (The Towers of Silence. p.167). No matter what the mistakes or the limitations of the parties involved, the authentic effort to enter into, to become part of each other in a real way would have redeemed the acts of cruelty, injustice, and prejudice between the two nations.[6]

If England and India would not live together as brothers it was better for both if they parted: "in a world grown suddenly dull because the beloved, thank God, has gone, offering his killing and unpredictable and selfish affections elsewhere" (The Jewel in the Crown, p.476). The crime of the raj is the lament of the son whose prince-father desired a singer from afar: "Such is the fate of love never made manifest" (Ibid., p.147). Even Ronald Merrick, in one brief, unbearable moment of honesty, knew that India could make him happy (A Division of the Spoils, p.594). But to bow to that realization would mean surrendering all the safe, small cubicles fortified by prejudice and fear; to step out of the collective role and live life freely and joyfully and invite everyone else to do the same.

Scott's message is that men must learn from the past, which enriches and influences everyone. Events of the past are frozen but lessons of the past are not. The lesson of Bibighar is that men must see into each other, past class or skin color and into the heart (The Jewel in the Crown, p.73, and The Day of the Scorpion, p.424), into the terrific thing that makes each person (The Towers of Silence, p.175). For the English or Indian nations to be truly great and truly civilized, they must find a place, a condition, an ability to appreciate and foster the individual person so that each man would feel the truth Hari Kumar suffered so much to understand: "I wasn't to be compared, I was myself" (The Day of the Scorpion, p.314). As Ahmed tried to explain to his father:

> The country's here, and so am I, and shouldn't we stop squabbling over it and start living in it? What does it really matter who runs it, or who believes in Allah, or Christ, or the avatars of Hindu mythology, or who has a dark face and who has a light?" (Ibid., p.475)

* * *

Illusion vs. reality is one of the major themes in the Raj Quartet. The most important examples are developed in each successive volume, such as what really constitutes a person's value and identity. Duleep Kumar's tragic illusion was that if a black man could be English in language, manner, and way of thinking, he would be recognized and advance in an Anglo-Indian world. This illusion had far-reaching effects for his son. Only after years of humiliation and suffering did Hari realize that external trapping did not determine his identity. This illusion was directly fostered by the British liberal tradition. Hari was "the loose end of our reign" (The Jewel in the Crown, p.475).

Within its own ranks the raj fostered illusions about how a person "counted." Susan Layton believed that if she followed the code, embodied the all-important tradition, she would find the secret garden of happy center. But in reality the code mattered more than any one person, and the collective survival of the raj mattered more than Susan's personal survival. Often the raj's survival was a direct threat to the individual. Life in the cantonment was an ingrown, hateful little world which masqueraded as part of the terrible enchantment of inherited identity (A Division of the Spoils, p.137). The raj family, single cell of the white community, did not signify a "geometric pattern of light and the circle of safety" (The Day of the Scorpion, p.230) because survival did not mean change but petrification. Preserved in "perpetual Edwardian sunlight," the raj hung on like grim death (Ibid., p.16). The raj wrote their code in stone instead of guaranteeing a vital and rewarding life experience and a world untroubled by sadness. A dead hand lay on the entire enterprise.

The primary illusion was that the raj inhabited a "world morally untroubled" (Ibid., p.346) because they came to India for the "good of their souls and the uplift of the native" (A Division of the Spoils, p.217). Such "kiplingesque double-talk" functioned like a cloak of legitimacy which disguised plain, ordinary Englishmen who entered into exile because of their own greed, or because they could not stand the commercial pace at home. No one really believed this "God-the-father-God-the-raj" "insular middle-and lower-class shit" (Ibid., p.217) except men like Ronald Merrick and the liberal historians who refused to recognize the real animus of British/Indian history (Ibid., p.314). Behind the smokescreen of moral responsibility, based on illusory assumptions of moral superiority, festered the primitive instinct to attack and destroy what they didn't understand. The moral issue, as Daphne realized, had gone sour, and rhetoric about sacred mission meant safeguarding racial superiority through biological purity. The raj's moral frame of reference was no better than Merrick's "line" which was defined by self-righteous and bigoted presumptions of superiority. England's "savagely practical and greedy policy" (Ibid., p.476) was not humane, enlightened, or moral. It did not mark the triumph of right reason or guarantee the moral drift of history, if there be such a thing. All the problems the British found when they first came to India had not been solved, only trapped in Pandora's Box to be released--without hope--when the white man left (A Division of the Spoils, p.546). Indian independence marked the moral failing rather than the moral triumph of the British people (Ibid., p.318).

References to illusion vs. reality crescendo to
an almost fever pitch in the final volume. There are
dozens of such references. Some refer to false hopes
and unfulfilled desires, such as Sarah's illusion of
serenity at the prospect of peace (A Division of the
Spoils, p.119) which was threatened by her return to
Pankot (Ibid., p.135); Perron's idea of India which
did not correspond to the real India (Ibid.,
pp.12-13); the Nawab's illusion that the British
would honor their promise to protect the autonomy of
the princely states even after they withdrew (Ibid.,
p.173); Perron's illusion of imminent escape from
Merrick while waiting for Bunbury (Ibid., p.233)
which seemed like an Indian ocean dream (Ibid.,
p.344); Millie Layton's illusion of youth (Ibid.,
p.283); the Layton's trip to Calcutta and Darjeeling
which gave the illusory impression that all was well
(Ibid., p.390); Merrick's perceptions of the raj's
real and imagined virtues (Ibid., p.584).

There are the "uneasy distances" between the
present and the past which caused memories to appear
illusory. Rowan was afraid that Hari's recollections
once laid bare in the unedited transcript, would be
judged as the fantasies of a bitter man with a grudge
(Ibid., pp.322,328). Perron suspected that Sarah's
memories of the governor's summer residence no longer
seemed real to her (Ibid., p.349), but to Perron, who
did not share these memories, Sarah seemed like a
prisoner of this unreality (Ibid., p.349). Hari's
memories of England seemed like illusions, "as
dreams, never fulfilled, never to be fulfilled"
(Ibid., p.557).

There are references to aspects of reality that
could not be mistaken for illusion: England's harsh
possession of India (Ibid., p.109); the poverty and
stench of black Mayapore (Ibid., p.308); Perron's
return to India ("India, he thought. India. I'm
back. Really back") (Ibid., p.498). There are
references that seem almost too minor for Scott to
even mention: the Count's imagined (anticipated)
persecution (Ibid., p.170); the illusion of coziness
in Governor Malcolm's office (Ibid., p.187); Perron's
illusion that if he left Merrick alone for even a day
the man would be promoted again (Ibid., p.214);
Pinky's impression that his night of horror was real
but he himself was not (Ibid., p.265); the illusion

of blindness and blankness in prison (Ibid., p.301);
the ordor of unreality which surrounded the summer
residence which only exile made seem real (Ibid.,
p.320); the metallic-grey specter of pale Maisie
Trehearne which gave an illusion of cooling breezes
(Ibid., p.361); the familiar courtroom where MAK
spoke with Sayed which did not have meaning or
dimensions of reality (Ibid., p.451).

Whatever the apparent source of illusion--the
perceiving and recollecting mind or the outside
world--the total effect is to make all of India
appear illusory, just as the material order is
illusory for the Hindu. It is the end of the Quartet
and the end of the British as they were. They are
withdrawing, and soon India will be only a memory
much like England was an illusion, a dream for Hari
Kumar. Most English would regard India as only a
repository of England's past (The Jewel in the Crown,
p.480). As Perron realized, history could often
appear irrelevant "to the things that people wanted
for themselves" (A Division of the Spoils, p.88). It
had been difficult for native Englishmen to regard
India as relevant to their lives while they still
ruled. It would be improbable that they would
envision a future stemming from their British/Indian
experience when they no longer beheld India in their
reflection. But the reflection was there--Perron
perceived it: "in the skulls and the bones of the
body. It's possession had helped nourish the flesh,
warm the blood of every man" (Ibid., p.107).

Whether the English see Indian independence as a
triumph of liberalism or as a moral failure, the
connection between England and India is still a
reality. In Scott's complicated structural nest of
boxes and converging circles, Hari Kumar's longing
for England is the inner box, the smallest circle out
of which the larger circles spiral. Hari's longing
signifies Scott's own longing for India, a longing he
hopes to instill in his countrymen. The great and
final illusion would be to think that just because
India is part of England's past that the connection
is over. The disaster would be not to rejoice that
it is still there: "bone of my bone, flesh of my
flesh."

258

FOOTNOTES CHAPTER V

[1] While Merrick was a man of the past, Perron was a man of the present who, as a scholar, was interested in the past (A Division of the Spoils, p.584).

[2] There is a time continuum within minds who are open to other people's experiences. Sr. Ludmila shared in English autumns through Hari Kumar's memories. The continuum of time is real in the mind of Barbie Batchelor, who in meditating on Edwina's heroic gestures at Muzzafirabad and then on the road from Dibrapur, recognized "a distance measurable in miles, in years, but between the occasions there was no distance" (The Towers of Silence, p.74). But there is no time continuum when people remain willfully ignorant or indifferent.

[3] Sometimes Scott traces only the outer perimeters of these outlying circles, as when he treats Susan's alarming action of placing her baby in a ring of fire, or only hints about the depths of Ronald Merrick's interior deformity. He leaves the rich center of mystery untouched.

[4] For an example of diplomatic circumnavigation of the point, see Rowan's and Bronowsky's discussion on the train (A Division of the Spoils, pp.169-178).

[5] This phrase suggests Genesis 2:23, when Adam says of Eve, "This at last is bone of my bone and flesh of my flesh." The fact of co-mingling is irrefutable although the circumstances not ideal: India was there, in the English face, in "the skull, and the bones of the body" (A Division of the Spoils, p.107).

[6] There are often places and people that seem alien on the surface, but as Daphne Manners knew, are underneath proof of something general and universal (The Jewel in the Crown, p.413).

265

270